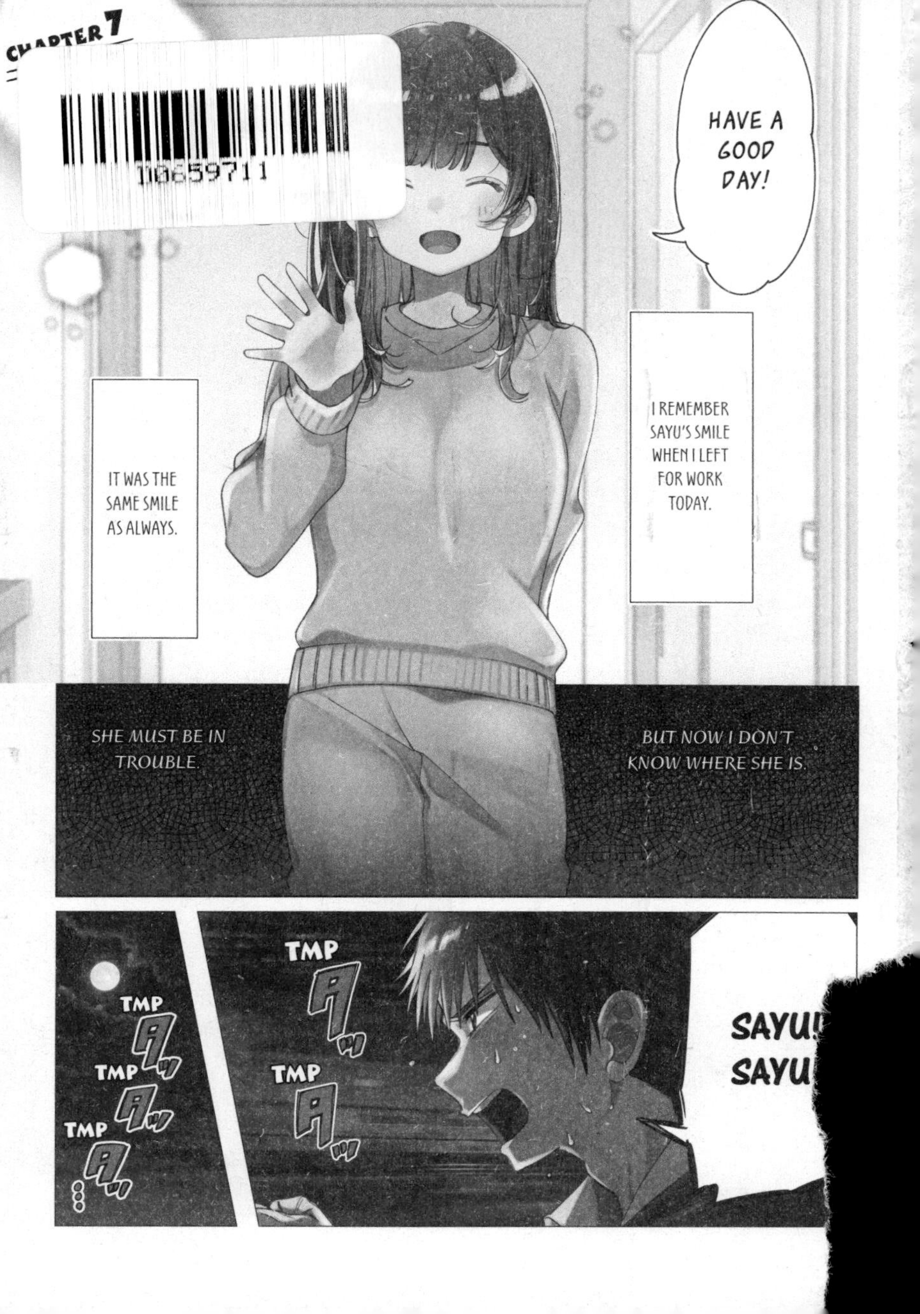
CHAPTER 7
HAVE A GOOD DAY!
I REMEMBER SAYU'S SMILE WHEN I LEFT FOR WORK TODAY.
IT WAS THE SAME SMILE AS ALWAYS.
BUT NOW I DON'T KNOW WHERE SHE IS.
SHE MUST BE IN TROUBLE.
SAYU! SAYU!
TMP
TMP
TMP
TMP
TMP

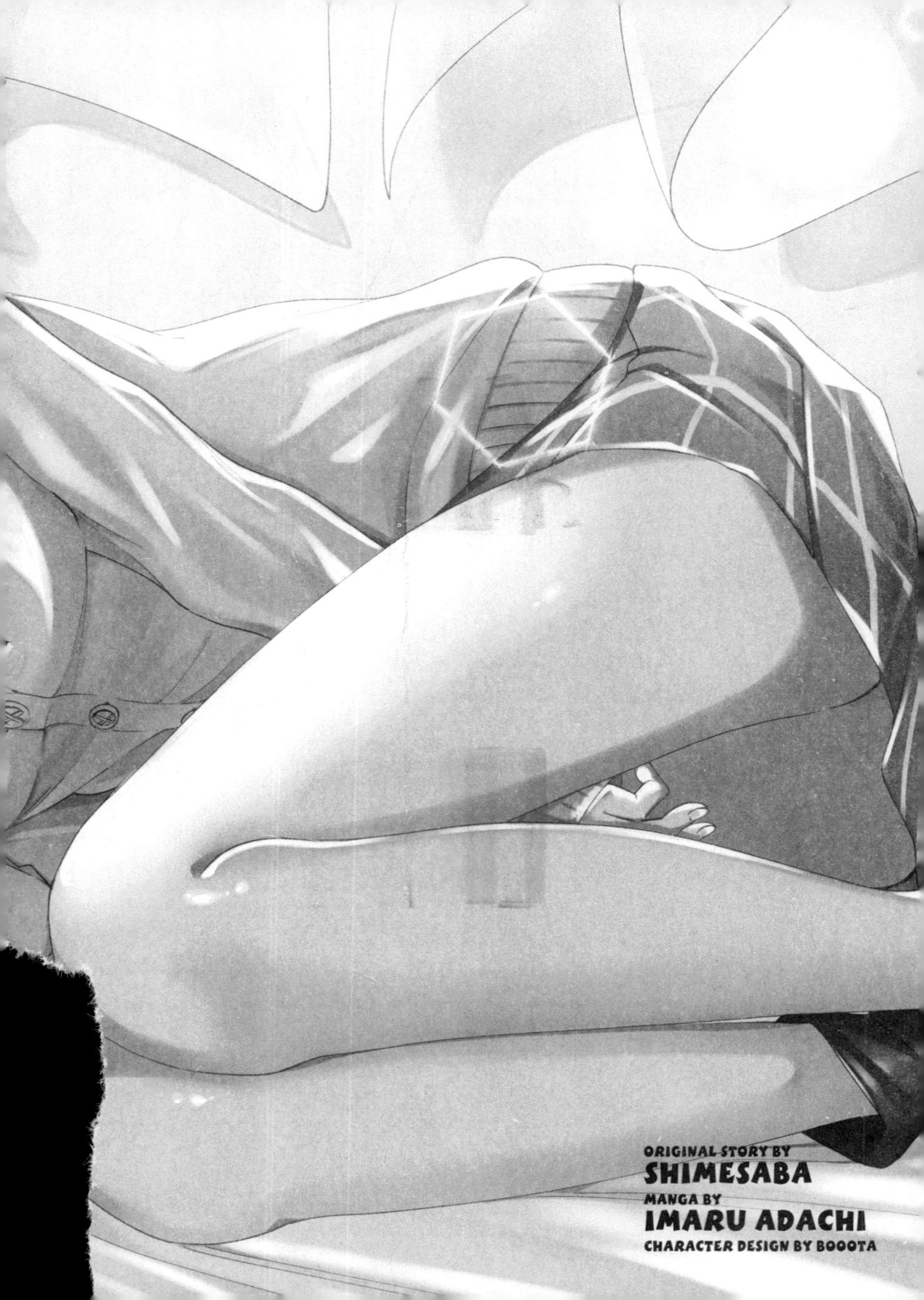

ORIGINAL STORY BY
SHIMESABA
MANGA BY
IMARU ADACHI
CHARACTER DESIGN BY BOOOTA

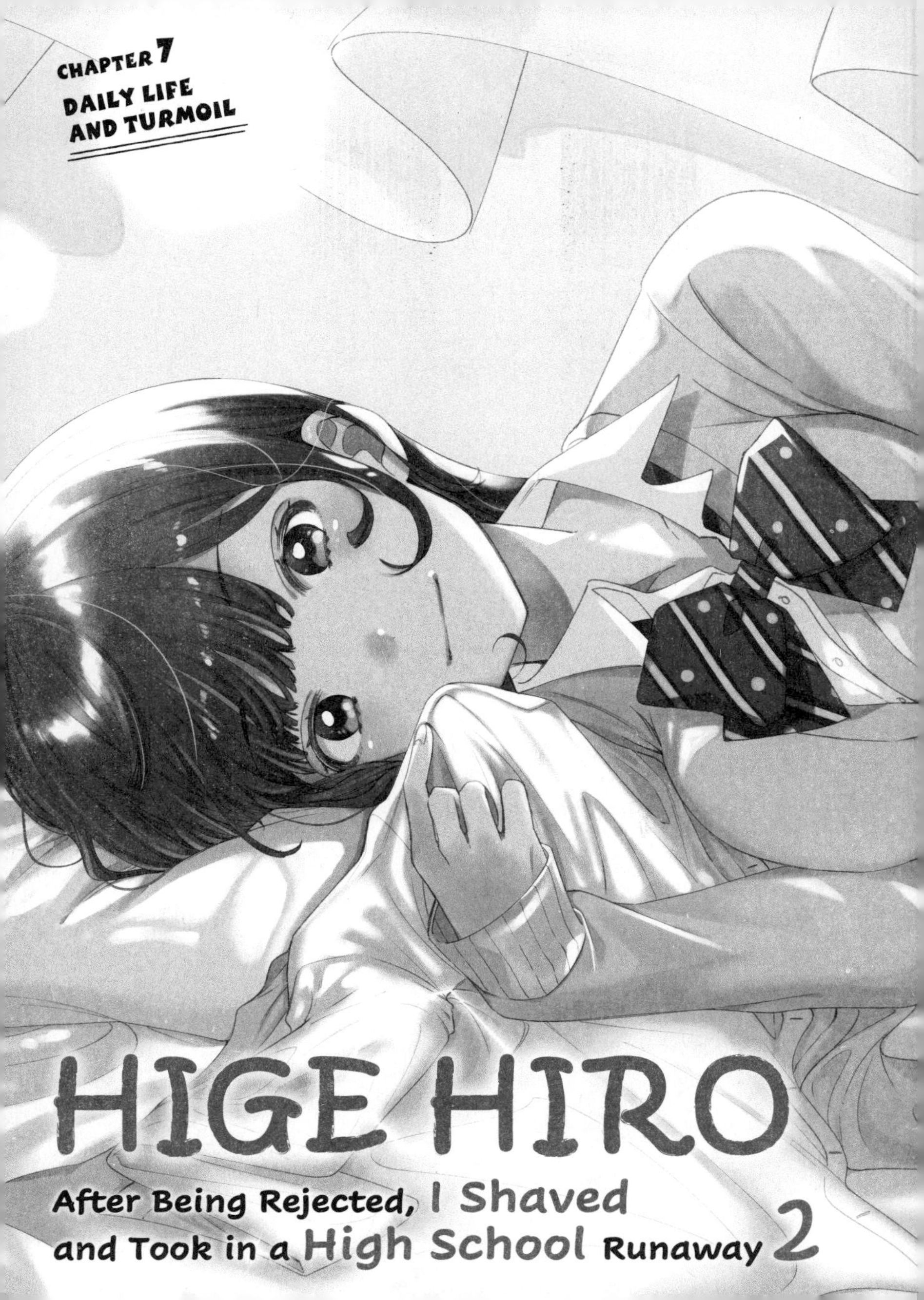
CHAPTER 7
DAILY LIFE AND TURMOIL
HIGE HIRO
After Being Rejected, I Shaved and Took in a High School Runaway 2

HIGEHIRO

**After Being Rejected,
I Shaved and Took
in a High School Runaway 2**

TABLE OF CONTENTS

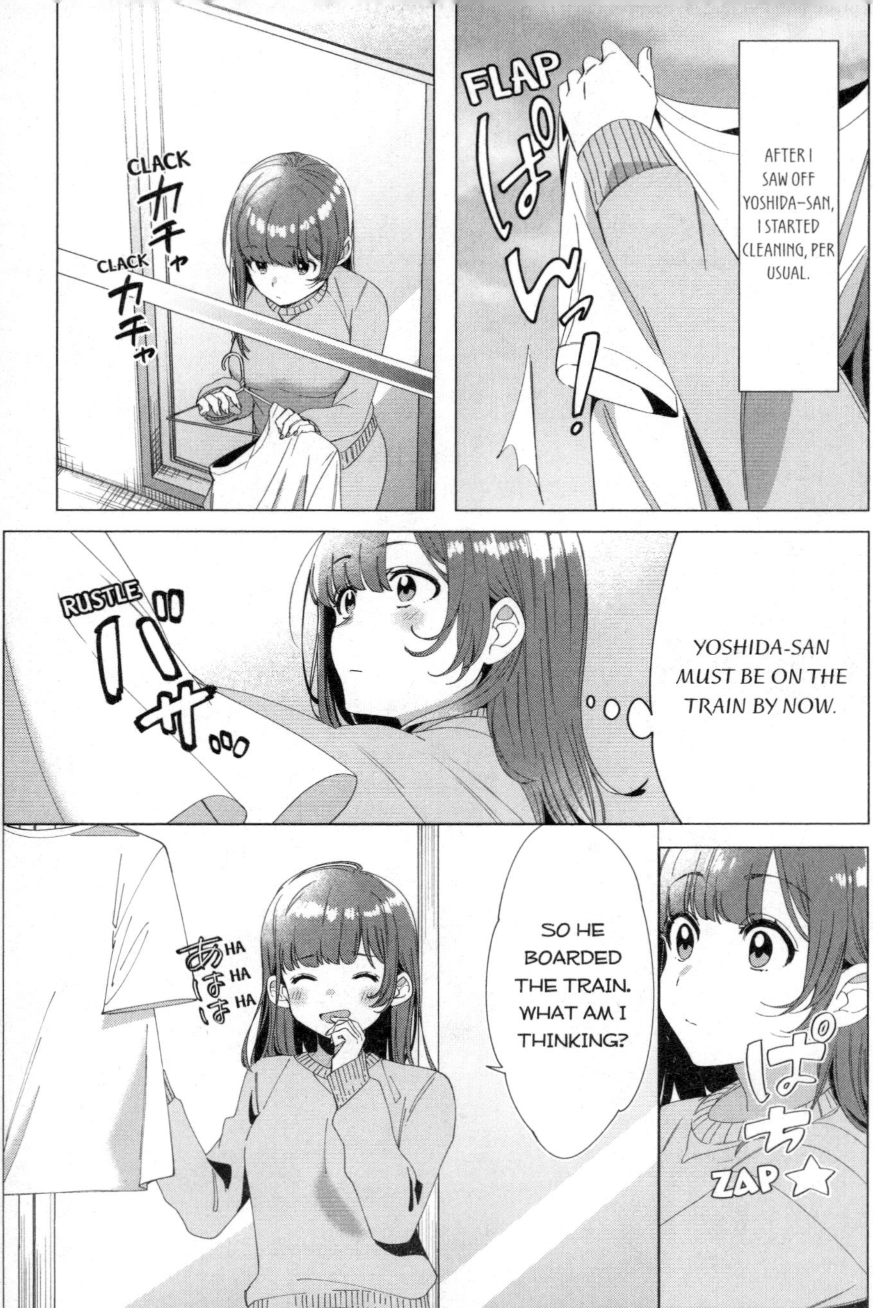

FLAP
ぱんっ!
AFTER I SAW OFF YOSHIDA-SAN, I STARTED CLEANING, PER USUAL.
CLACK
カチャ
CLACK
カチャ
RUSTLE
バサッ
YOSHIDA-SAN MUST BE ON THE TRAIN BY NOW.
ぱちっ
ZAP ☆
SO HE BOARDED THE TRAIN. WHAT AM I THINKING?
あははは
HA HA HA

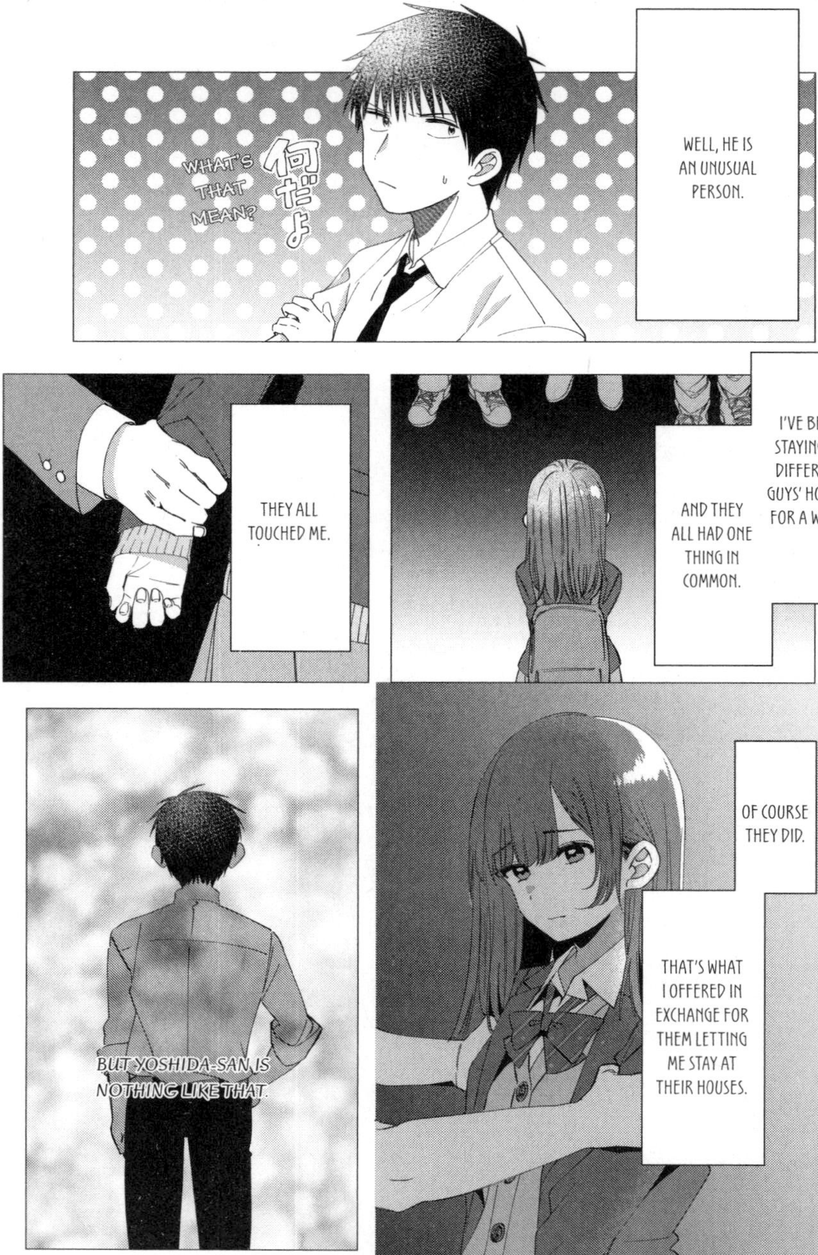
WELL, HE IS AN UNUSUAL PERSON.
何だよ
WHAT'S THAT MEAN?
I'VE BEEN STAYING AT DIFFERENT GUYS' HOUSES FOR A WHILE
AND THEY ALL HAD ONE THING IN COMMON.
THEY ALL TOUCHED ME.
OF COURSE THEY DID.
THAT'S WHAT I OFFERED IN EXCHANGE FOR THEM LETTING ME STAY AT THEIR HOUSES.
BUT YOSHIDA-SAN IS NOTHING LIKE THAT.

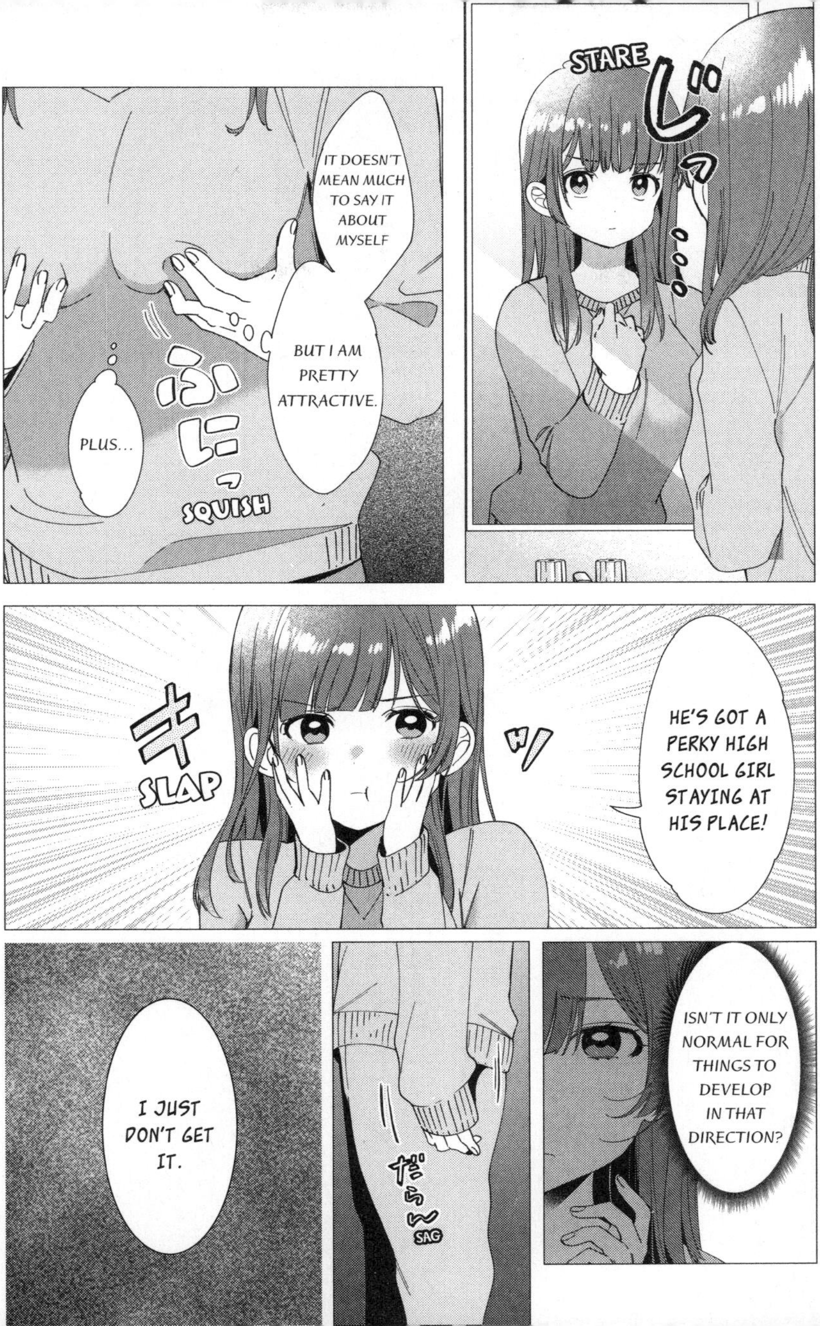
STARE
じっ
IT DOESN'T MEAN MUCH TO SAY IT ABOUT MYSELF
BUT I AM PRETTY ATTRACTIVE.
PLUS…
ふにっ
SQUISH
HE'S GOT A PERKY HIGH SCHOOL GIRL STAYING AT HIS PLACE!
SLAP
ISN'T IT ONLY NORMAL FOR THINGS TO DEVELOP IN THAT DIRECTION?
だらん
SAG
I JUST DON'T GET IT.

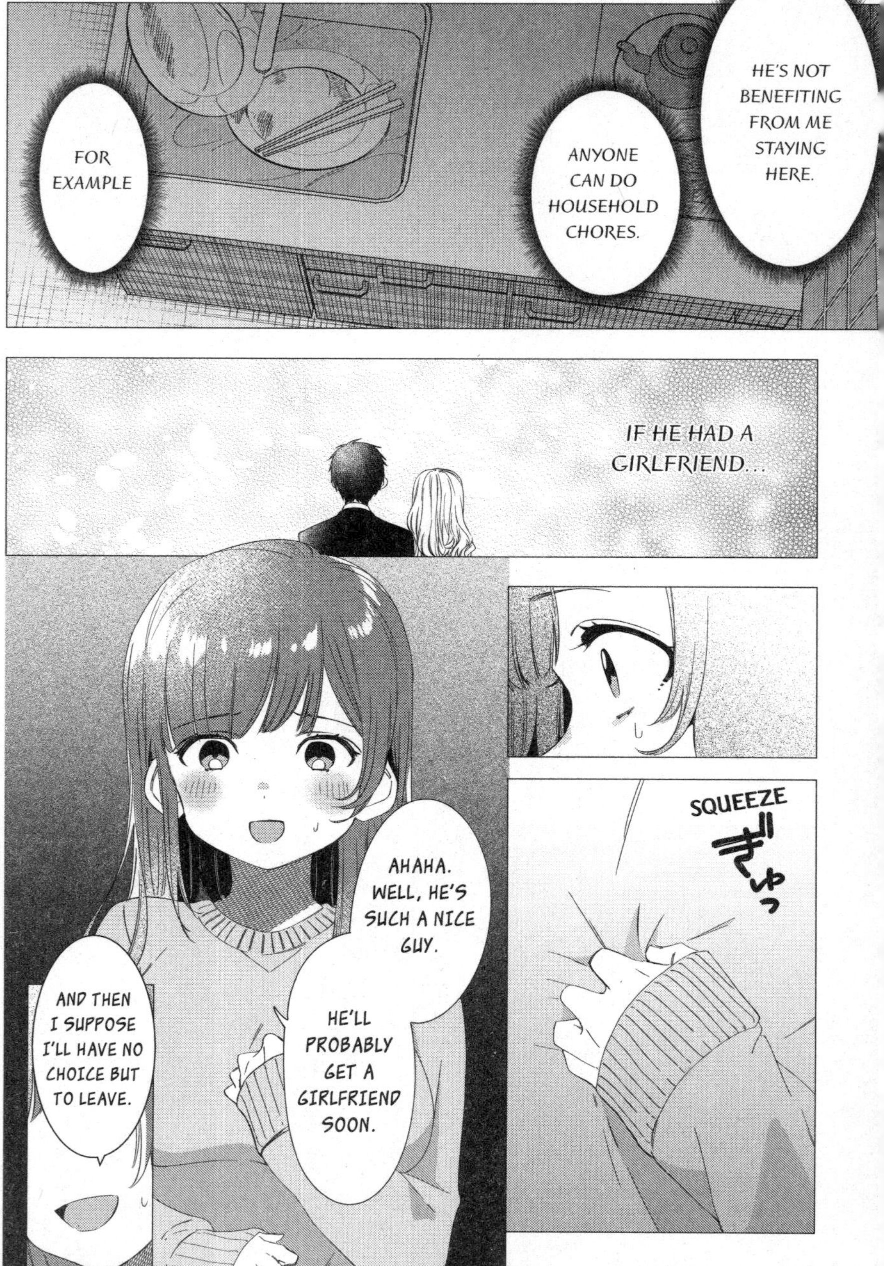
HE'S NOT BENEFITING FROM ME STAYING HERE.
ANYONE CAN DO HOUSEHOLD CHORES.
FOR EXAMPLE
IF HE HAD A GIRLFRIEND...
SQUEEZE
ぎゅっ
AHAHA. WELL, HE'S SUCH A NICE GUY.
HE'LL PROBABLY GET A GIRLFRIEND SOON.
AND THEN I SUPPOSE I'LL HAVE NO CHOICE BUT TO LEAVE.

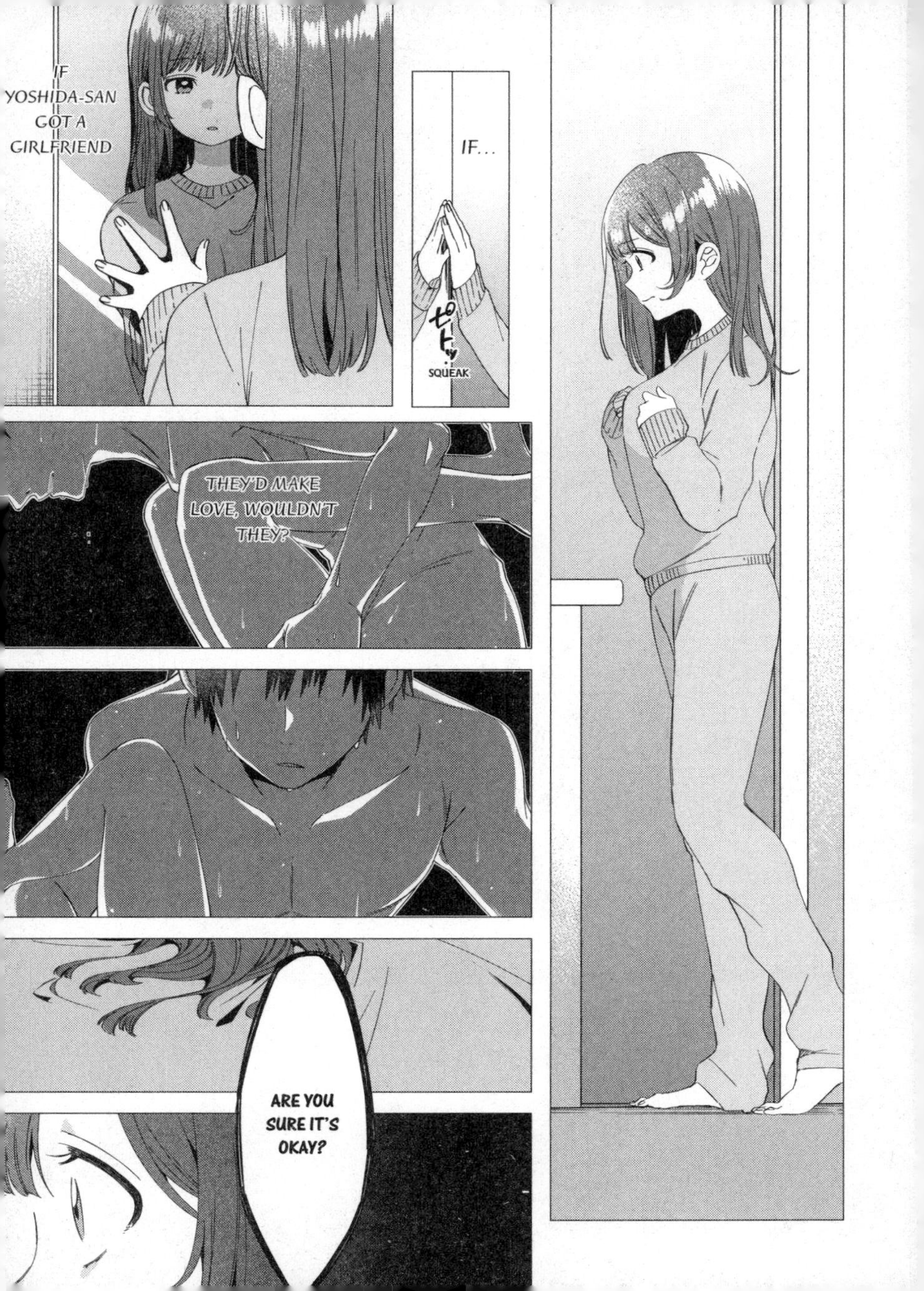
IF...
SQUEAK
IF YOSHIDA-SAN GOT A GIRLFRIEND
THEY'D MAKE LOVE, WOULDN'T THEY?
ARE YOU SURE IT'S OKAY?

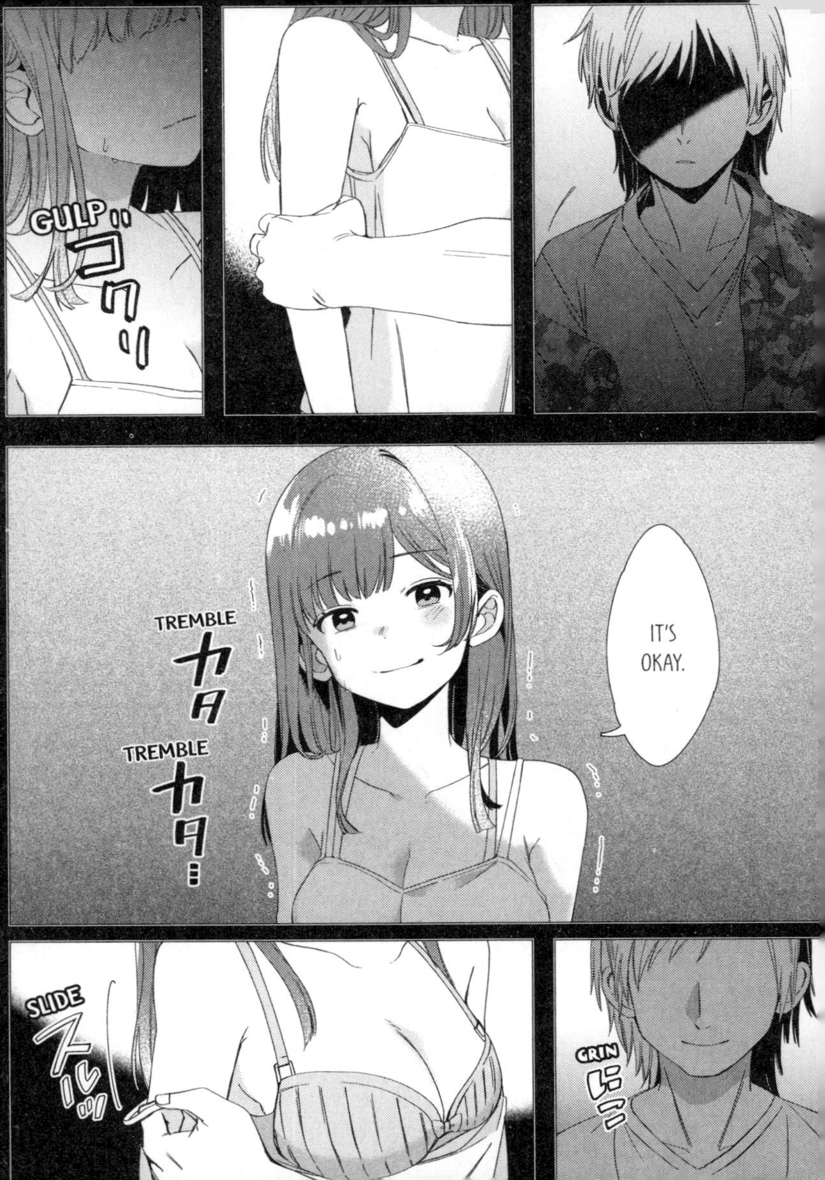
GULP
ゴクッ
IT'S OKAY.
TREMBLE
カタ
TREMBLE
カタ…
GRIN
にこ
SLIDE
スルッ

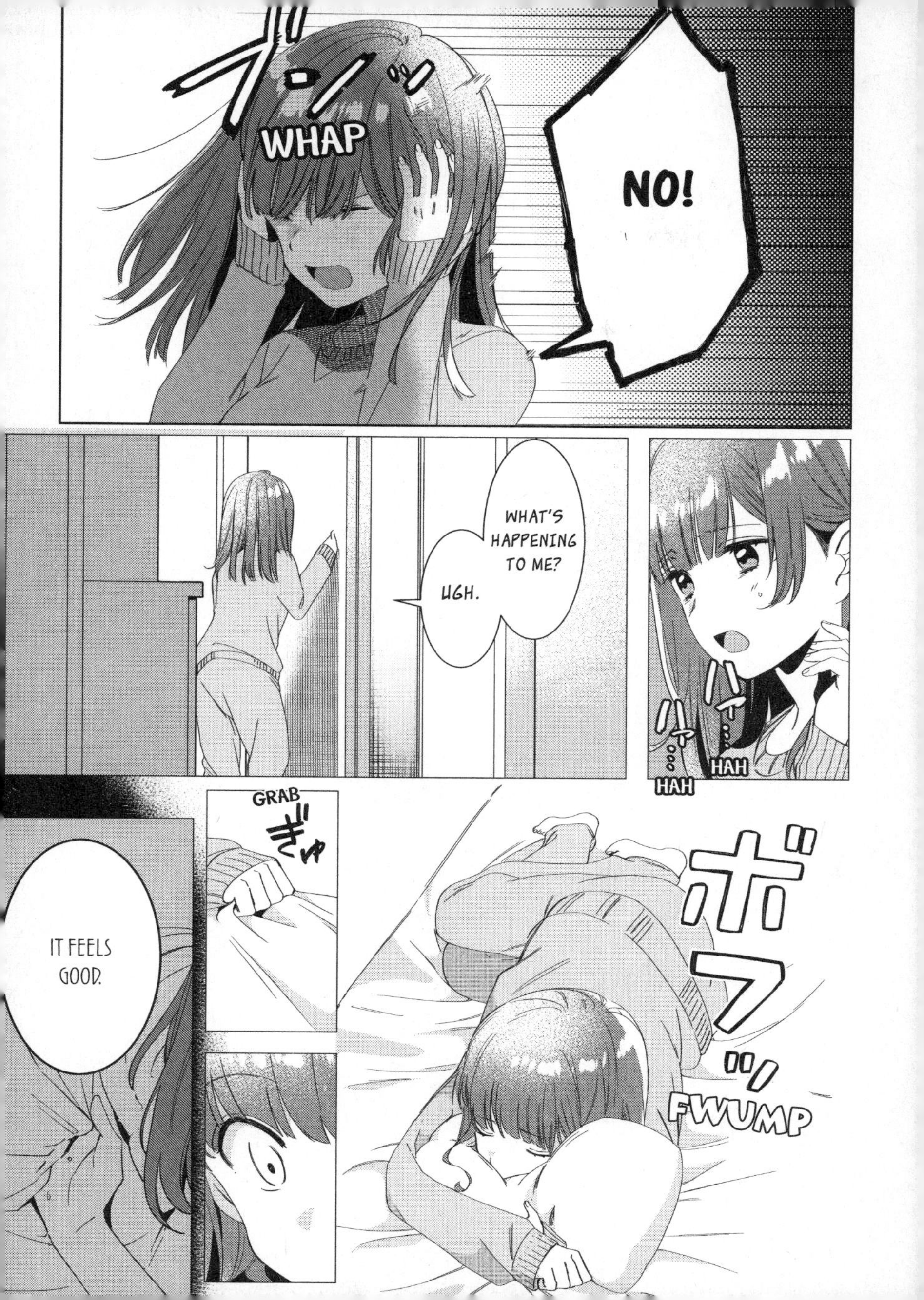
NO!
WHAP
HAH
HAH
WHAT'S HAPPENING TO ME?
UGH.
ボフッ
FWUMP
GRAB
ぎゅ
IT FEELS GOOD.

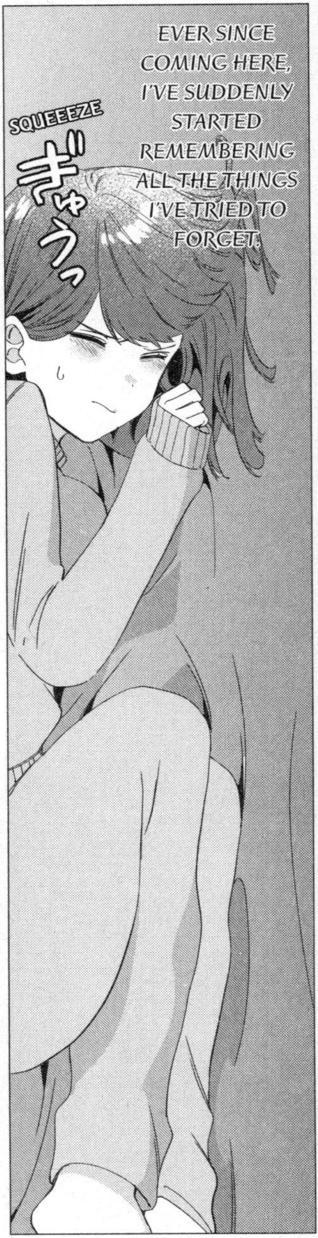
EVER SINCE COMING HERE, I'VE SUDDENLY STARTED REMEMBERING ALL THE THINGS I'VE TRIED TO FORGET.
SQUEEEZE
ぎゅうっ
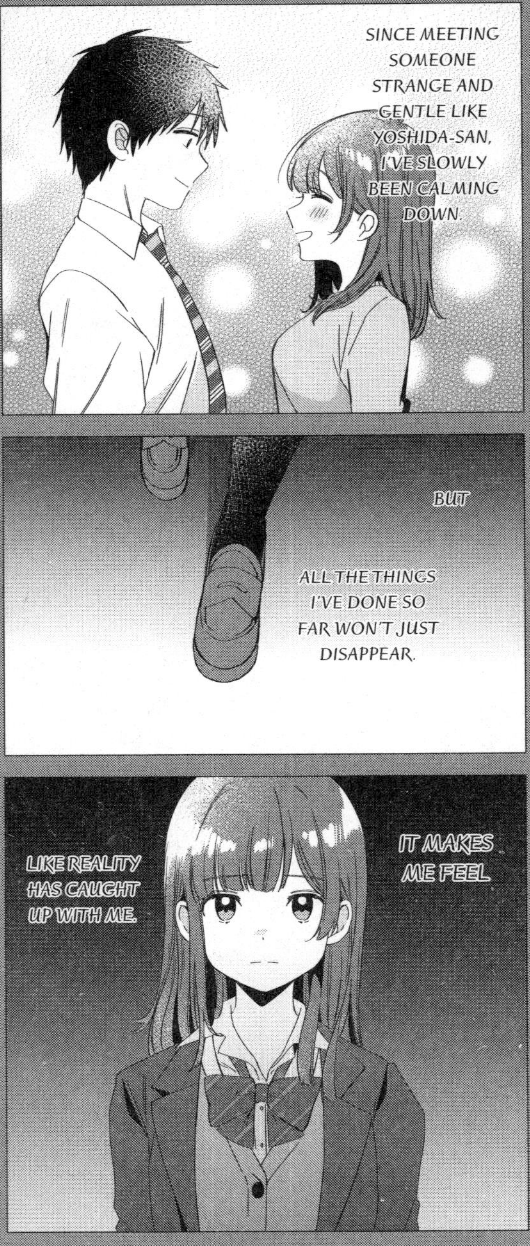
SINCE MEETING SOMEONE STRANGE AND GENTLE LIKE YOSHIDA-SAN, I'VE SLOWLY BEEN CALMING DOWN.
BUT
ALL THE THINGS I'VE DONE SO FAR WON'T JUST DISAPPEAR.
IT MAKES ME FEEL
LIKE REALITY HAS CAUGHT UP WITH ME.

YOSHIDA-
SAN.

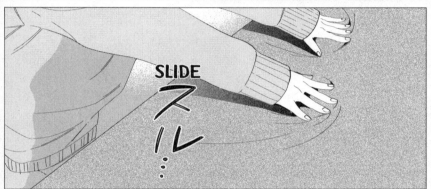

SLIDE
スル
…

…YOSHIDA-
SAN.

DRIP

SQUEEZE

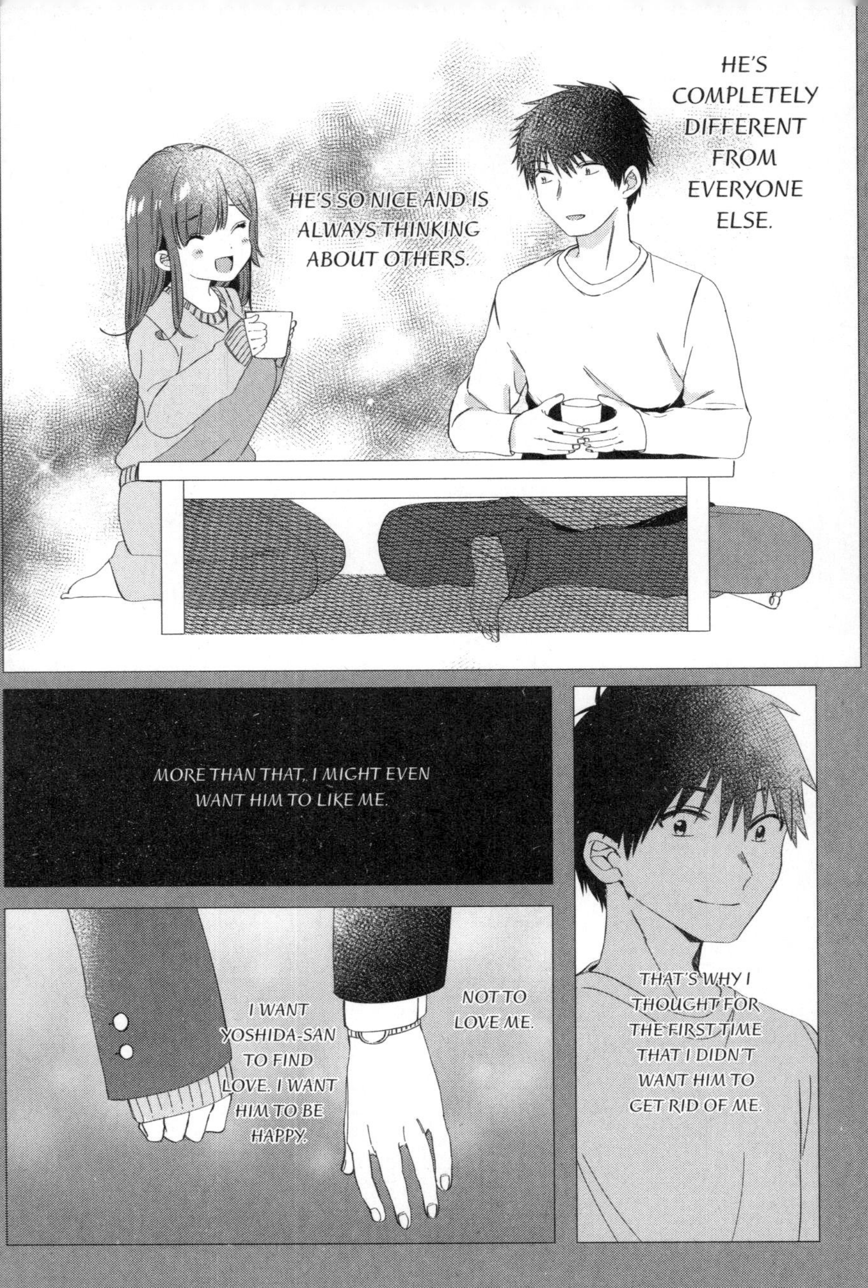
HE'S COMPLETELY DIFFERENT FROM EVERYONE ELSE.
HE'S SO NICE AND IS ALWAYS THINKING ABOUT OTHERS.
THAT'S WHY I THOUGHT FOR THE FIRST TIME THAT I DIDN'T WANT HIM TO GET RID OF ME.
MORE THAN THAT, I MIGHT EVEN WANT HIM TO LIKE ME.
NOT TO LOVE ME.
I WANT YOSHIDA-SAN TO FIND LOVE. I WANT HIM TO BE HAPPY.

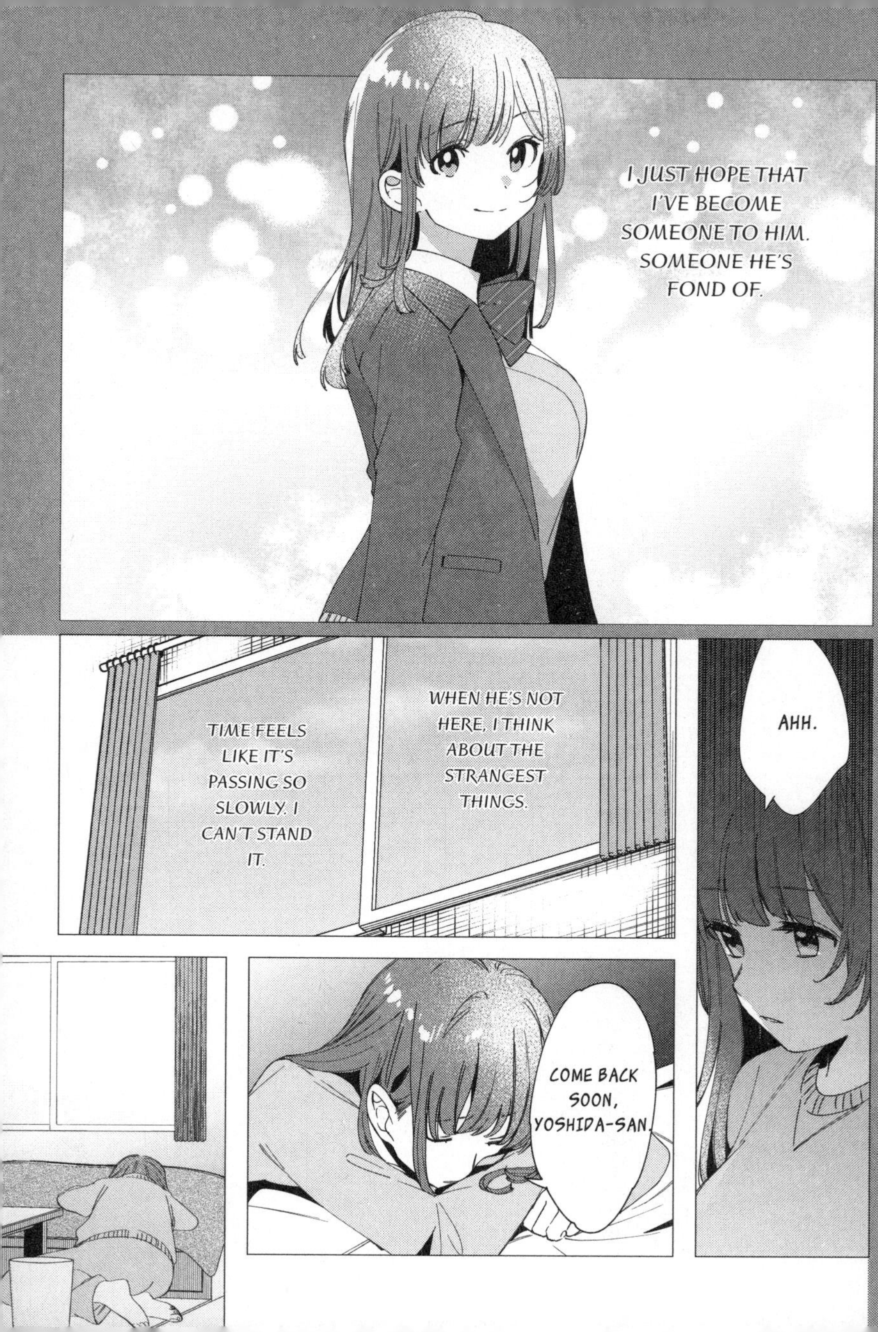
I JUST HOPE THAT I'VE BECOME SOMEONE TO HIM. SOMEONE HE'S FOND OF.
AHH.
WHEN HE'S NOT HERE, I THINK ABOUT THE STRANGEST THINGS.
TIME FEELS LIKE IT'S PASSING SO SLOWLY. I CAN'T STAND IT.
COME BACK SOON, YOSHIDA-SAN.

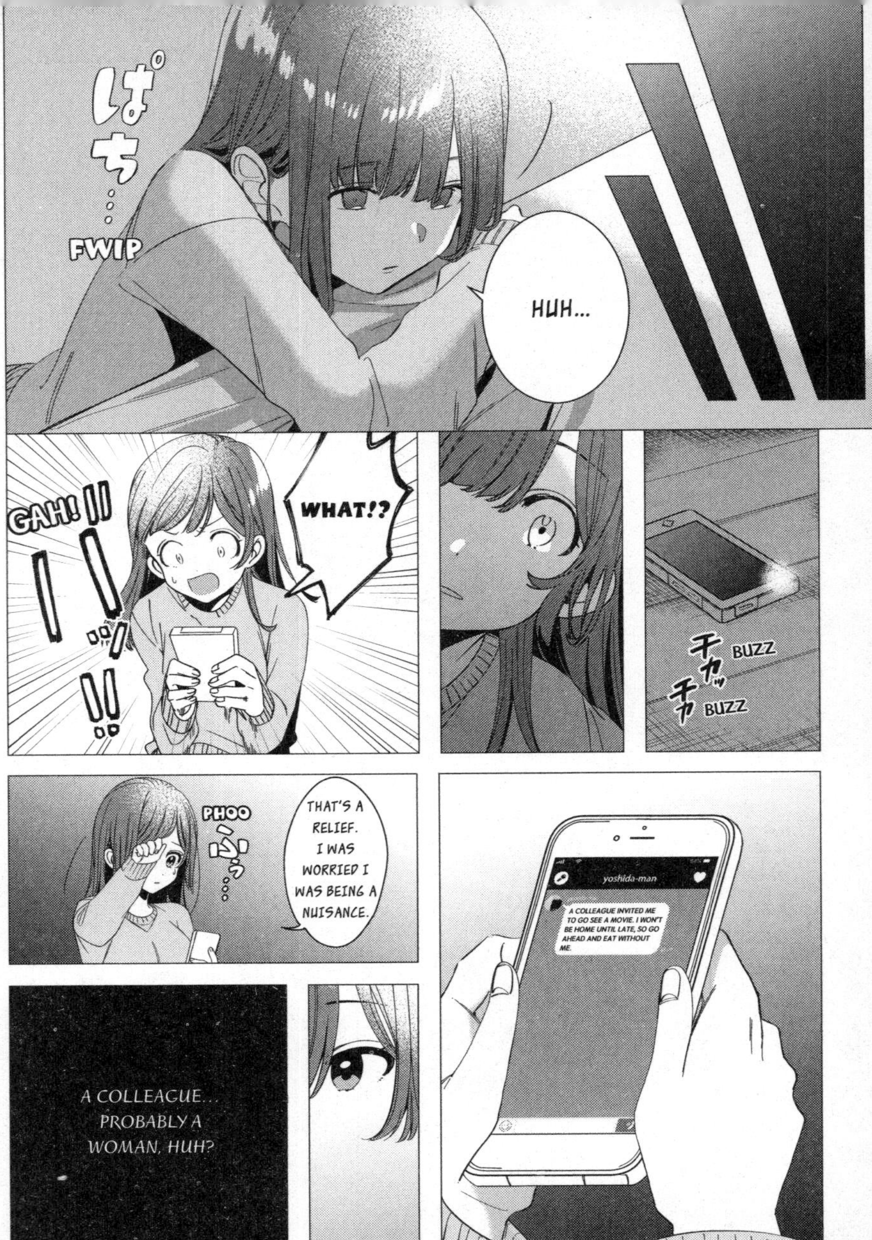
ぱち…
FWIP
HUH...
チカッ
BUZZ
チカ
BUZZ
WHAT!?
GAH!
yoshida-man
A COLLEAGUE INVITED ME TO GO SEE A MOVIE. I WON'T BE HOME UNTIL LATE, SO GO AHEAD AND EAT WITHOUT ME.
THAT'S A RELIEF. I WAS WORRIED I WAS BEING A NUISANCE.
PHOO
ふぅ…
A COLLEAGUE... PROBABLY A WOMAN, HUH?

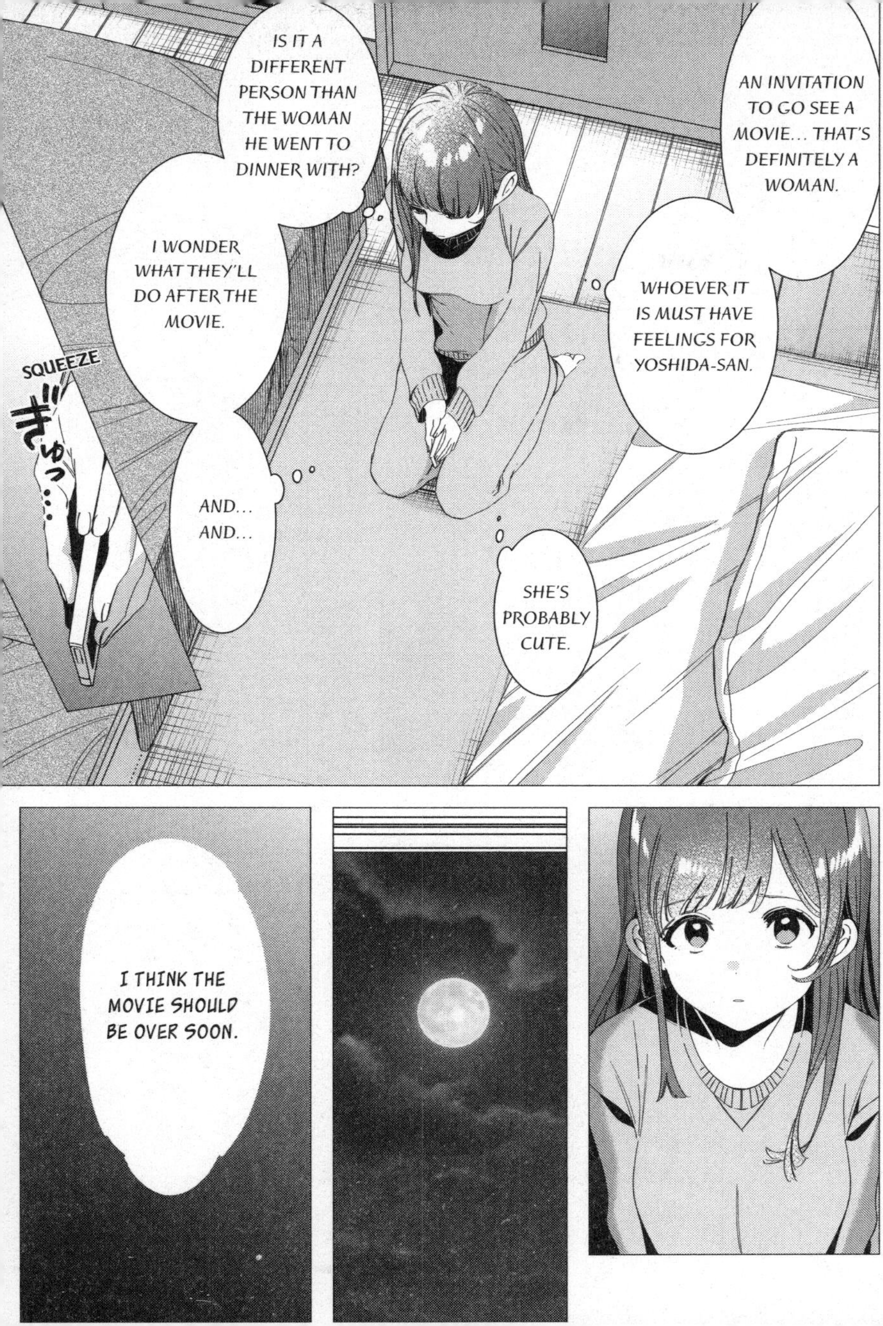
AN INVITATION TO GO SEE A MOVIE… THAT'S DEFINITELY A WOMAN.
WHOEVER IT IS MUST HAVE FEELINGS FOR YOSHIDA-SAN.
IS IT A DIFFERENT PERSON THAN THE WOMAN HE WENT TO DINNER WITH?
I WONDER WHAT THEY'LL DO AFTER THE MOVIE.
SQUEEZE
ぎゅっ…
AND… AND…
SHE'S PROBABLY CUTE.
I THINK THE MOVIE SHOULD BE OVER SOON.

I KNEW IT WAS STUPID.

CLICK
ガチャ

NORMALLY I WOULDN'T END UP THINKING LIKE THIS.

CLACK
ヤヤ

TAP
トン

TAP
トン

WIPE
グイッ

STEP
コツ

STEP
コツ

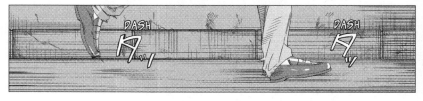

DASH
タッ

DASH
タッ

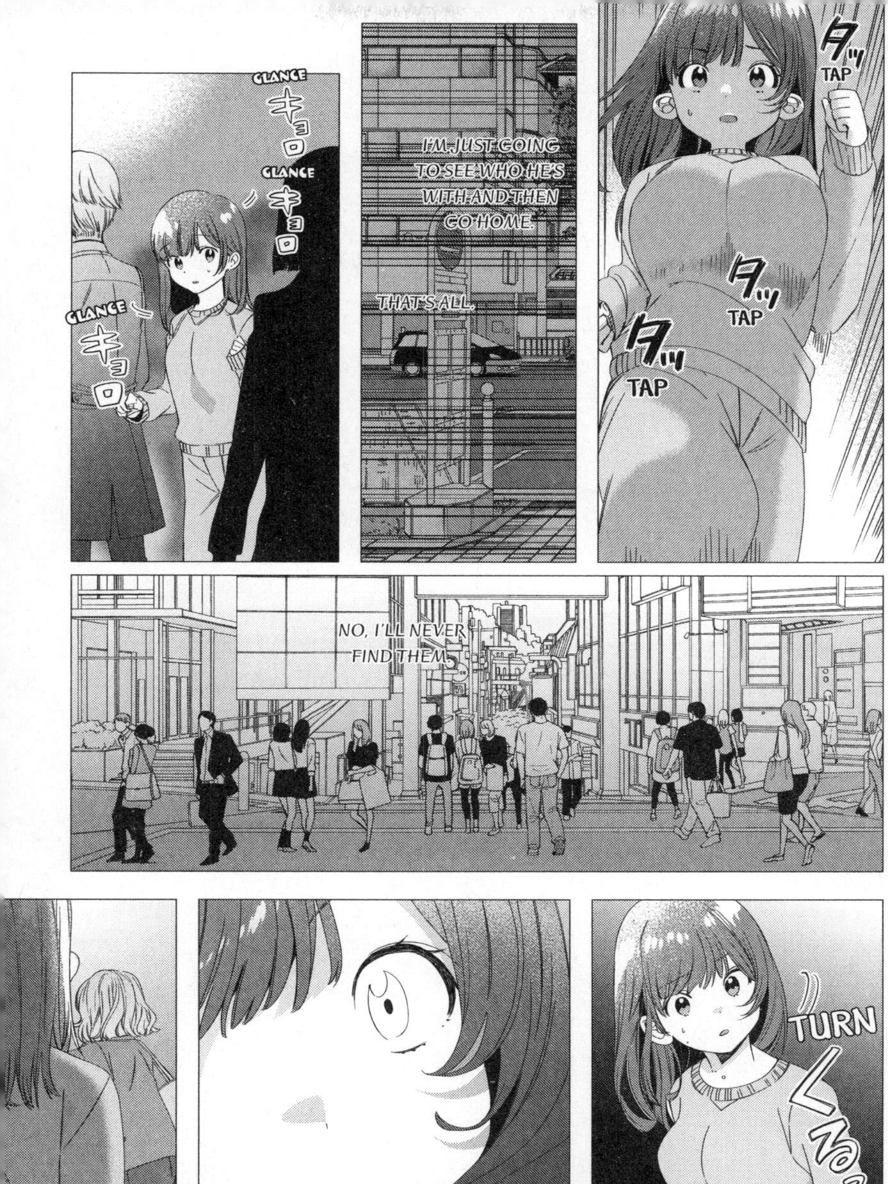
タッ
TAP
タッ
TAP
タッ
TAP
I'M JUST GOING TO SEE WHO HE'S WITH AND THEN GO HOME.
THAT'S ALL.
GLANCE
キョロ
GLANCE
キョロ
GLANCE
キョロ
NO, I'LL NEVER FIND THEM.
TURN
くるっ

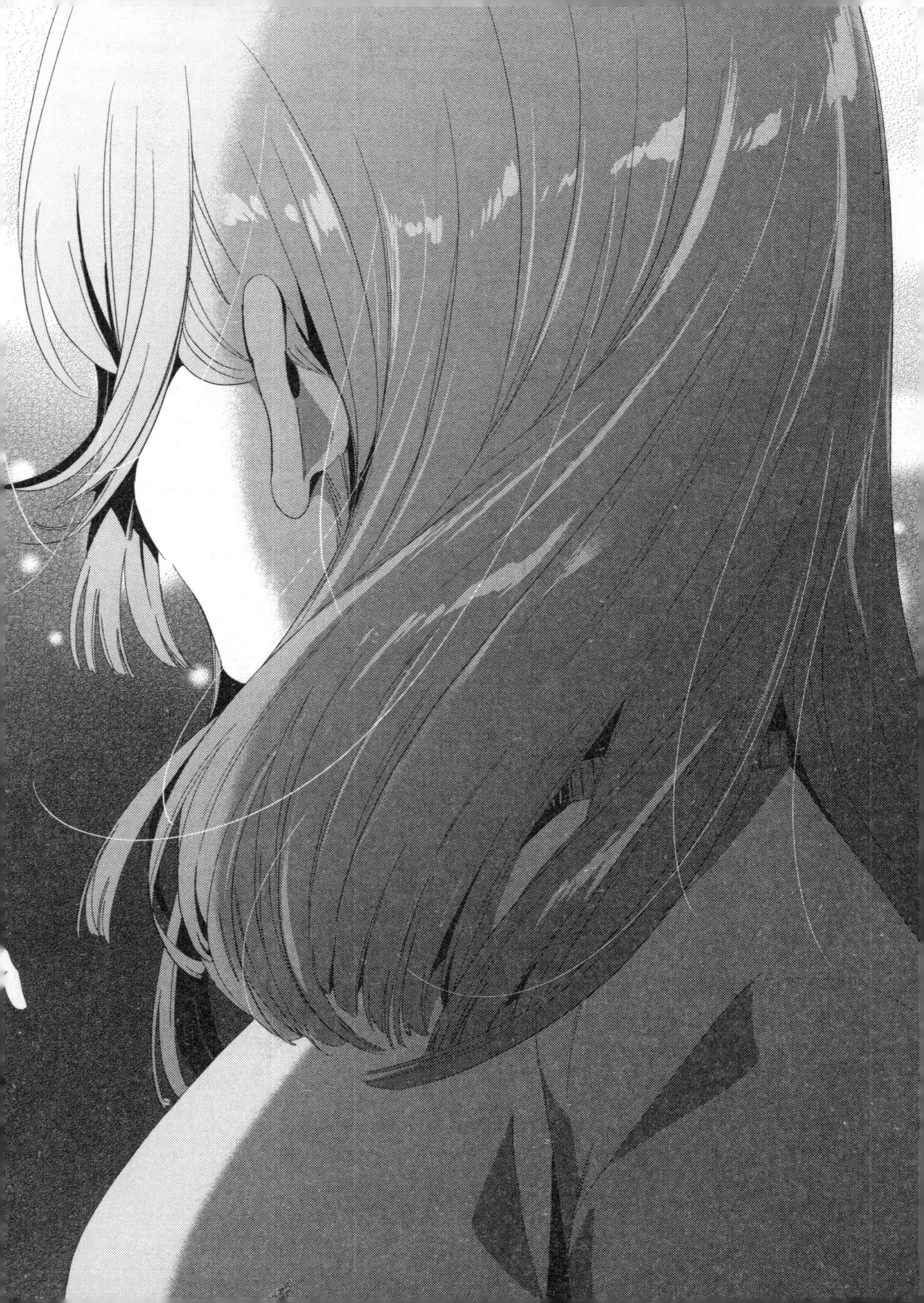

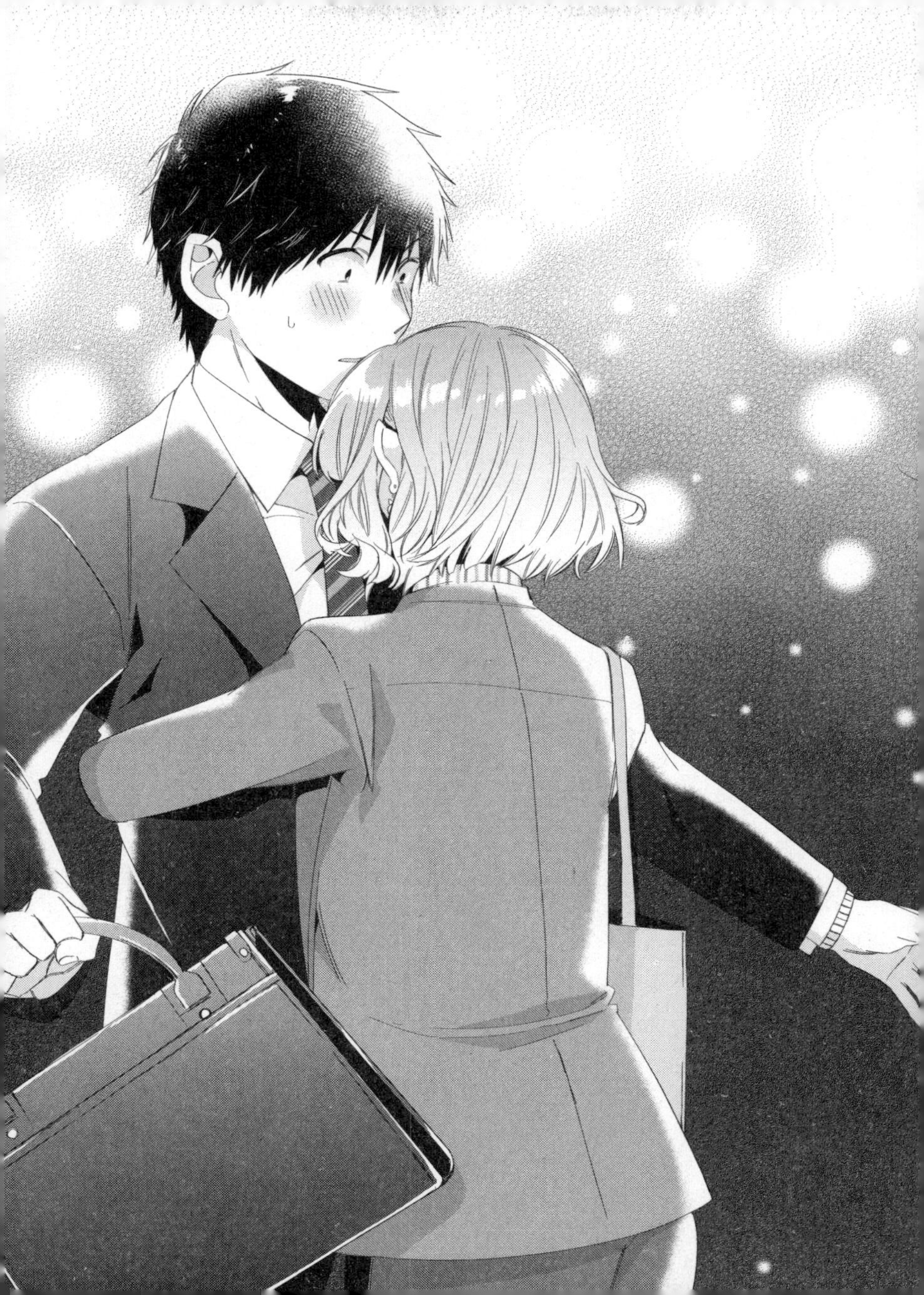

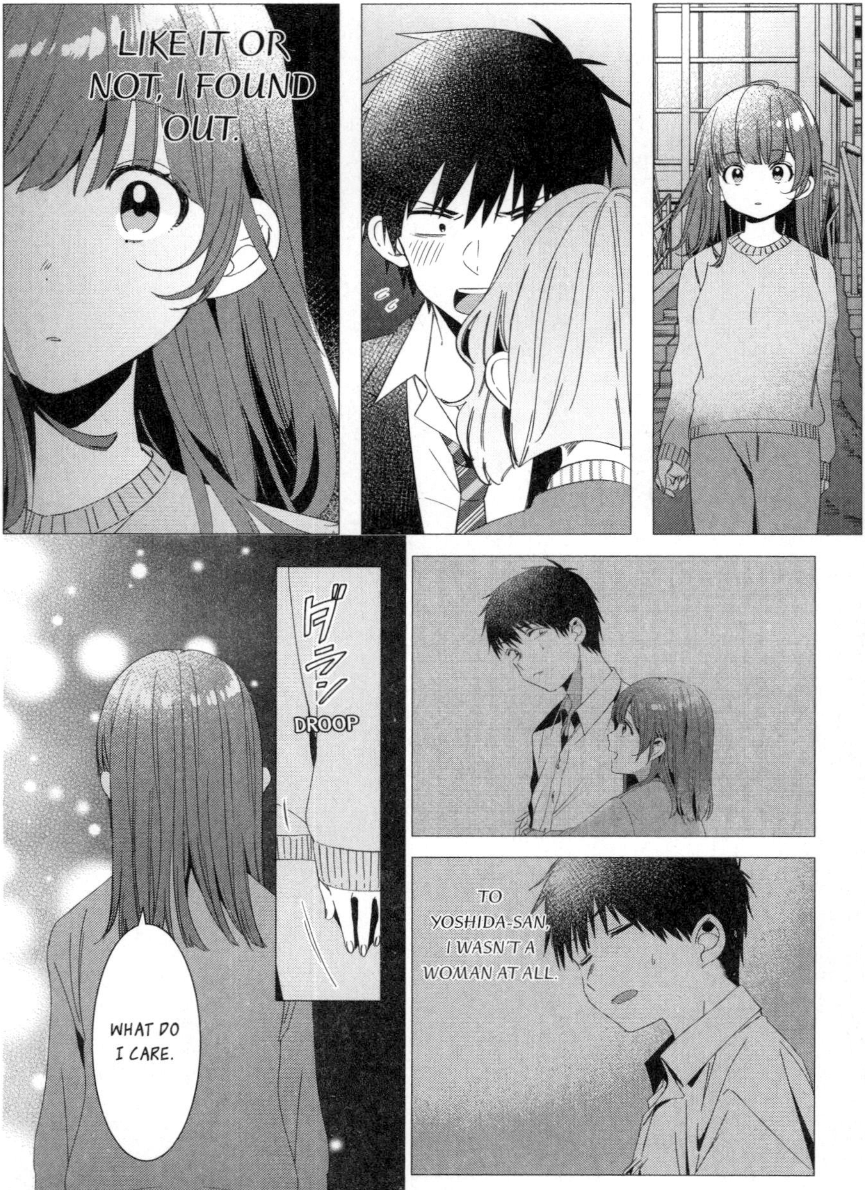
LIKE IT OR NOT, I FOUND OUT.
TO YOSHIDA-SAN, I WASN'T A WOMAN AT ALL.
ダラン
DROOP
WHAT DO I CARE.

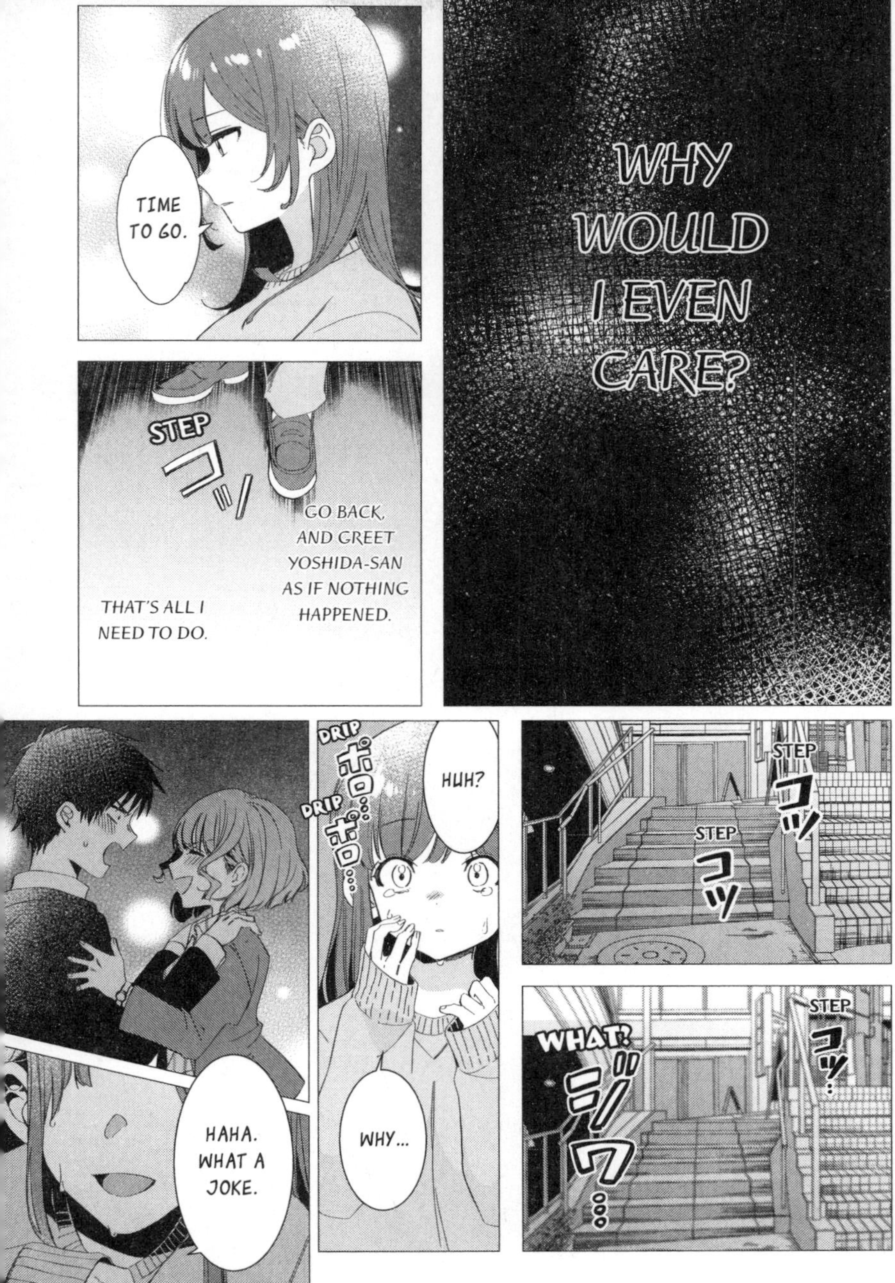

WHY WOULD I EVEN CARE?
TIME TO GO.
STEP
コッ
GO BACK, AND GREET YOSHIDA-SAN AS IF NOTHING HAPPENED.
THAT'S ALL I NEED TO DO.
STEP
コッ
STEP
コッ
STEP
コッ…
WHAT!?
ジワ…
DRIP
ポロ…
DRIP
ポロ…
HUH?
WHY…
HAHA. WHAT A JOKE.

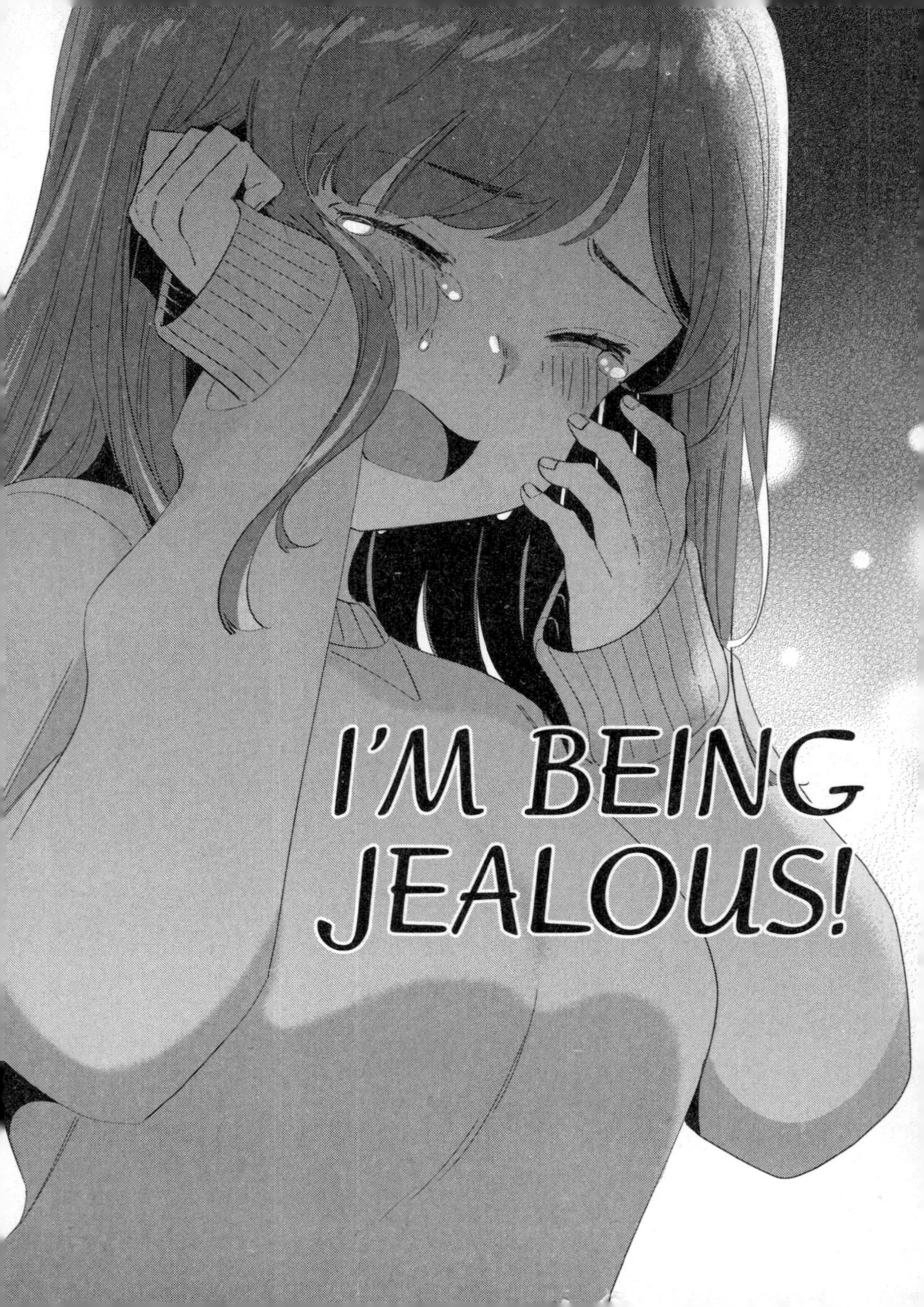
I'M BEING JEALOUS!

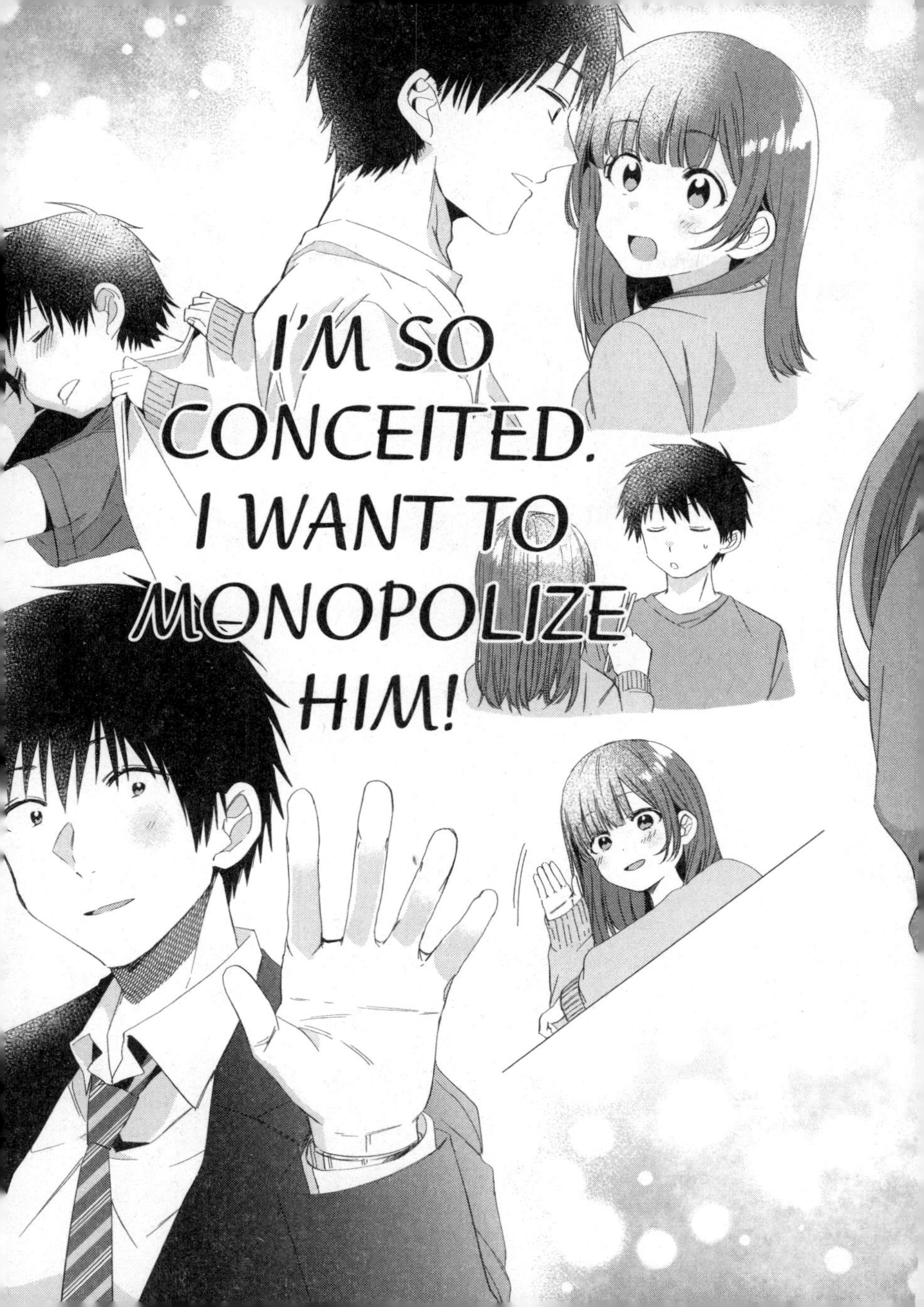
I'M SO CONCEITED. I WANT TO MONOPOLIZE HIM!

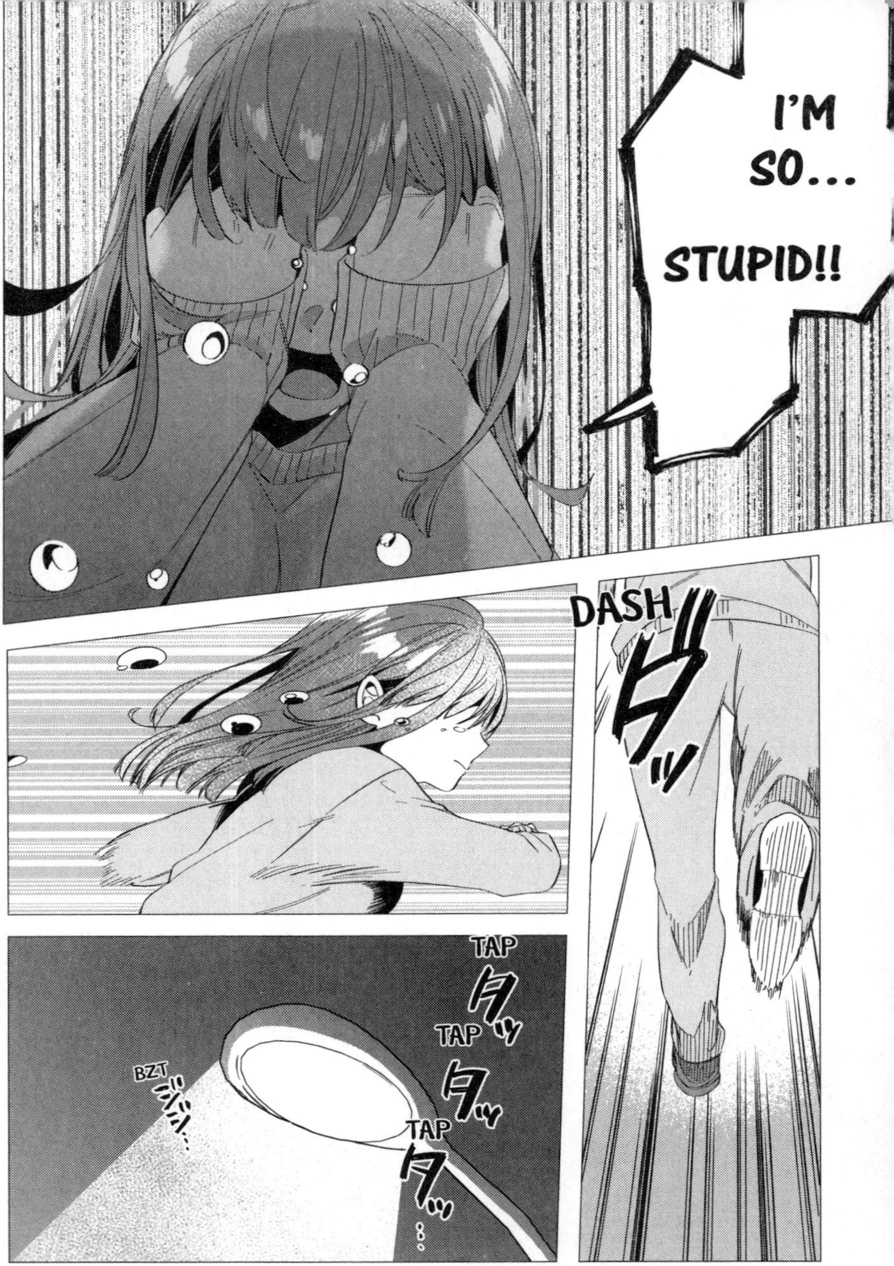
I'M SO... STUPID!!
DASH
TAP
TAP
TAP
BZT

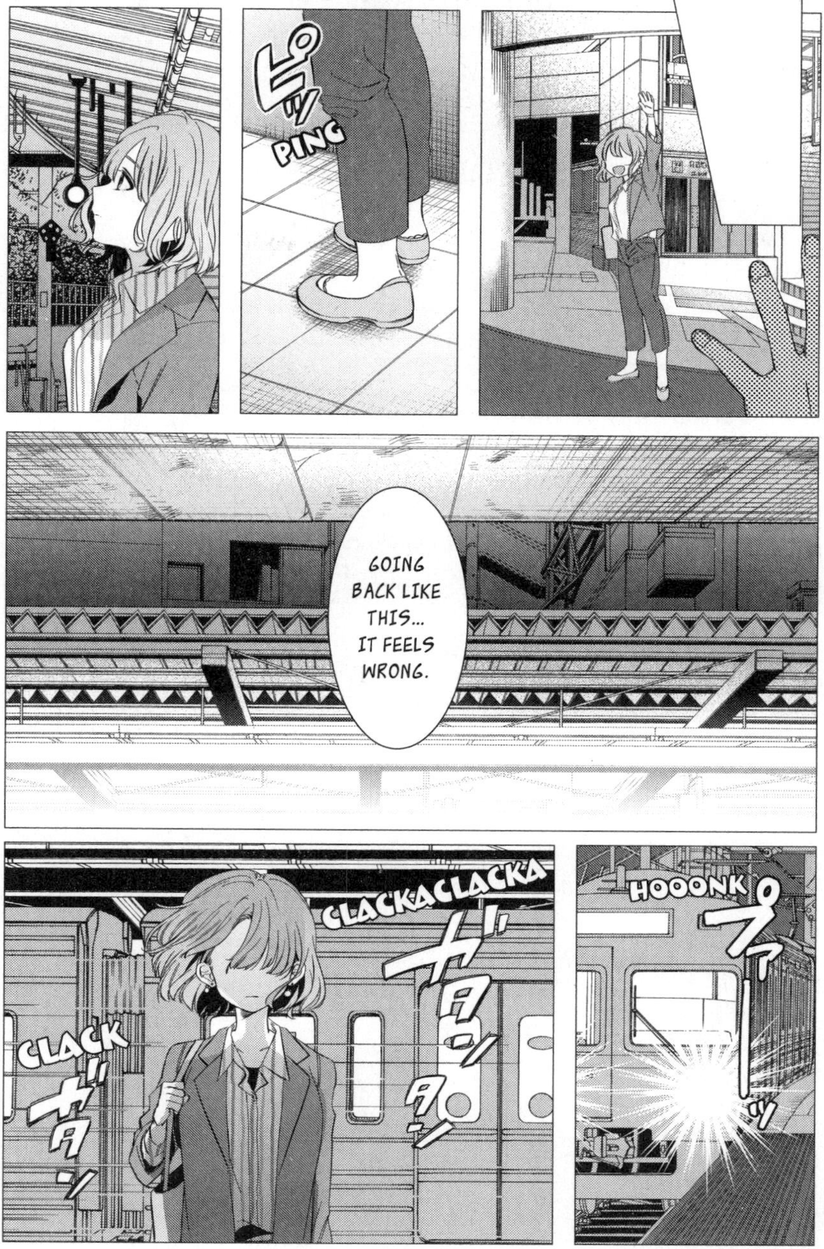
PING
GOING BACK LIKE THIS... IT FEELS WRONG.
HOOONK
CLACKACLACKA
CLACK

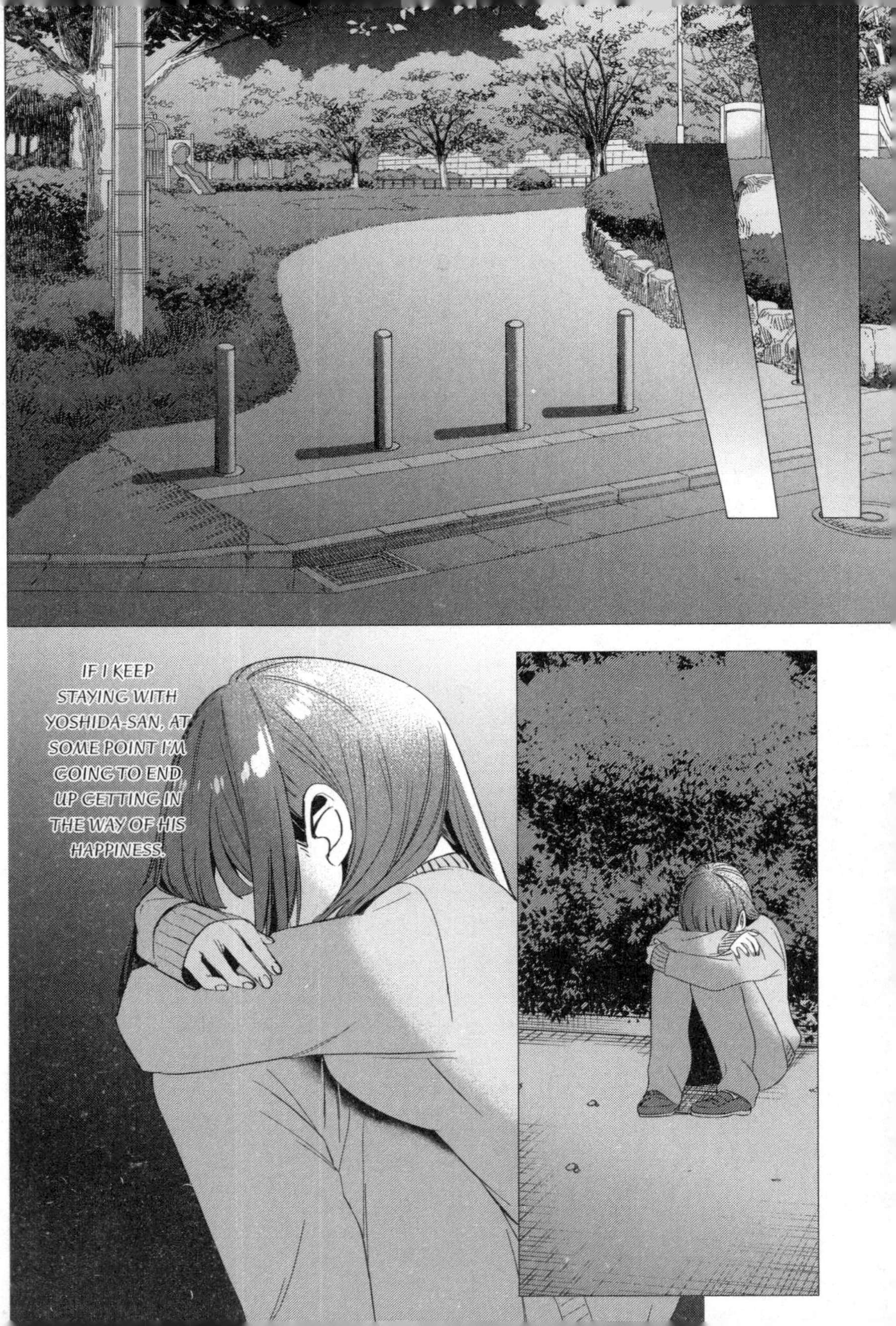
IF I KEEP STAYING WITH YOSHIDA-SAN, AT SOME POINT I'M GOING TO END UP GETTING IN THE WAY OF HIS HAPPINESS.

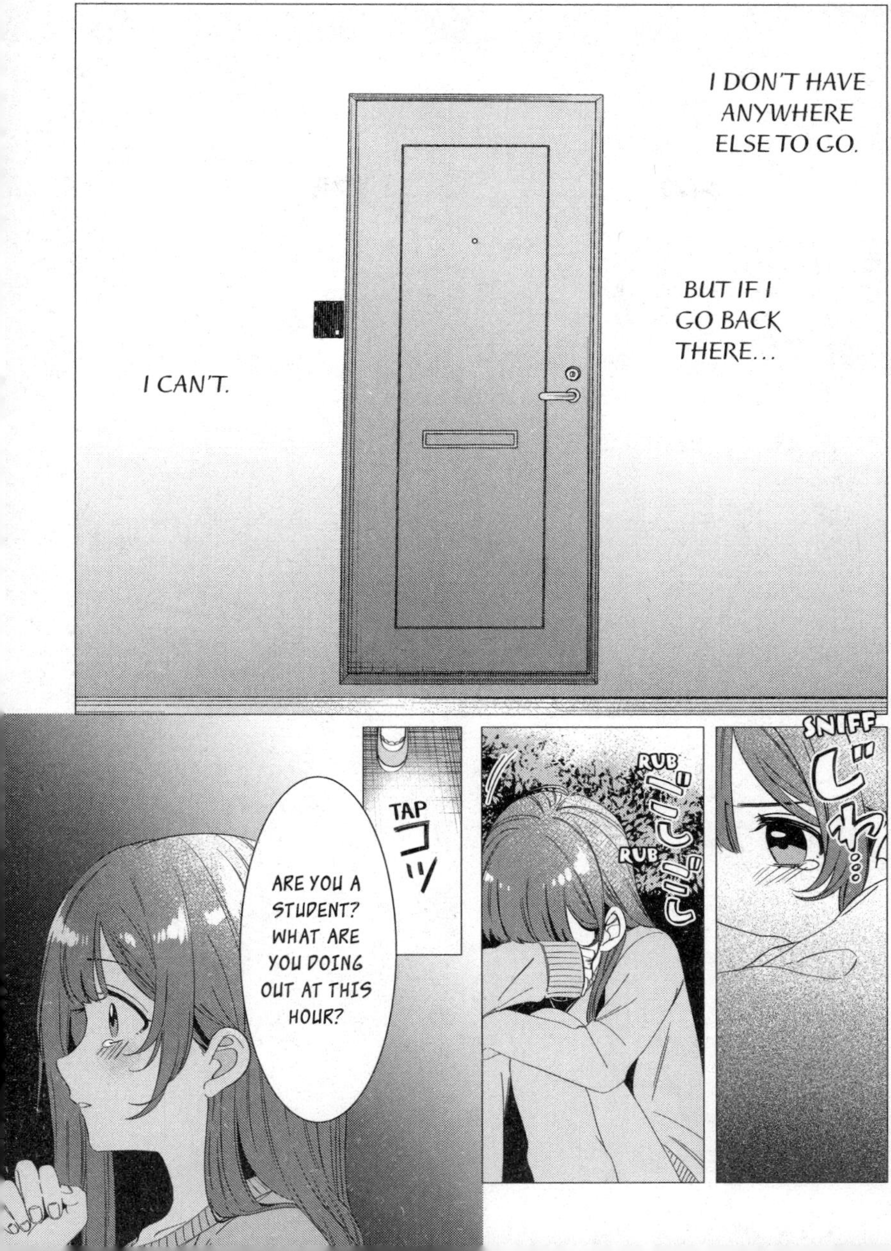
I DON'T HAVE ANYWHERE ELSE TO GO.
BUT IF I GO BACK THERE...
I CAN'T.
SNIFF
じわ…
RUB
RUB
ごしごし
TAP
コツ
ARE YOU A STUDENT? WHAT ARE YOU DOING OUT AT THIS HOUR?

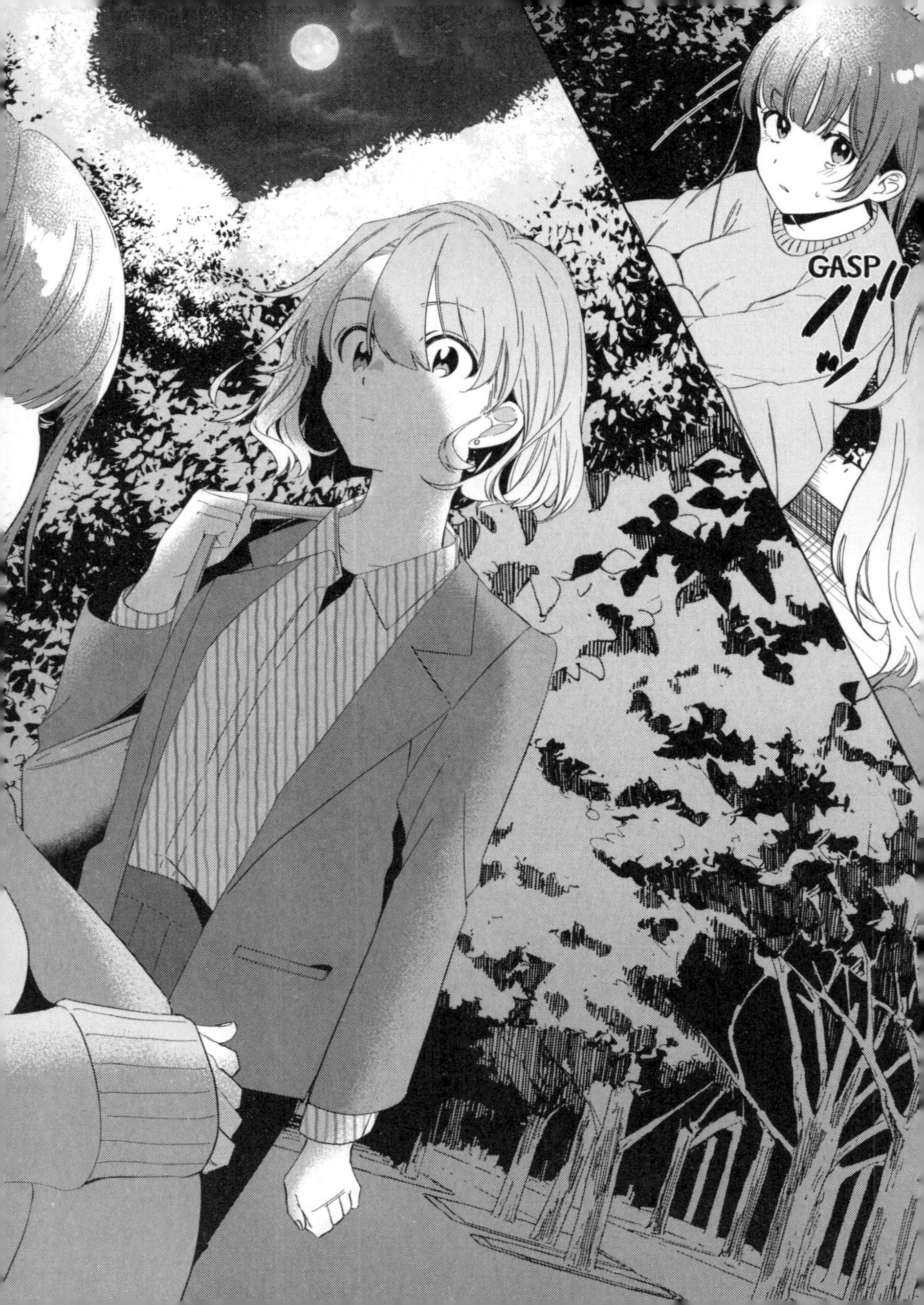
GASP

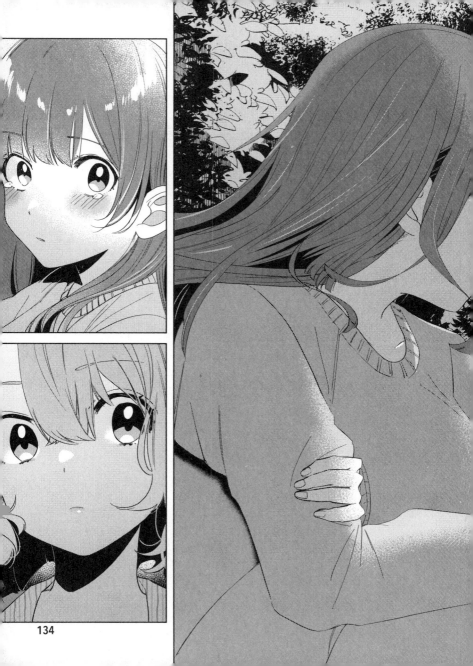

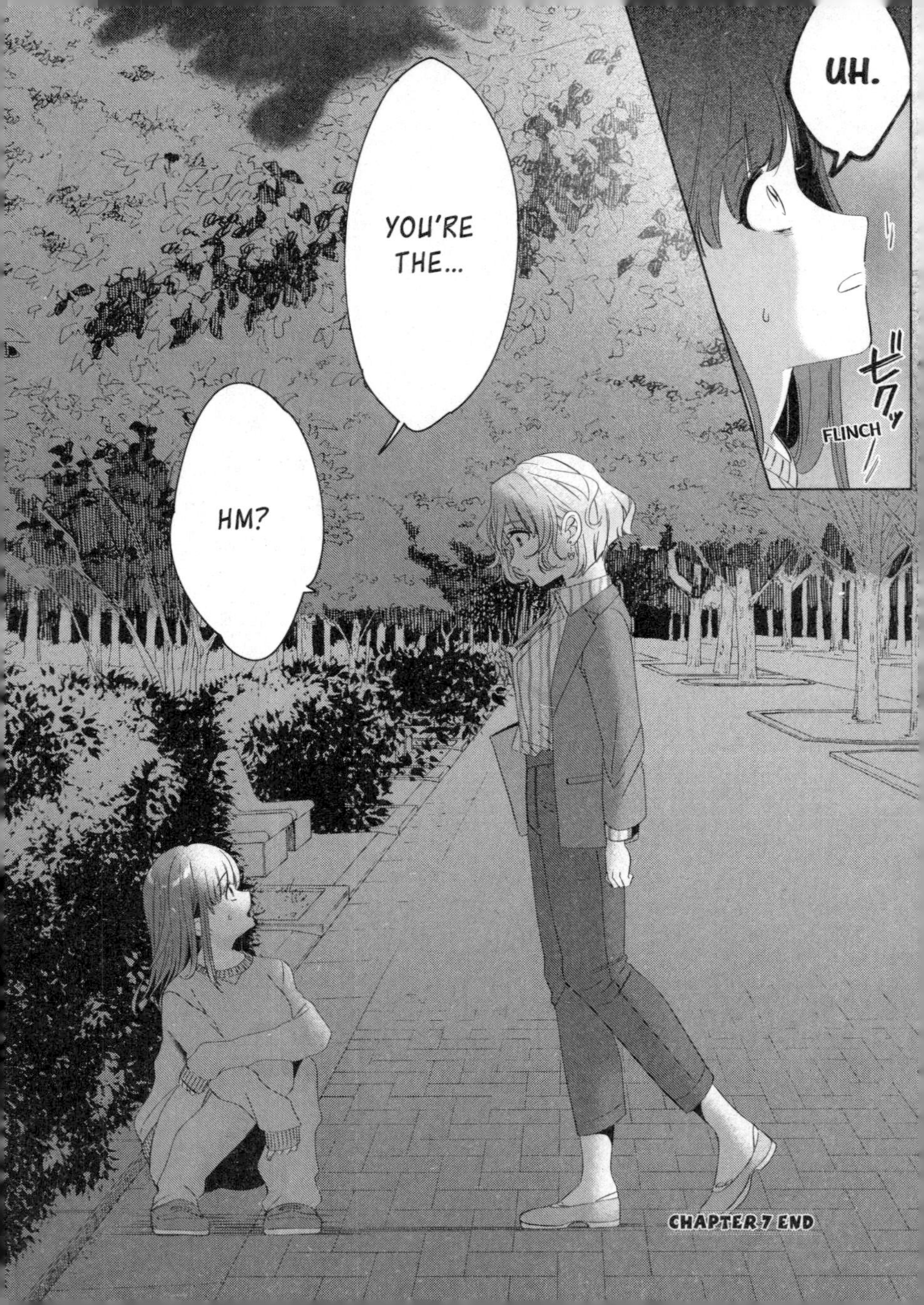
UH.
ビクッ
FLINCH
YOU'RE THE...
HM?
CHAPTER 7 END

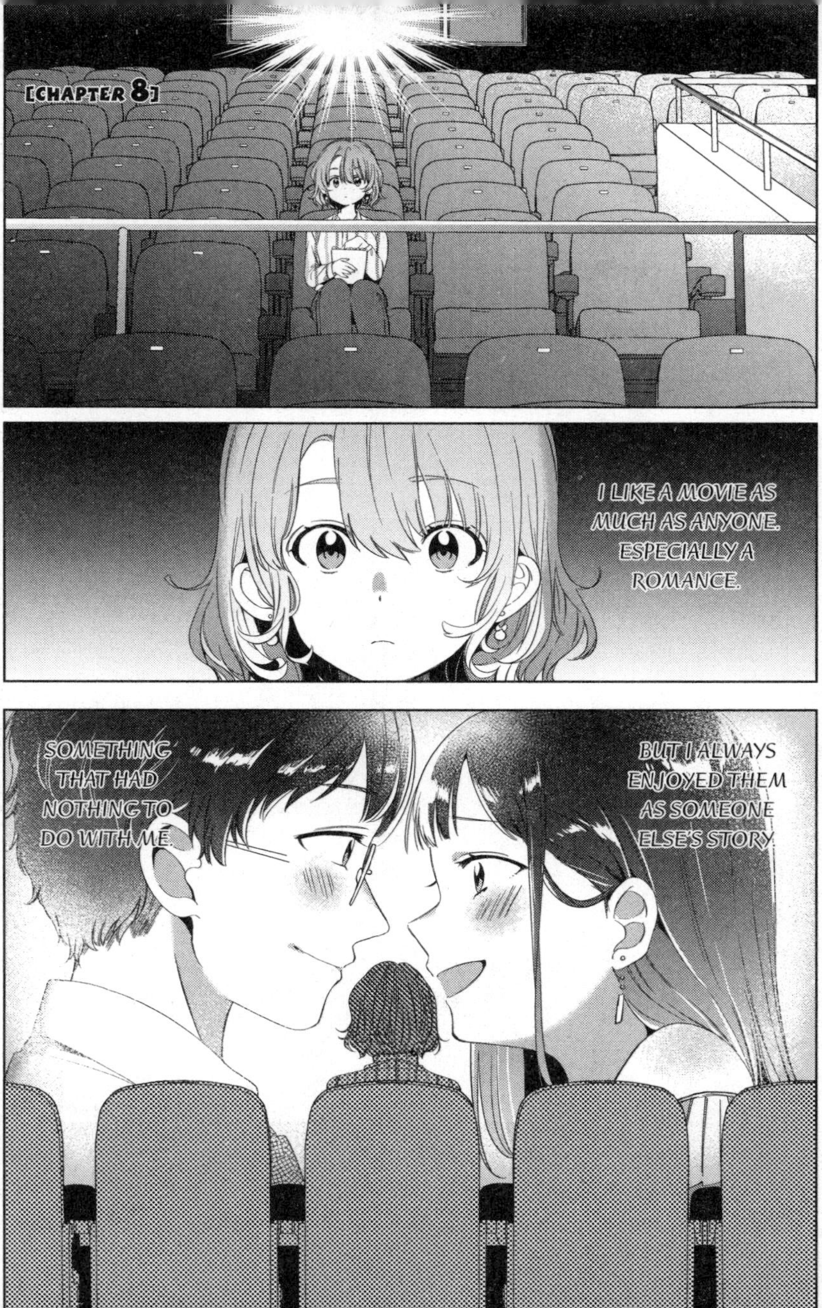
[CHAPTER 8]
I LIKE A MOVIE AS MUCH AS ANYONE. ESPECIALLY A ROMANCE.
BUT I ALWAYS ENJOYED THEM AS SOMEONE ELSE'S STORY.
SOMETHING THAT HAD NOTHING TO DO WITH ME.

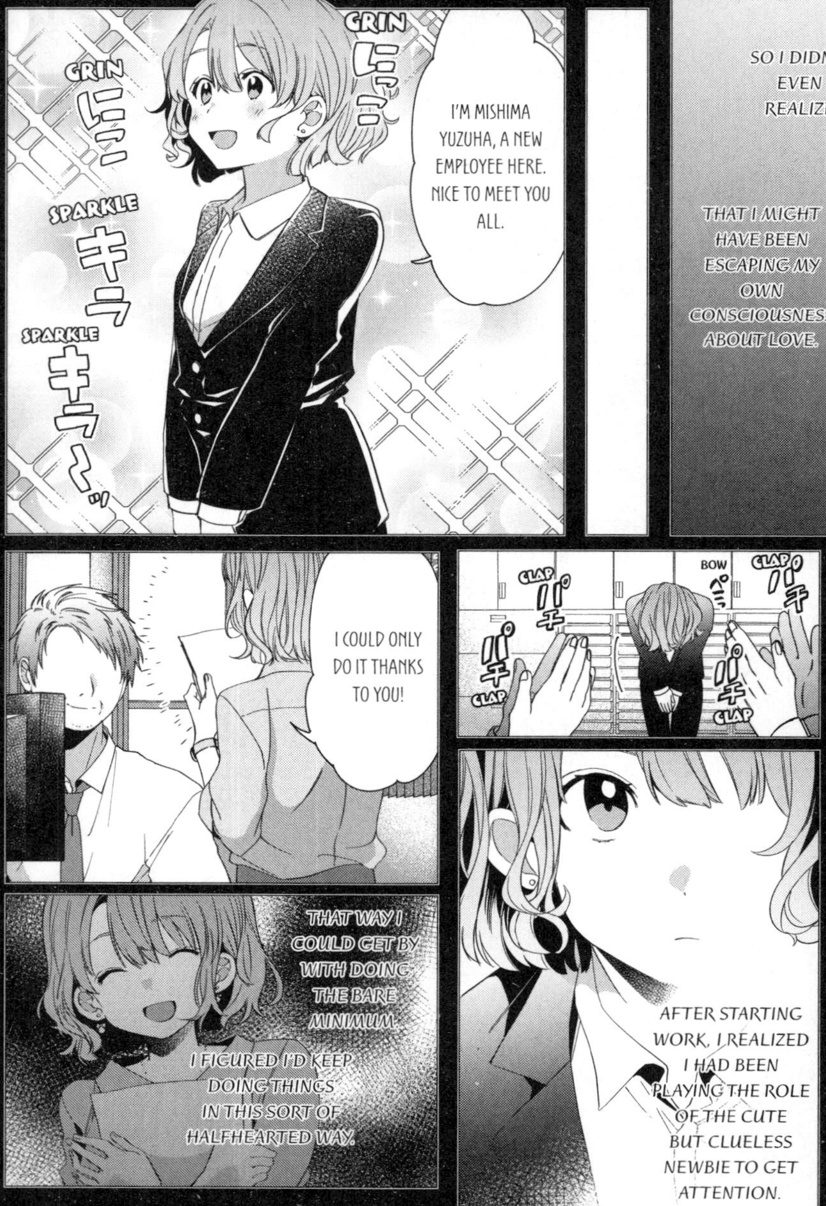
SO I DIDN'T EVEN REALIZE
THAT I MIGHT HAVE BEEN ESCAPING MY OWN CONSCIOUSNESS ABOUT LOVE.
GRIN
I'M MISHIMA YUZUHA, A NEW EMPLOYEE HERE. NICE TO MEET YOU ALL.
GRIN
SPARKLE
SPARKLE
CLAP
BOW
CLAP
CLAP
CLAP
AFTER STARTING WORK, I REALIZED I HAD BEEN PLAYING THE ROLE OF THE CUTE BUT CLUELESS NEWBIE TO GET ATTENTION.
I COULD ONLY DO IT THANKS TO YOU!
THAT WAY I COULD GET BY WITH DOING THE BARE MINIMUM.
I FIGURED I'D KEEP DOING THINGS IN THIS SORT OF HALFHEARTED WAY.

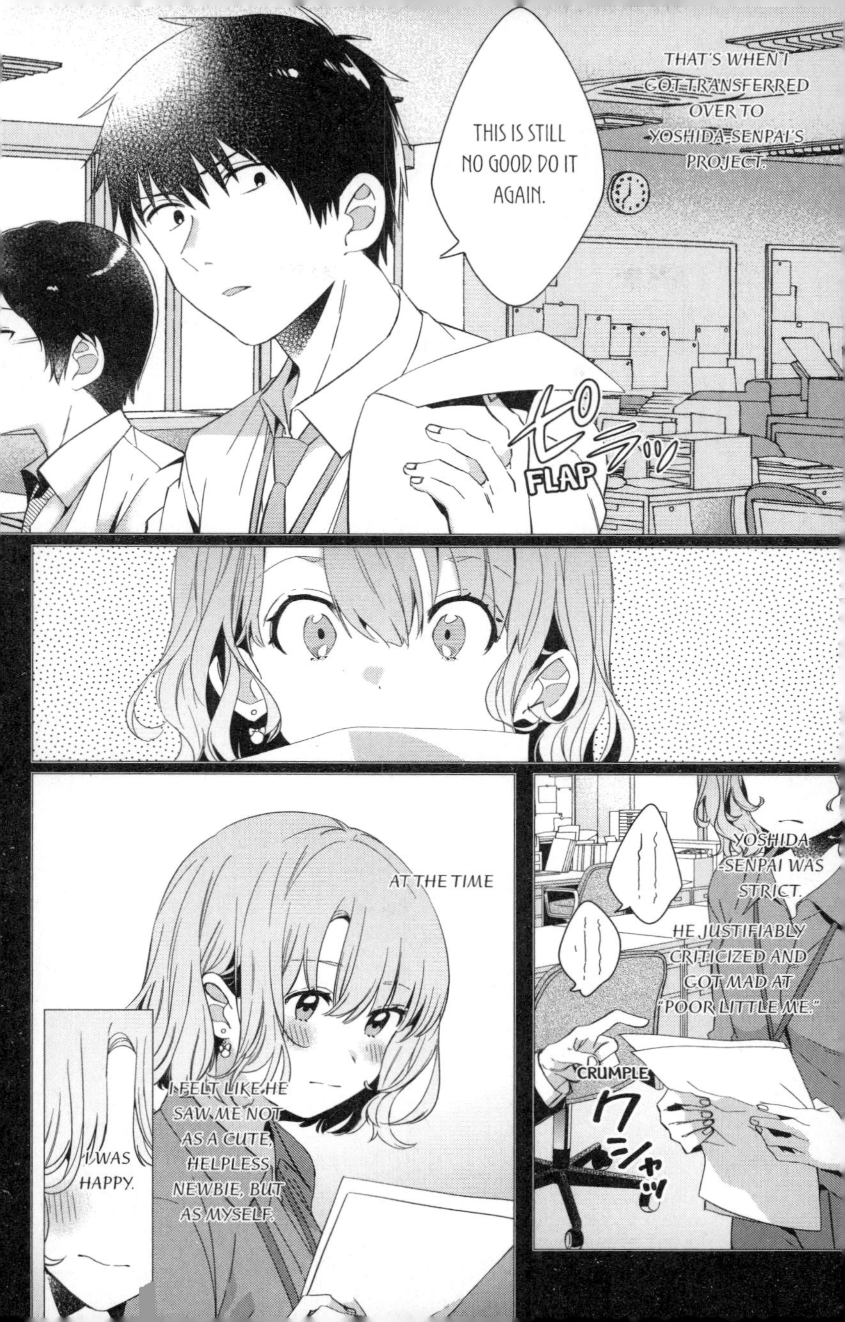
THAT'S WHEN I GOT TRANSFERRED OVER TO YOSHIDA-SENPAI'S PROJECT.
THIS IS STILL NO GOOD. DO IT AGAIN.
FLAP
YOSHIDA-SENPAI WAS STRICT.
HE JUSTIFIABLY CRITICIZED AND GOT MAD AT "POOR LITTLE ME."
CRUMPLE
AT THE TIME
I FELT LIKE HE SAW ME NOT AS A CUTE, HELPLESS NEWBIE, BUT AS MYSELF.
I WAS HAPPY.

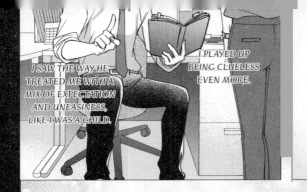

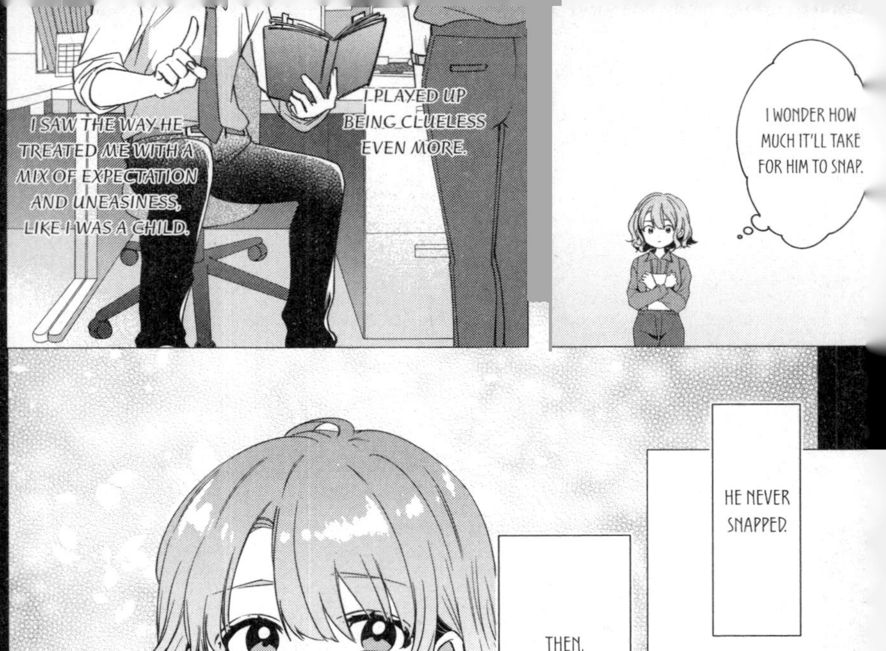

I WONDER HOW MUCH IT'LL TAKE FOR HIM TO SNAP.
I PLAYED UP BEING CLUELESS EVEN MORE.
I SAW THE WAY HE TREATED ME WITH A MIX OF EXPECTATION AND UNEASINESS, LIKE I WAS A CHILD.
HE NEVER SNAPPED.
THEN, SOMEWHERE ALONG THE LINE, I STARTED
TO FALL FOR HIM.

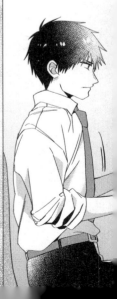

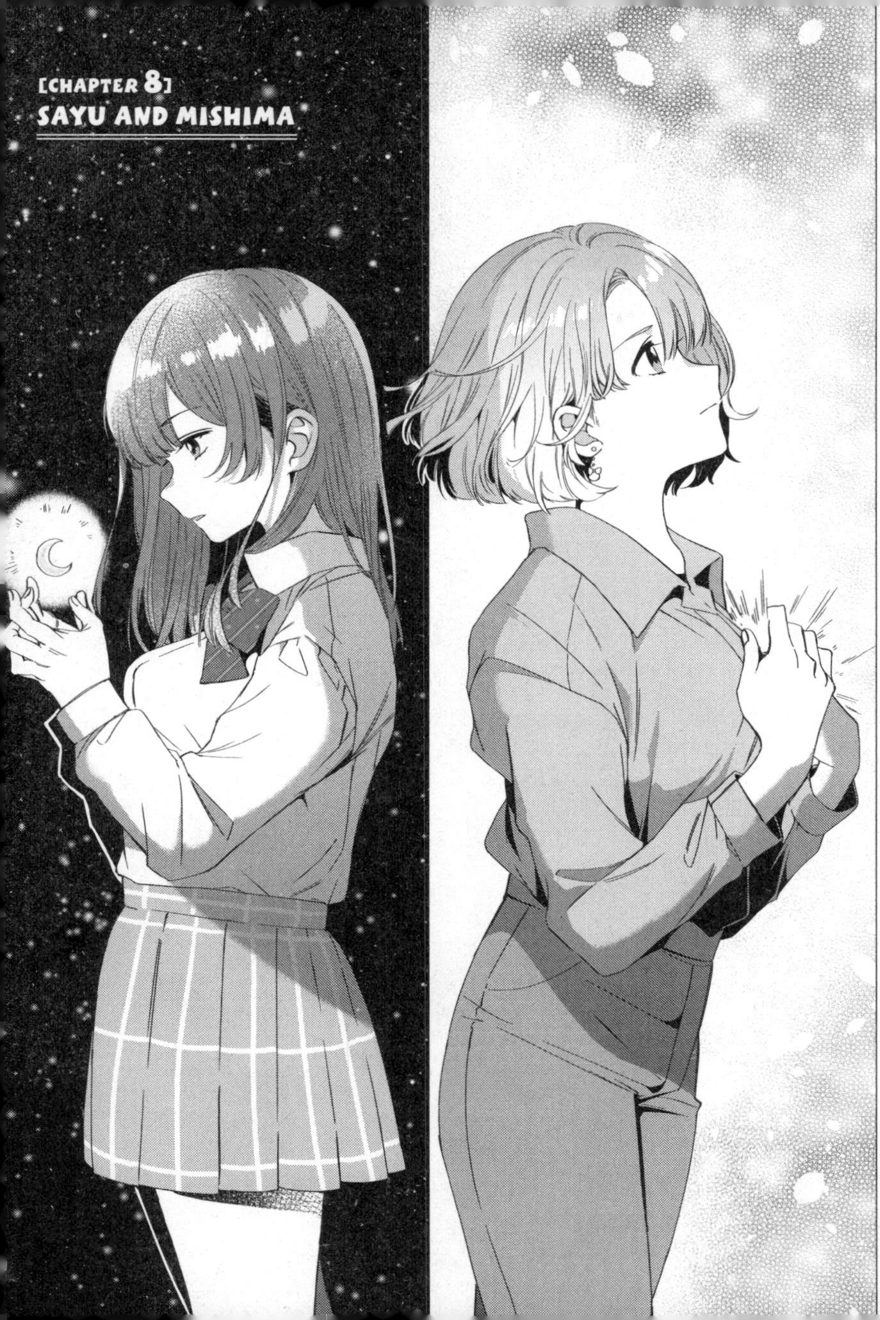
[CHAPTER 8]
SAYU AND MISHIMA

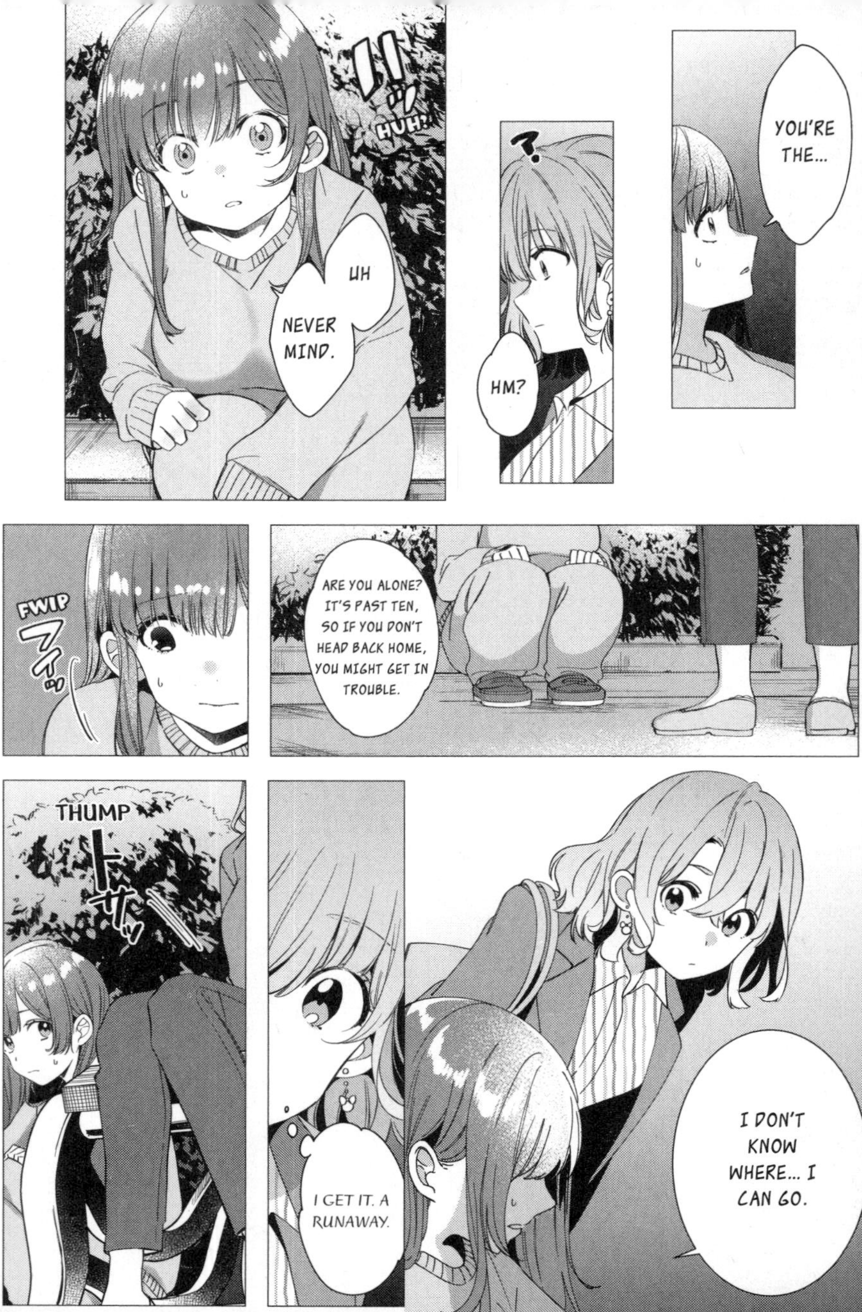
YOU'RE THE...
?
HM?
HUH?!
UH
NEVER MIND.
ARE YOU ALONE? IT'S PAST TEN, SO IF YOU DON'T HEAD BACK HOME, YOU MIGHT GET IN TROUBLE.
FWIP
I DON'T KNOW WHERE... I CAN GO.
I GET IT. A RUNAWAY.
THUMP

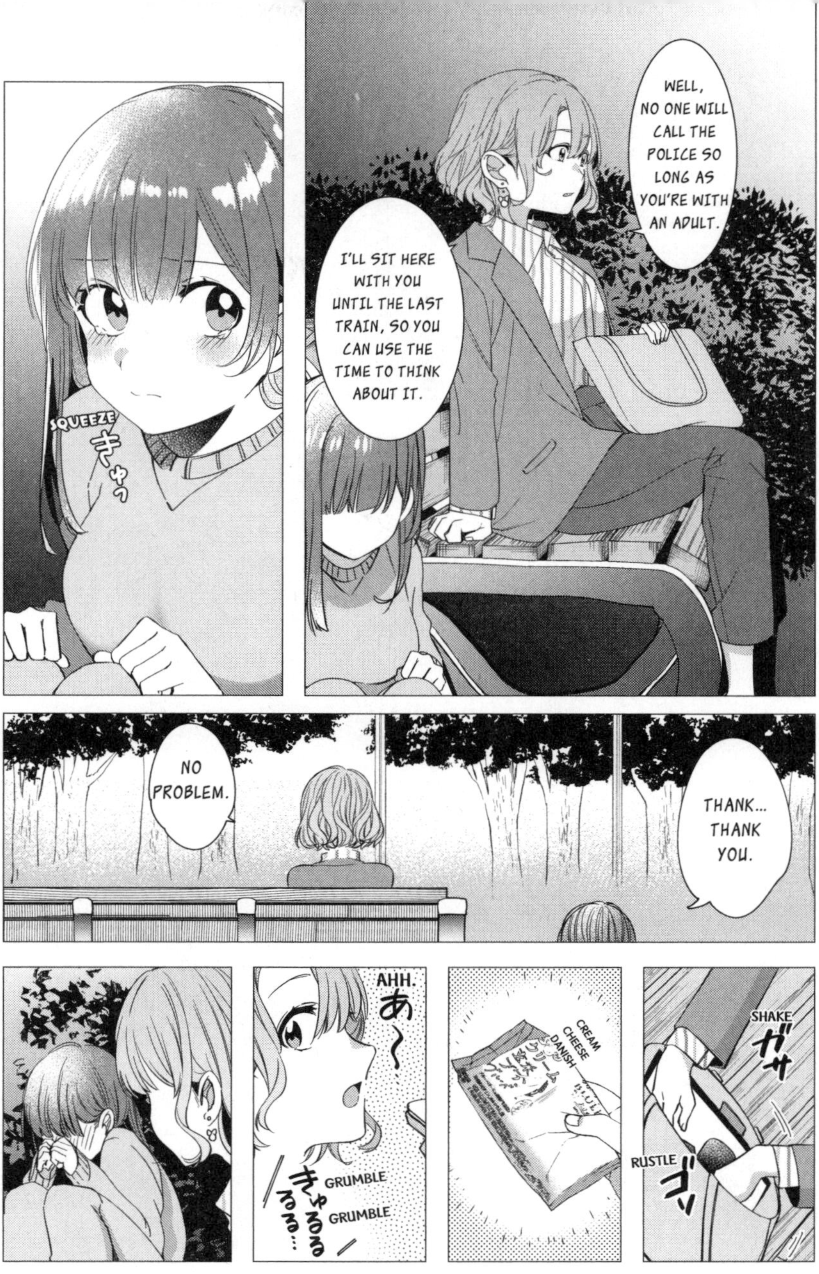
WELL, NO ONE WILL CALL THE POLICE SO LONG AS YOU'RE WITH AN ADULT.
I'LL SIT HERE WITH YOU UNTIL THE LAST TRAIN, SO YOU CAN USE THE TIME TO THINK ABOUT IT.
SQUEEZE
きゅっ
THANK... THANK YOU.
NO PROBLEM.
SHAKE
ガサ
RUSTLE
ゴソ
CREAM CHEESE DANISH
AHH.
あ〜
GRUMBLE GRUMBLE
きゅるるるるる…

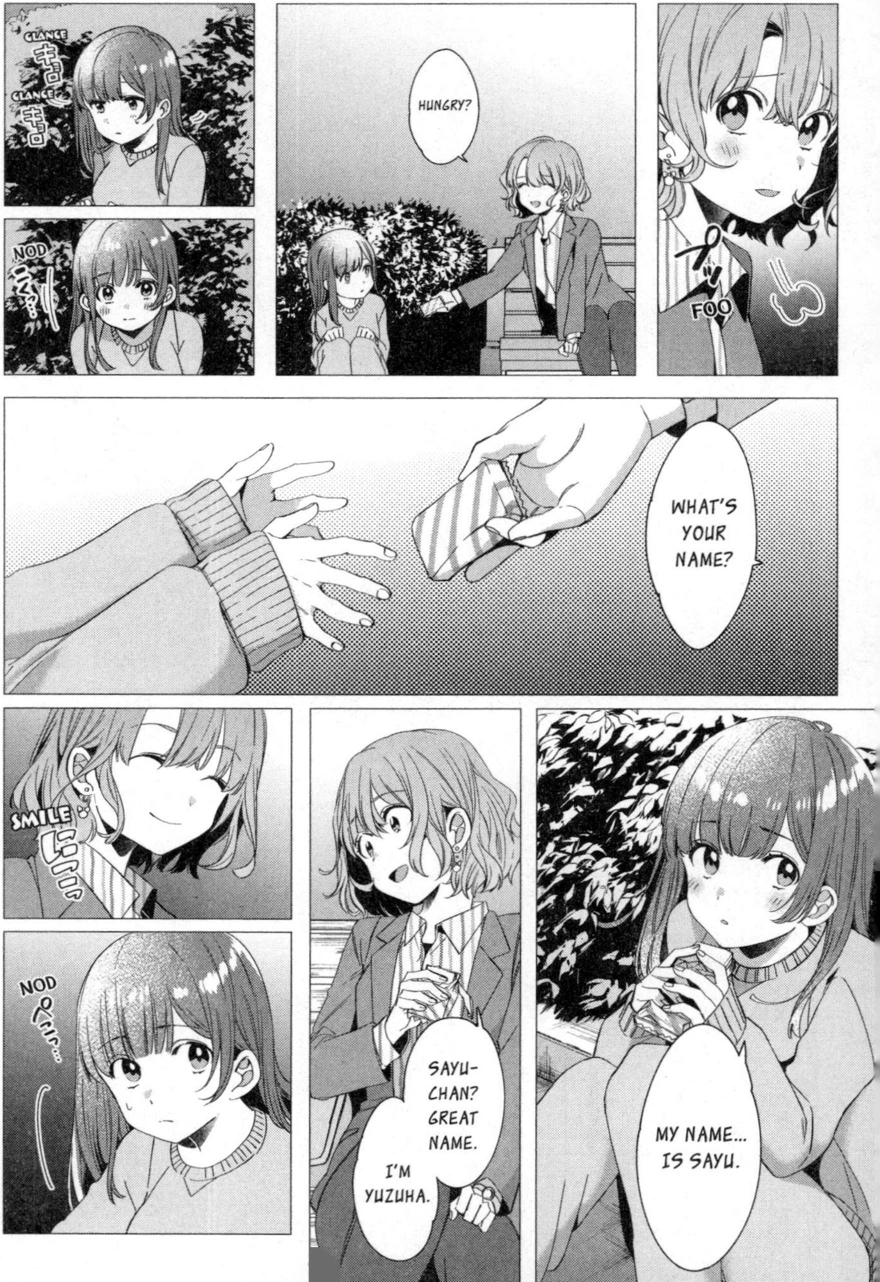
FOO
HUNGRY?
GLANCE キョロ
GLANCE キョロ
NOD
WHAT'S YOUR NAME?
MY NAME... IS SAYU.
SAYU-CHAN? GREAT NAME.
I'M YUZUHA.
SMILE
NOD

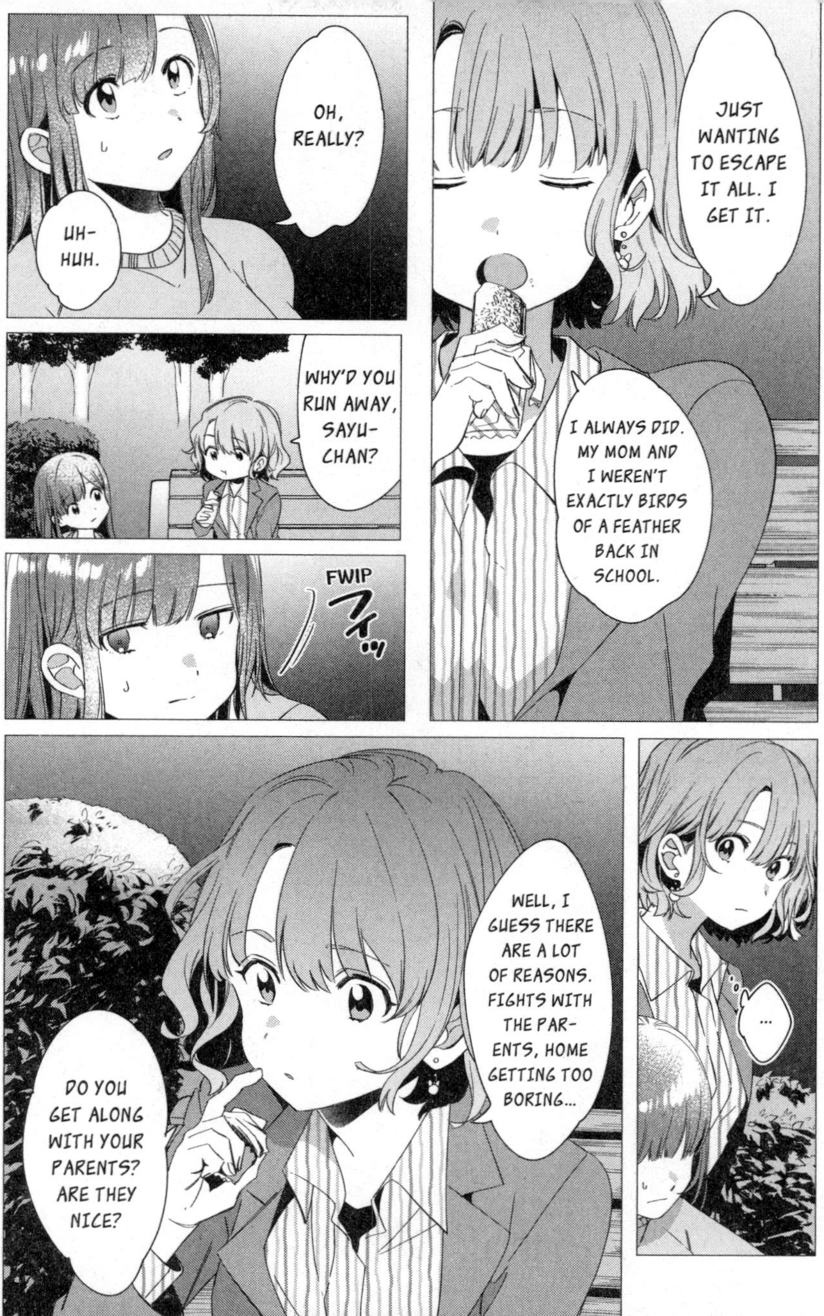
JUST WANTING TO ESCAPE IT ALL. I GET IT.
I ALWAYS DID. MY MOM AND I WEREN'T EXACTLY BIRDS OF A FEATHER BACK IN SCHOOL.
OH, REALLY?
UH-HUH.
WHY'D YOU RUN AWAY, SAYU-CHAN?
FWIP
...
WELL, I GUESS THERE ARE A LOT OF REASONS. FIGHTS WITH THE PAR-ENTS, HOME GETTING TOO BORING...
DO YOU GET ALONG WITH YOUR PARENTS? ARE THEY NICE?

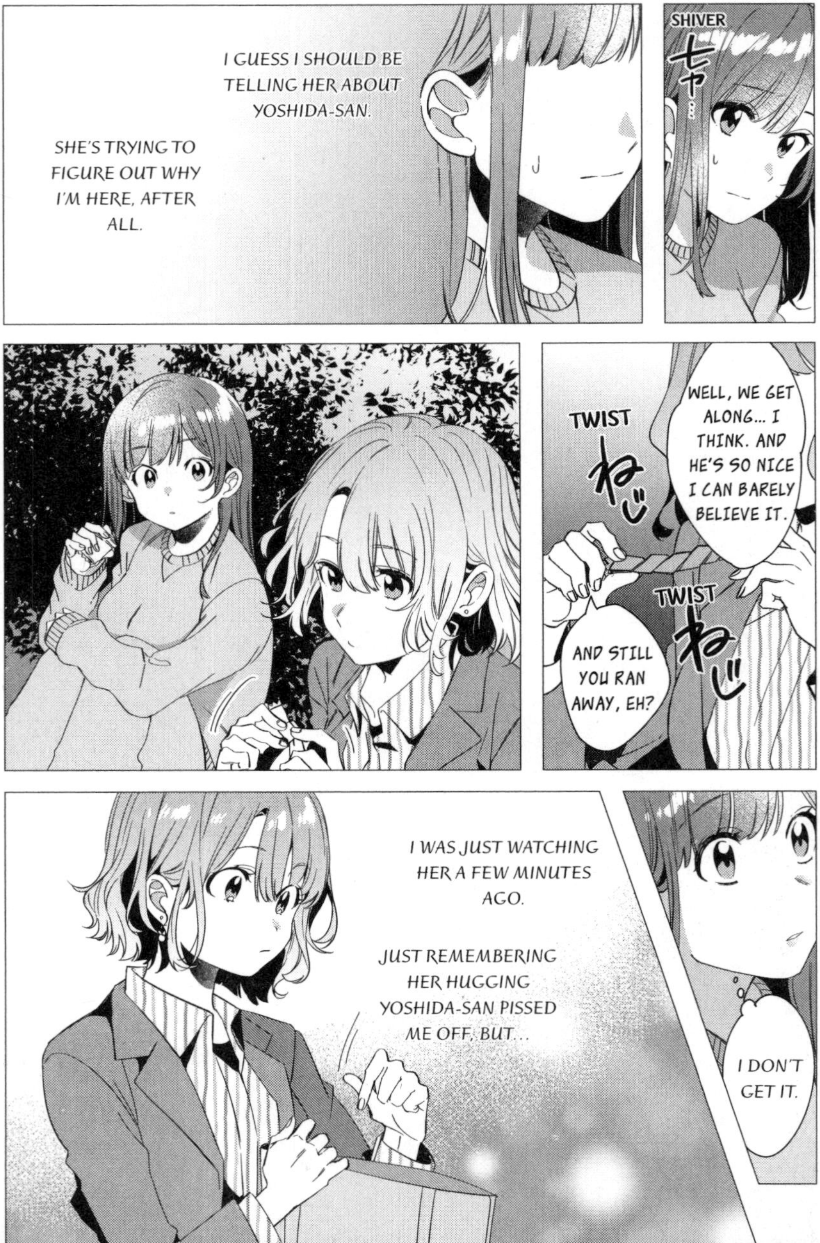
SHIVER
ヒヤ…
I GUESS I SHOULD BE TELLING HER ABOUT YOSHIDA-SAN.
SHE'S TRYING TO FIGURE OUT WHY I'M HERE, AFTER ALL.
WELL, WE GET ALONG... I THINK. AND HE'S SO NICE I CAN BARELY BELIEVE IT.
TWIST
ねじ
TWIST
ねじ
AND STILL YOU RAN AWAY, EH?
I DON'T GET IT.
I WAS JUST WATCHING HER A FEW MINUTES AGO.
JUST REMEMBERING HER HUGGING YOSHIDA-SAN PISSED ME OFF, BUT...

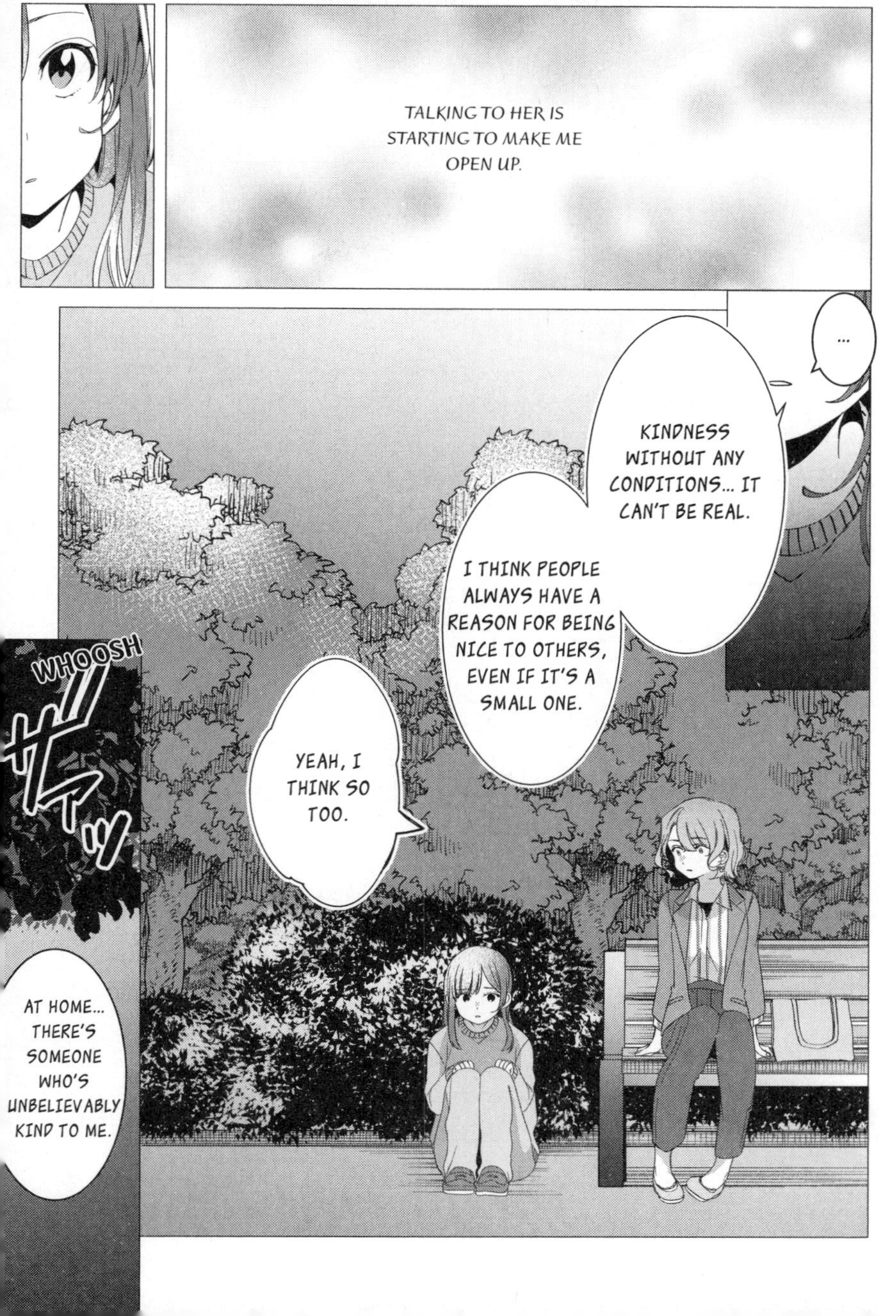
TALKING TO HER IS STARTING TO MAKE ME OPEN UP.
...
KINDNESS WITHOUT ANY CONDITIONS... IT CAN'T BE REAL.
I THINK PEOPLE ALWAYS HAVE A REASON FOR BEING NICE TO OTHERS, EVEN IF IT'S A SMALL ONE.
YEAH, I THINK SO TOO.
WHOOSH
ザァッ
AT HOME... THERE'S SOMEONE WHO'S UNBELIEVABLY KIND TO ME.

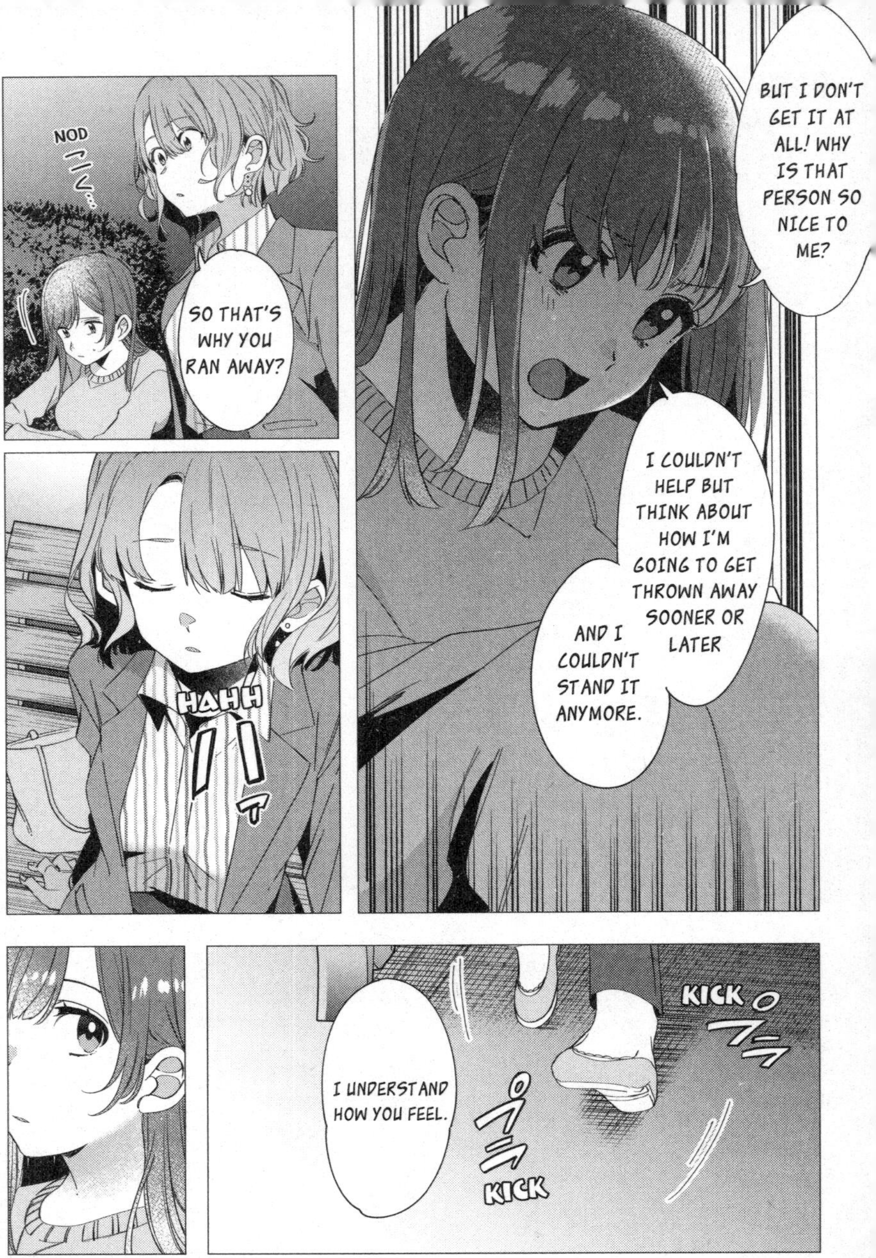
BUT I DON'T GET IT AT ALL! WHY IS THAT PERSON SO NICE TO ME?
I COULDN'T HELP BUT THINK ABOUT HOW I'M GOING TO GET THROWN AWAY SOONER OR LATER
AND I COULDN'T STAND IT ANYMORE.
NOD
SO THAT'S WHY YOU RAN AWAY?
HAHH
KICK
I UNDERSTAND HOW YOU FEEL.
KICK

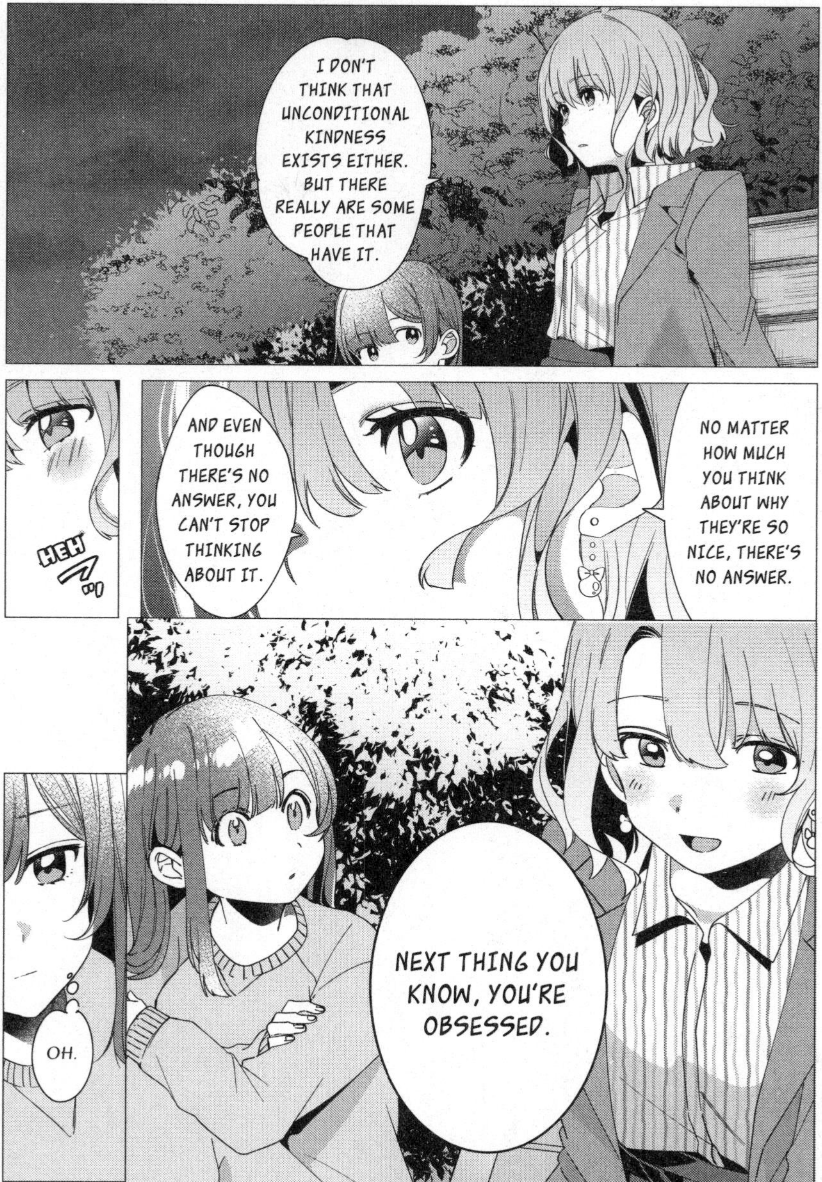
I DON'T THINK THAT UNCONDITIONAL KINDNESS EXISTS EITHER. BUT THERE REALLY ARE SOME PEOPLE THAT HAVE IT.
NO MATTER HOW MUCH YOU THINK ABOUT WHY THEY'RE SO NICE, THERE'S NO ANSWER.
AND EVEN THOUGH THERE'S NO ANSWER, YOU CAN'T STOP THINKING ABOUT IT.
HEH
NEXT THING YOU KNOW, YOU'RE OBSESSED.
OH.

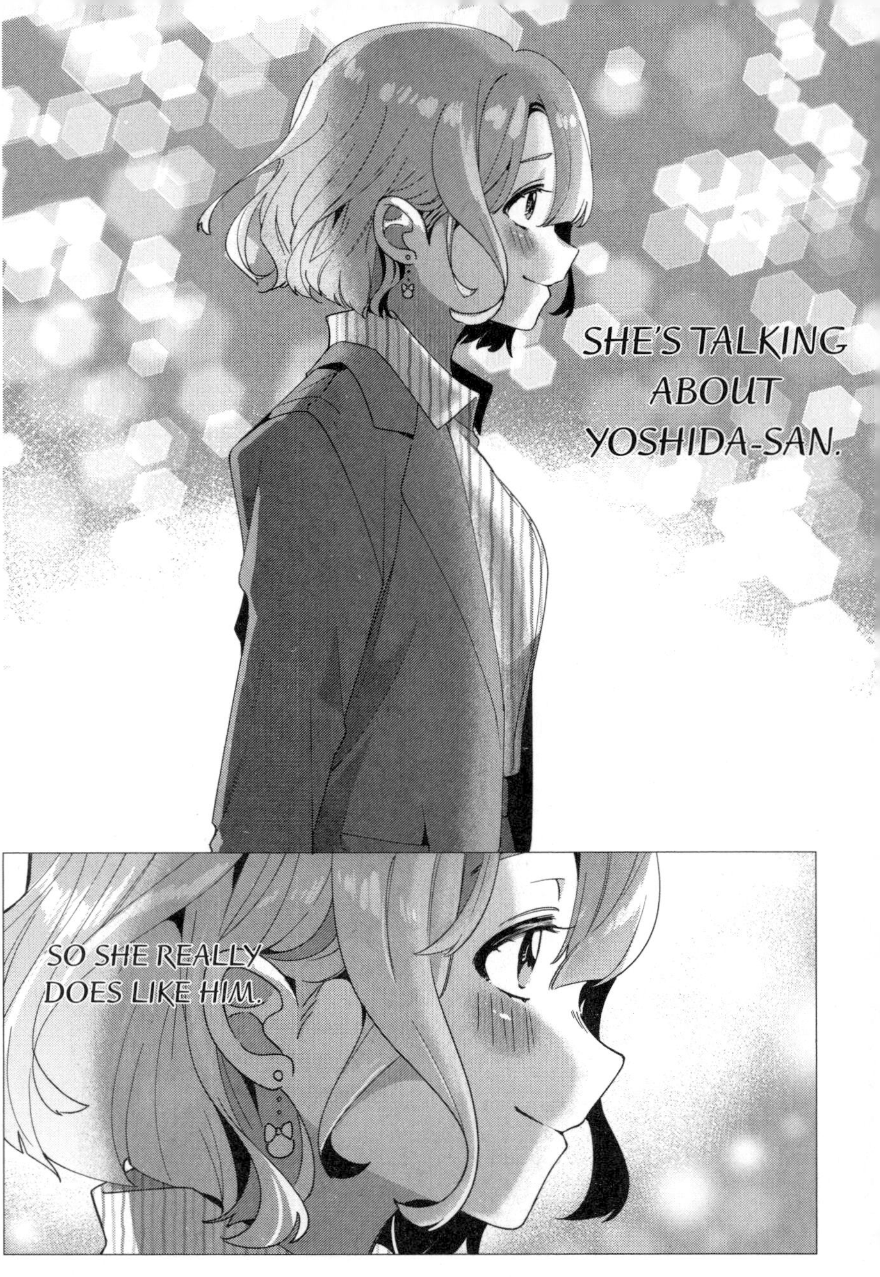
SHE'S TALKING ABOUT YOSHIDA-SAN.
SO SHE REALLY DOES LIKE HIM.

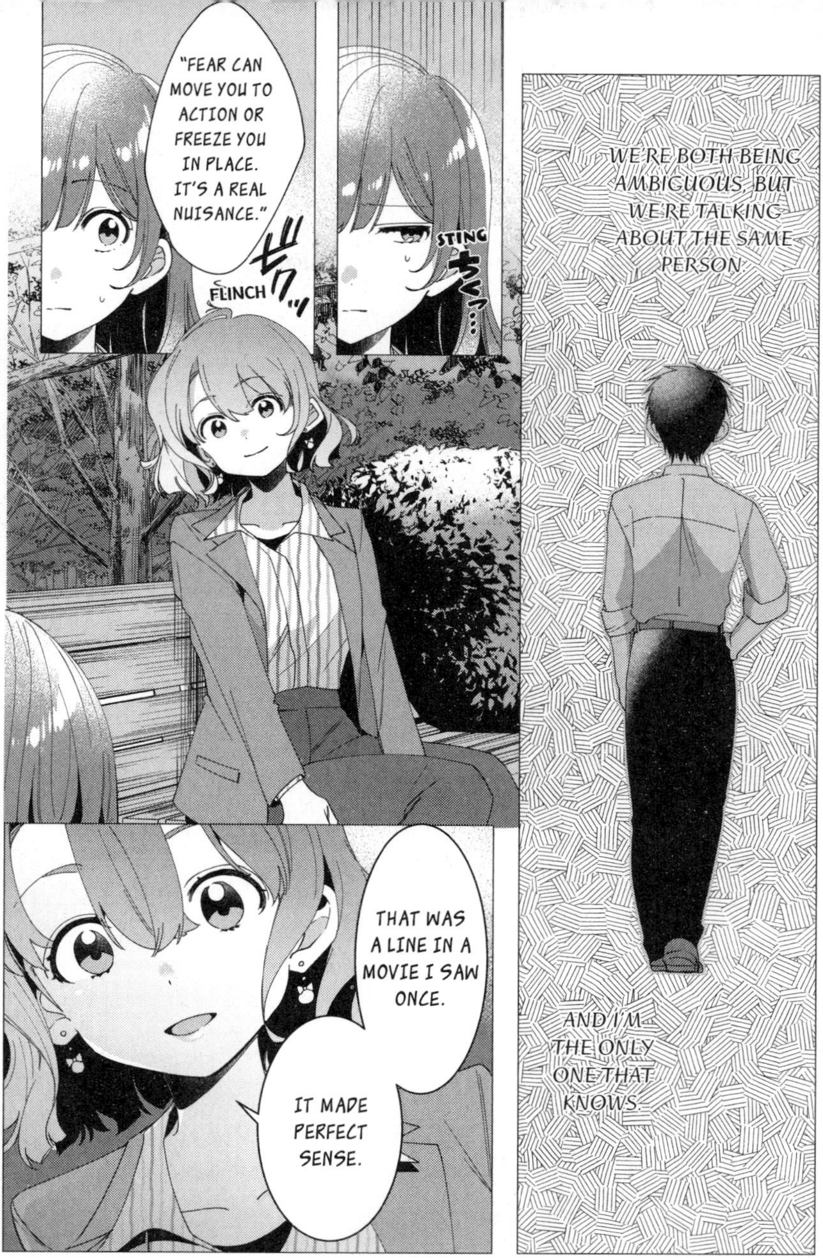
WE'RE BOTH BEING AMBICUOUS, BUT WE'RE TALKING ABOUT THE SAME PERSON.
AND I'M THE ONLY ONE THAT KNOWS.
STING
ちくっ…
"FEAR CAN MOVE YOU TO ACTION OR FREEZE YOU IN PLACE. IT'S A REAL NUISANCE."
FLINCH
ビクッ
THAT WAS A LINE IN A MOVIE I SAW ONCE.
IT MADE PERFECT SENSE.

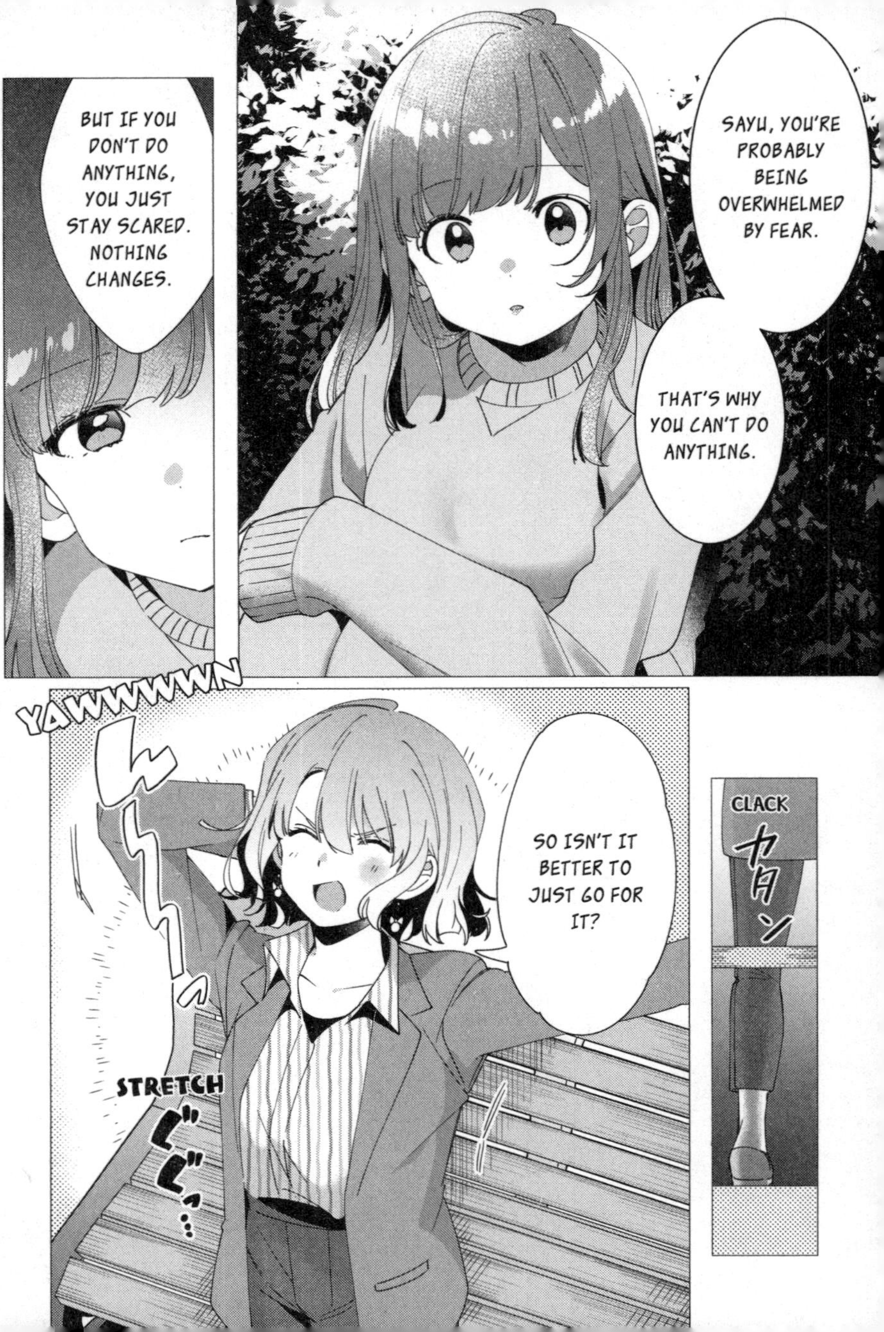
SAYU, YOU'RE PROBABLY BEING OVERWHELMED BY FEAR.
THAT'S WHY YOU CAN'T DO ANYTHING.
BUT IF YOU DON'T DO ANYTHING, YOU JUST STAY SCARED. NOTHING CHANGES.
CLACK
カタン
YAWWWWN
SO ISN'T IT BETTER TO JUST GO FOR IT?
STRETCH

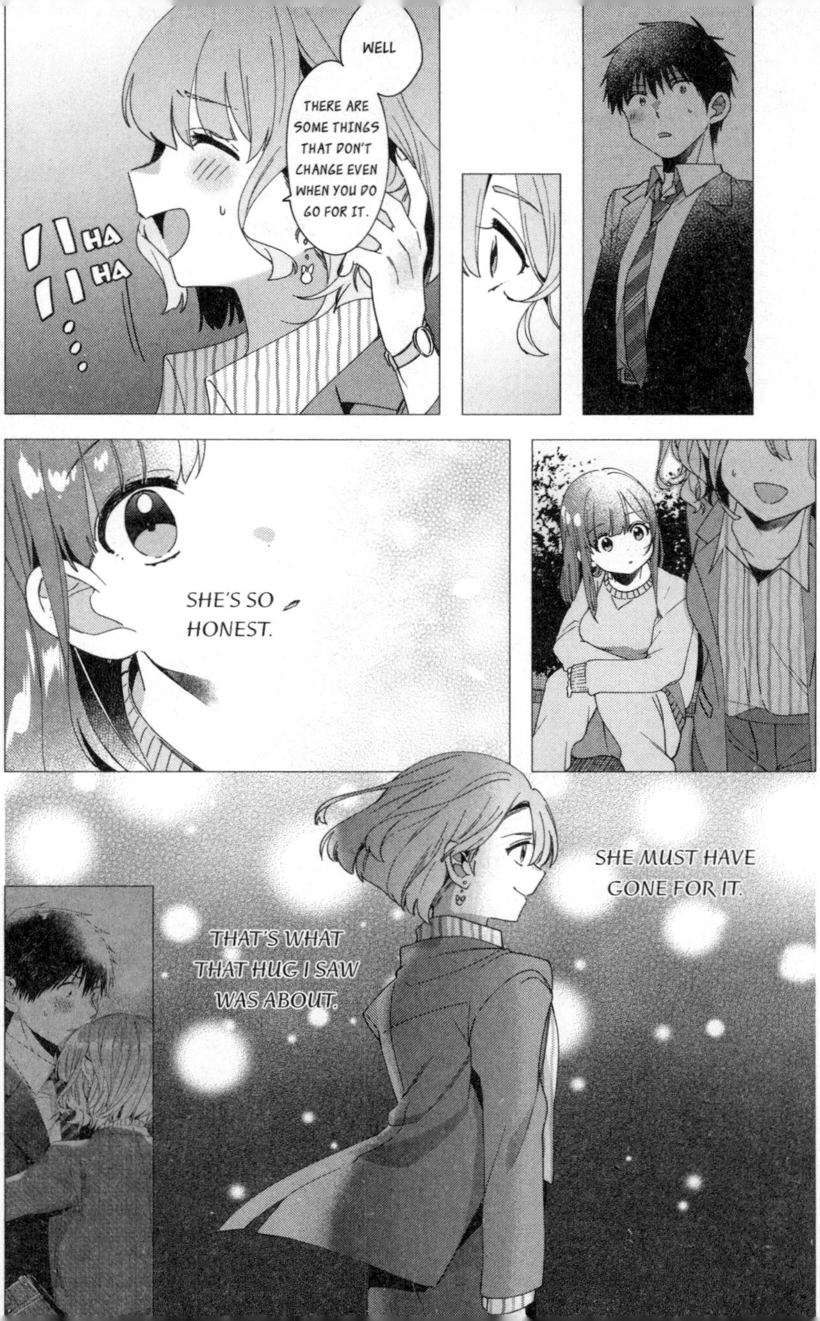
WELL
THERE ARE SOME THINGS THAT DON'T CHANGE EVEN WHEN YOU DO GO FOR IT.
HA HA
SHE'S SO HONEST.
SHE MUST HAVE GONE FOR IT.
THAT'S WHAT THAT HUG I SAW WAS ABOUT.

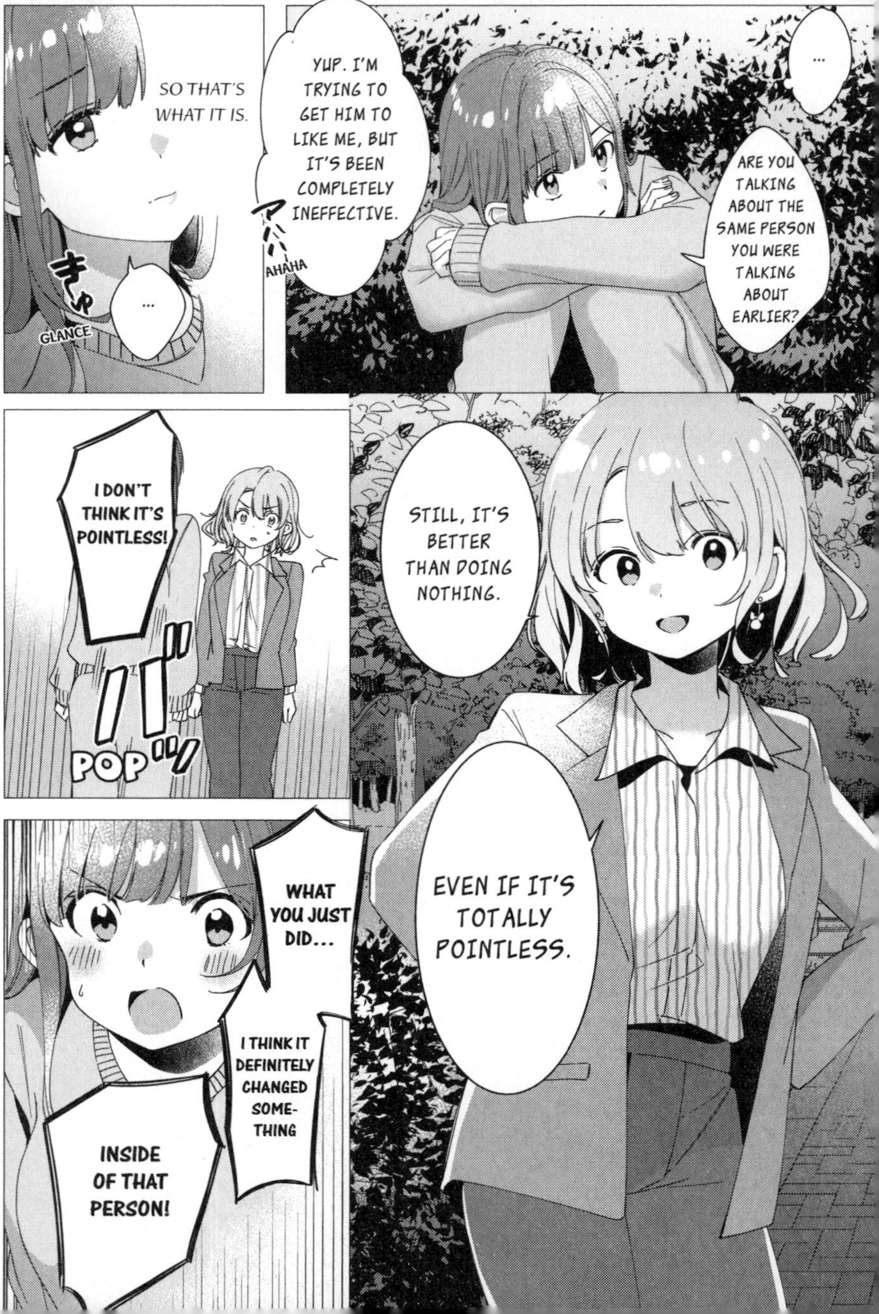
...
ARE YOU TALKING ABOUT THE SAME PERSON YOU WERE TALKING ABOUT EARLIER?
YUP. I'M TRYING TO GET HIM TO LIKE ME, BUT IT'S BEEN COMPLETELY INEFFECTIVE.
AHAHA
SO THAT'S WHAT IT IS.
GLANCE
...
STILL, IT'S BETTER THAN DOING NOTHING.
EVEN IF IT'S TOTALLY POINTLESS.
I DON'T THINK IT'S POINTLESS!
POP
WHAT YOU JUST DID...
I THINK IT DEFINITELY CHANGED SOME-THING
INSIDE OF THAT PERSON!

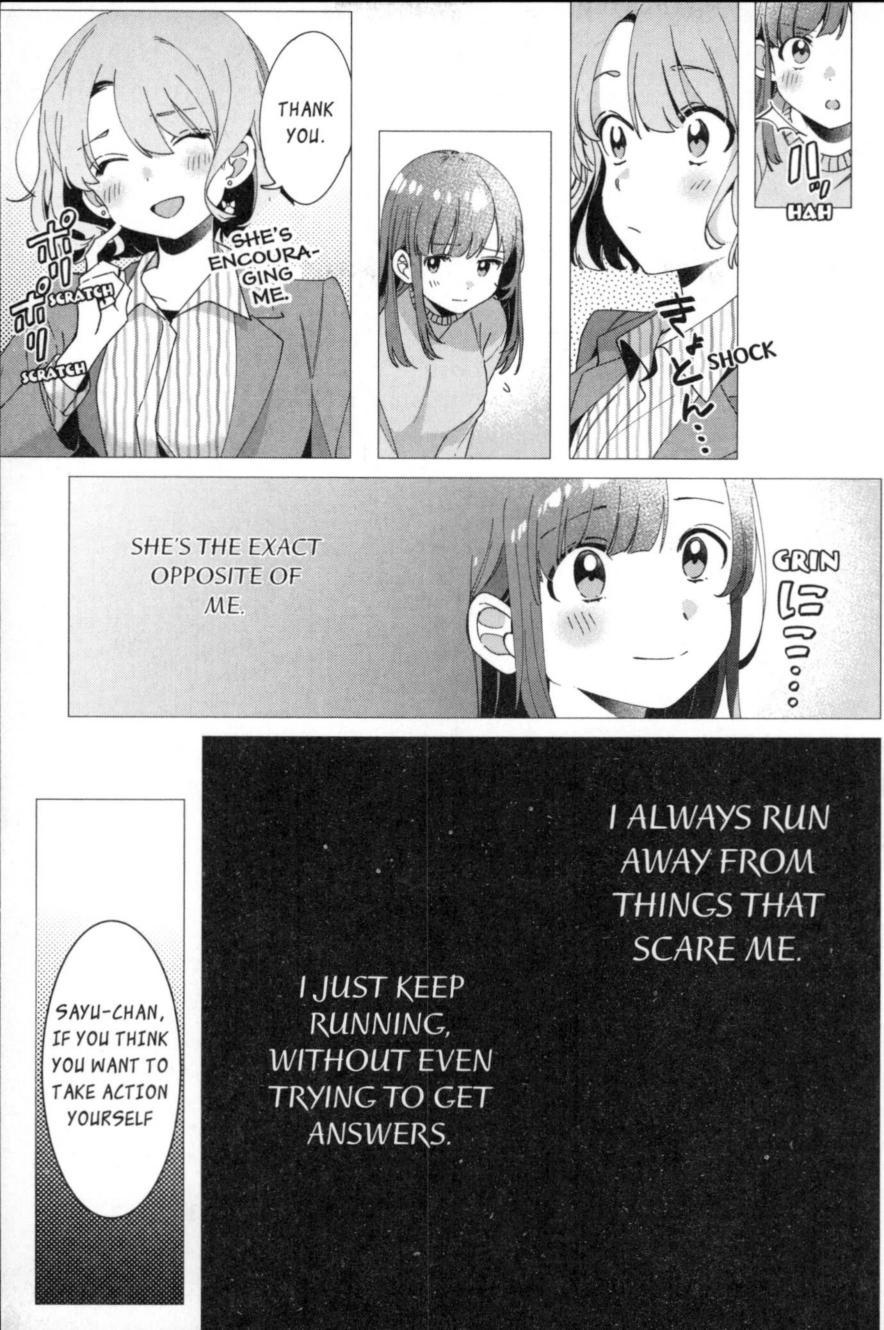
ハッ
HAH
きょとん…
SHOCK
THANK YOU.
SHE'S ENCOURAGING ME.
ポリ
SCRATCH
ポリ
SCRATCH
にこ…
GRIN
SHE'S THE EXACT OPPOSITE OF ME.
I ALWAYS RUN AWAY FROM THINGS THAT SCARE ME.
I JUST KEEP RUNNING, WITHOUT EVEN TRYING TO GET ANSWERS.
SAYU-CHAN, IF YOU THINK YOU WANT TO TAKE ACTION YOURSELF

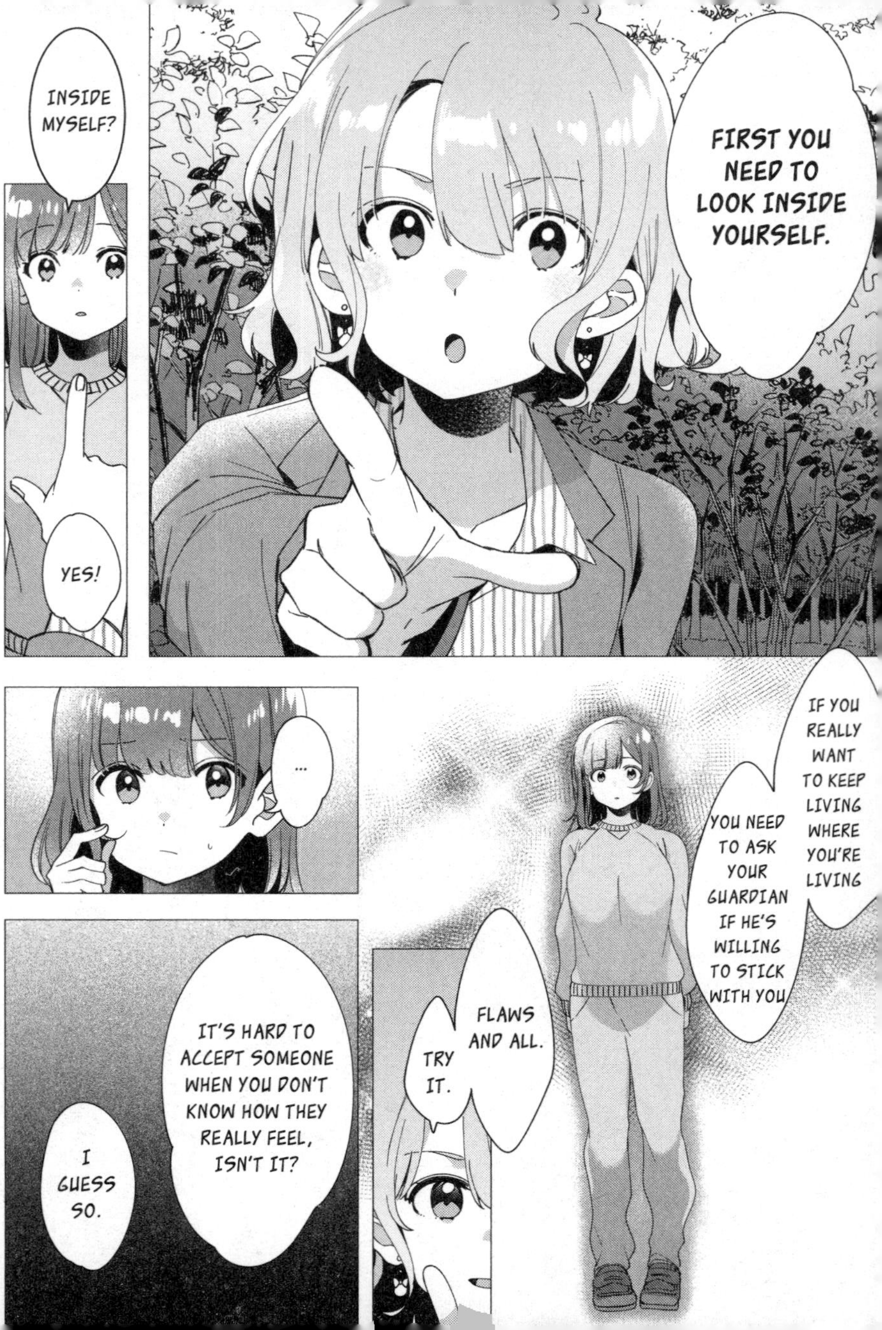
FIRST YOU NEED TO LOOK INSIDE YOURSELF.
INSIDE MYSELF?
YES!
IF YOU REALLY WANT TO KEEP LIVING WHERE YOU'RE LIVING
YOU NEED TO ASK YOUR GUARDIAN IF HE'S WILLING TO STICK WITH YOU
FLAWS AND ALL.
TRY IT.
...
IT'S HARD TO ACCEPT SOMEONE WHEN YOU DON'T KNOW HOW THEY REALLY FEEL, ISN'T IT?
I GUESS SO.

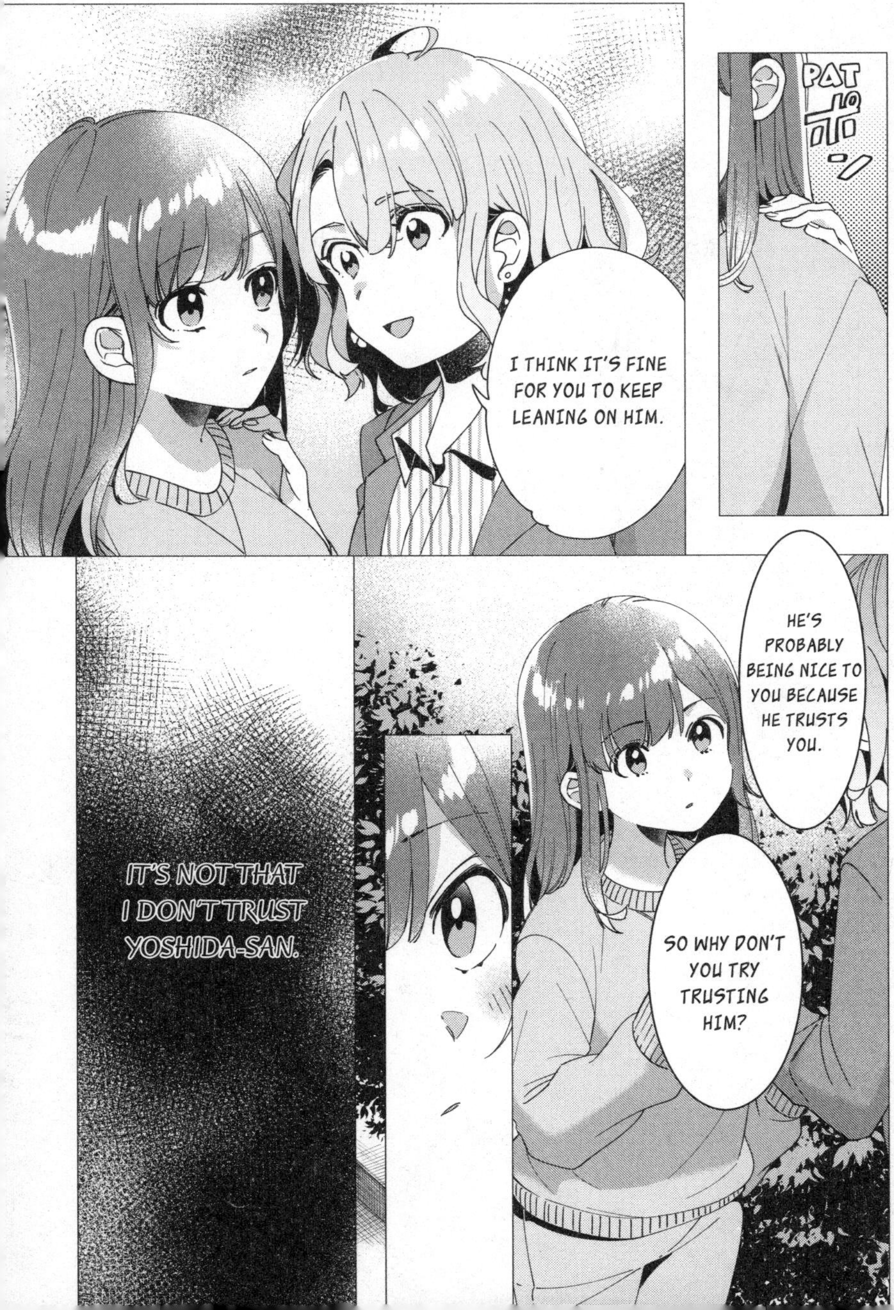
PAT
I THINK IT'S FINE FOR YOU TO KEEP LEANING ON HIM.
HE'S PROBABLY BEING NICE TO YOU BECAUSE HE TRUSTS YOU.
SO WHY DON'T YOU TRY TRUSTING HIM?
IT'S NOT THAT I DON'T TRUST YOSHIDA-SAN.

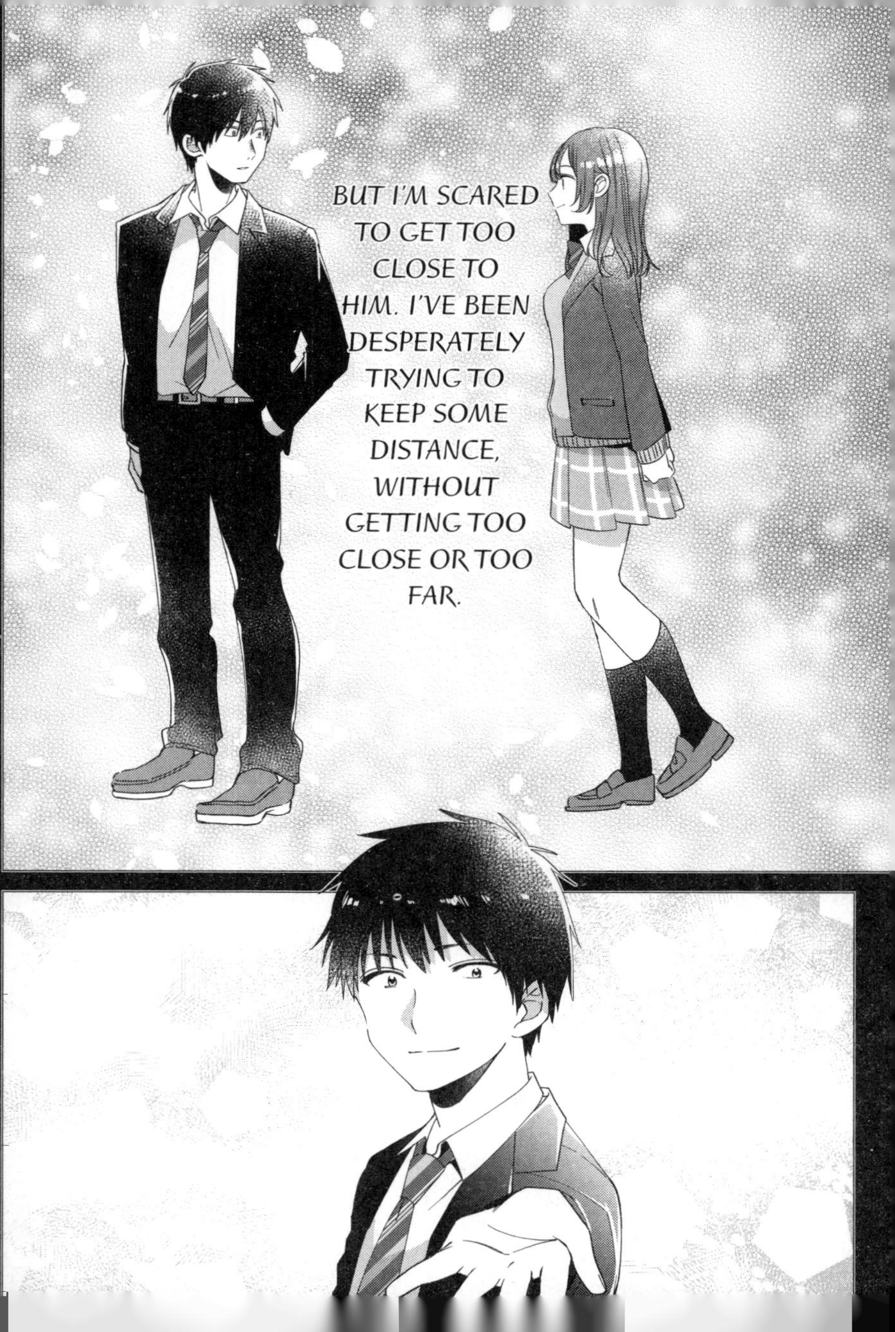
BUT I'M SCARED TO GET TOO CLOSE TO HIM. I'VE BEEN DESPERATELY TRYING TO KEEP SOME DISTANCE, WITHOUT GETTING TOO CLOSE OR TOO FAR.

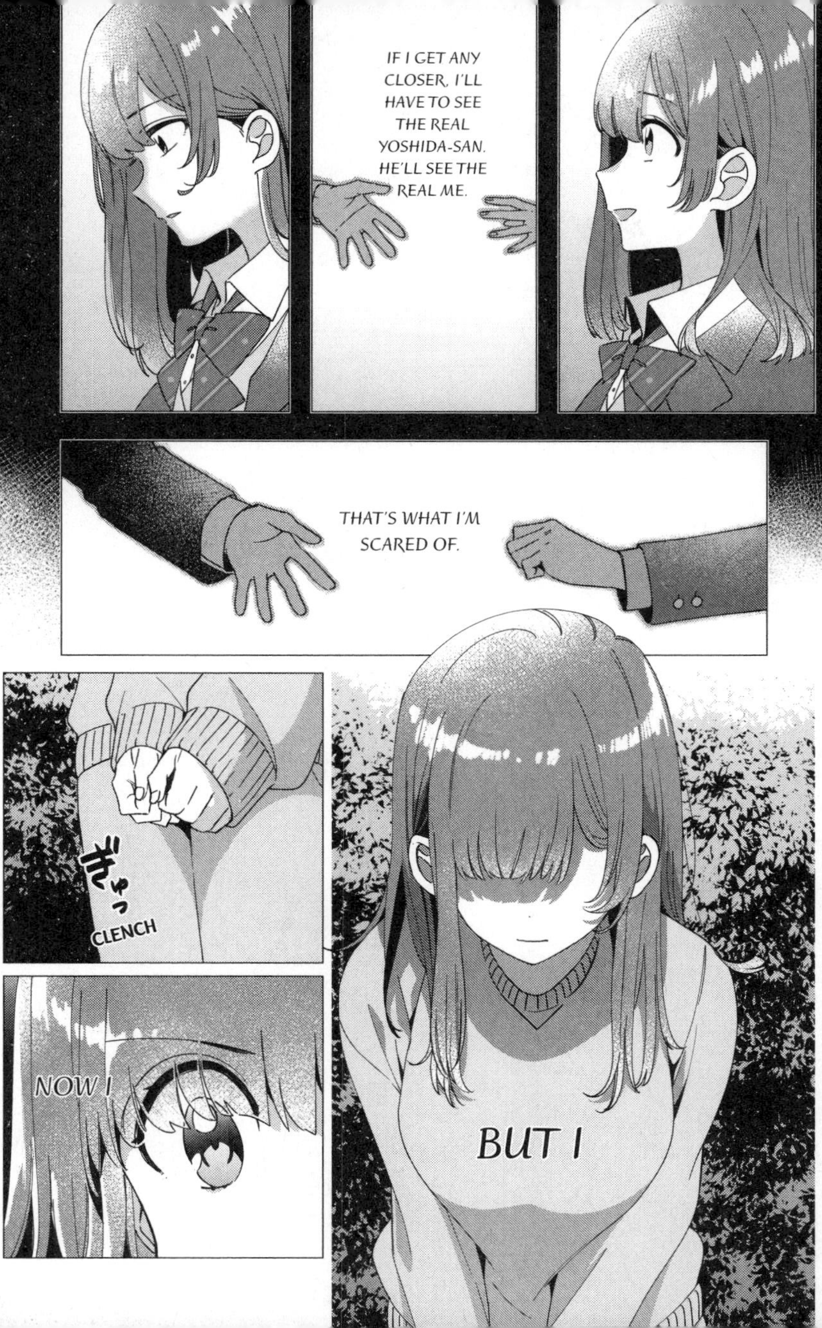
IF I GET ANY CLOSER, I'LL HAVE TO SEE THE REAL YOSHIDA-SAN. HE'LL SEE THE REAL ME.
THAT'S WHAT I'M SCARED OF.
BUT I
ぎゅっ
CLENCH
NOW I

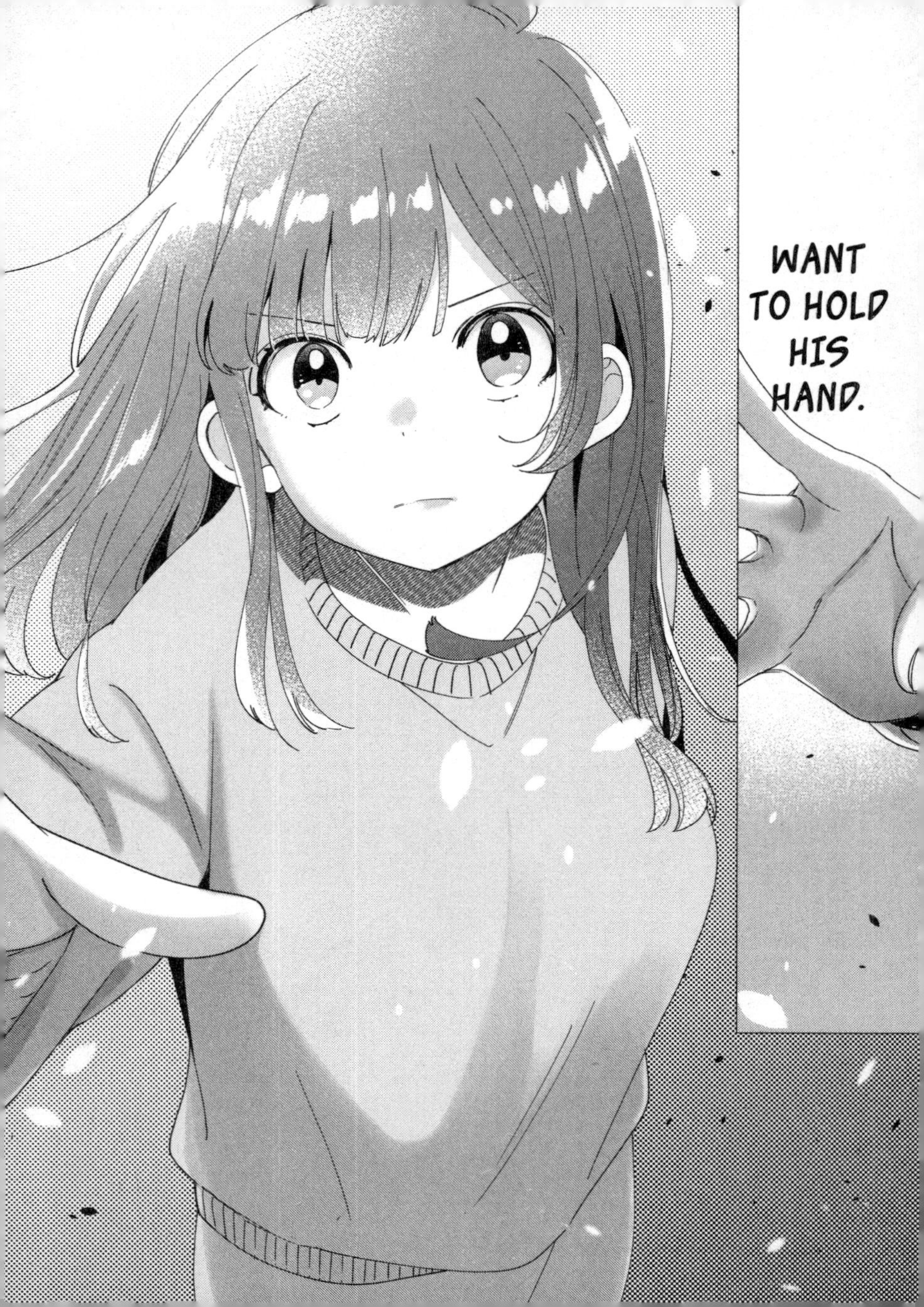
WANT TO HOLD HIS HAND.

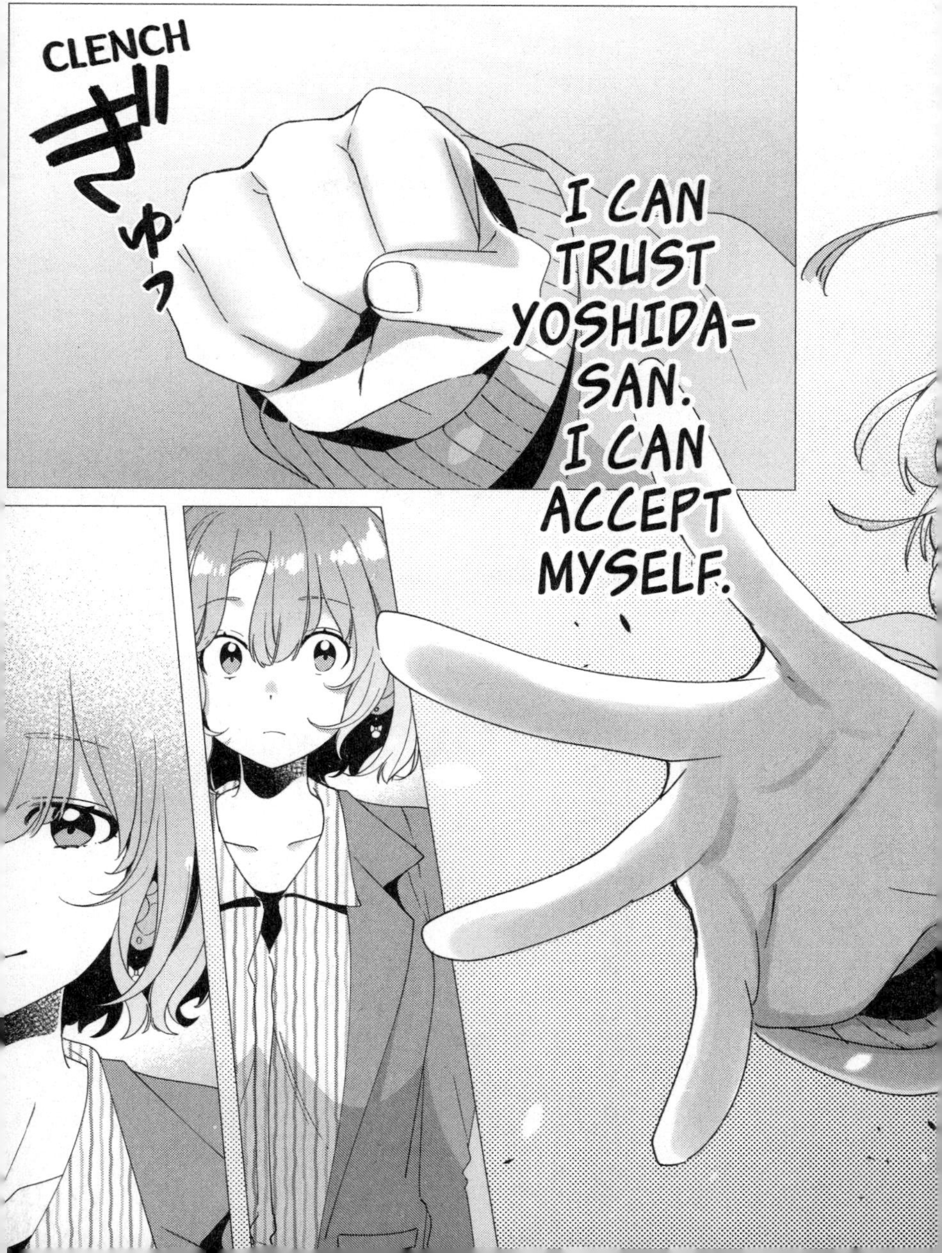
CLENCH
ぎゅっ
I CAN TRUST YOSHIDA-SAN. I CAN ACCEPT MYSELF.

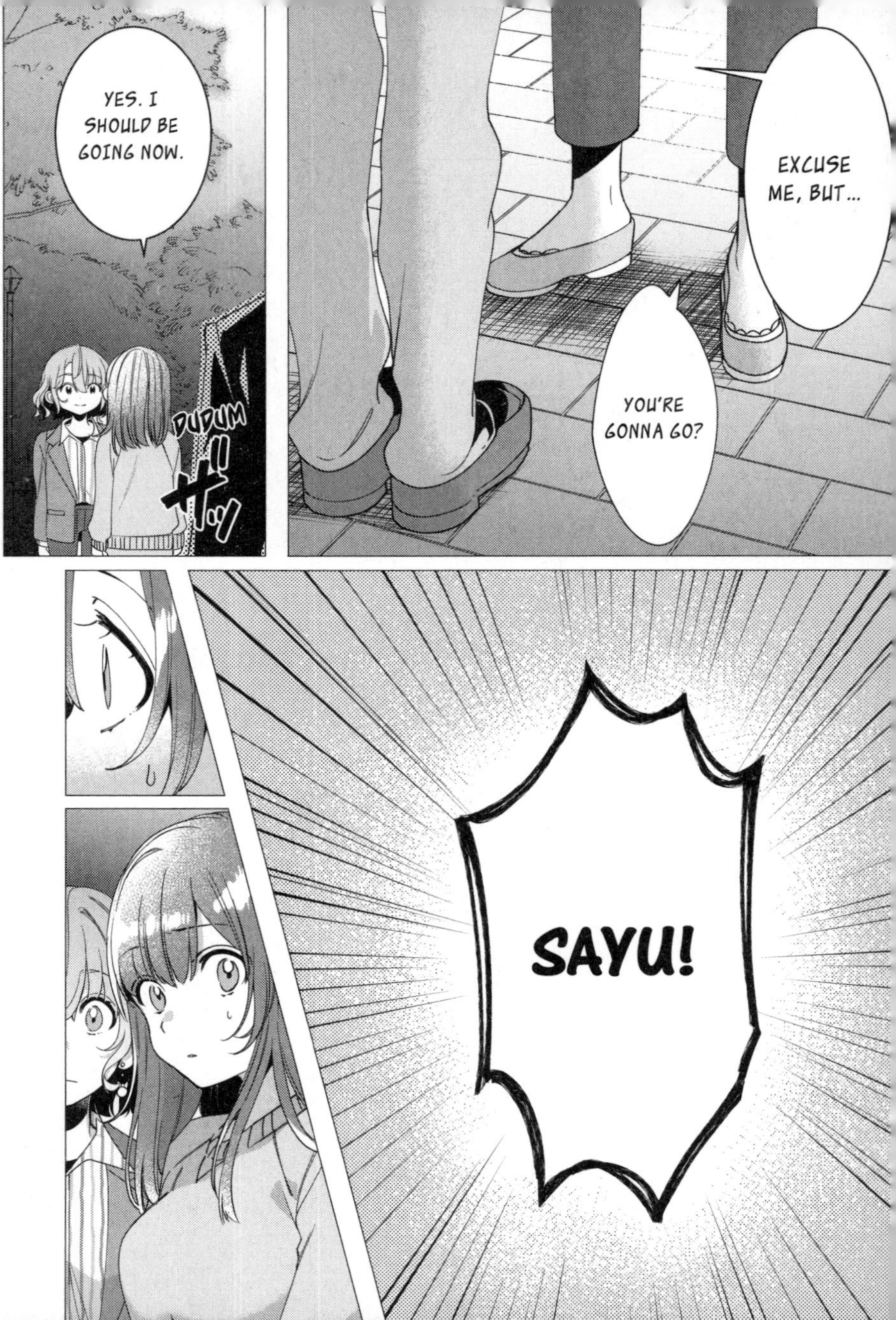
EXCUSE ME, BUT...
YOU'RE GONNA GO?
YES. I SHOULD BE GOING NOW.
DUDUM!!
SAYU!

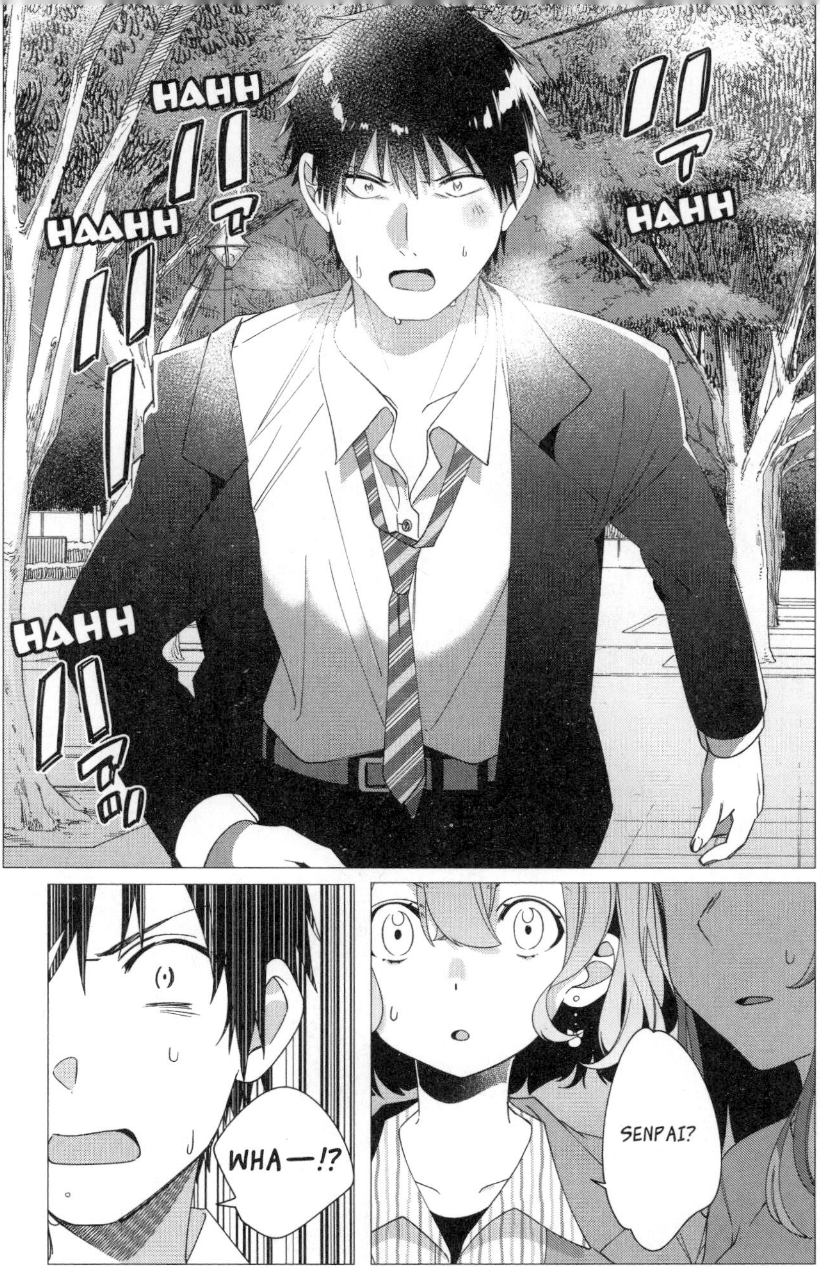
HAHH
HAHH
HAAHH
HAHH
SENPAI?
WHA—!?

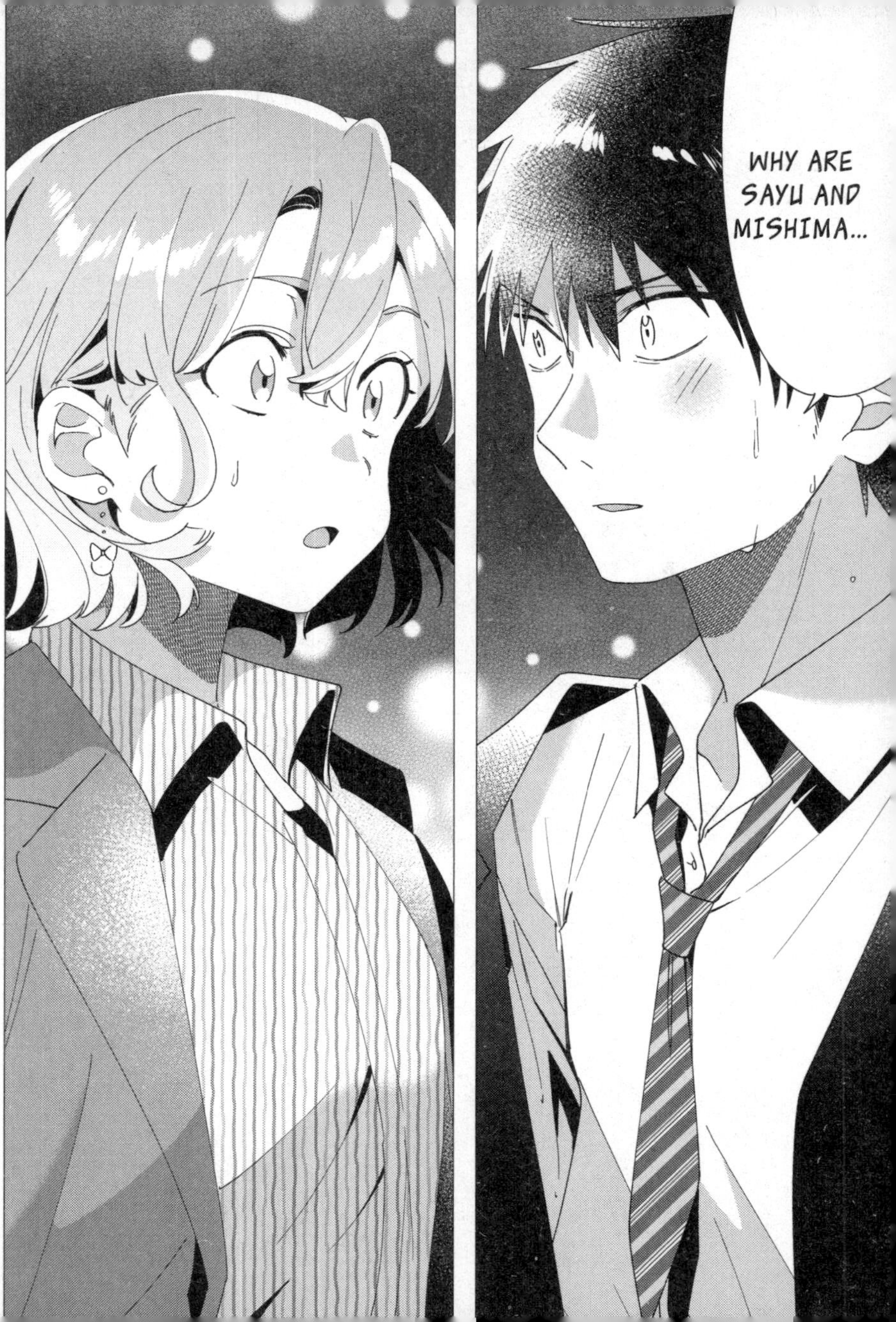
WHY ARE SAYU AND MISHIMA...

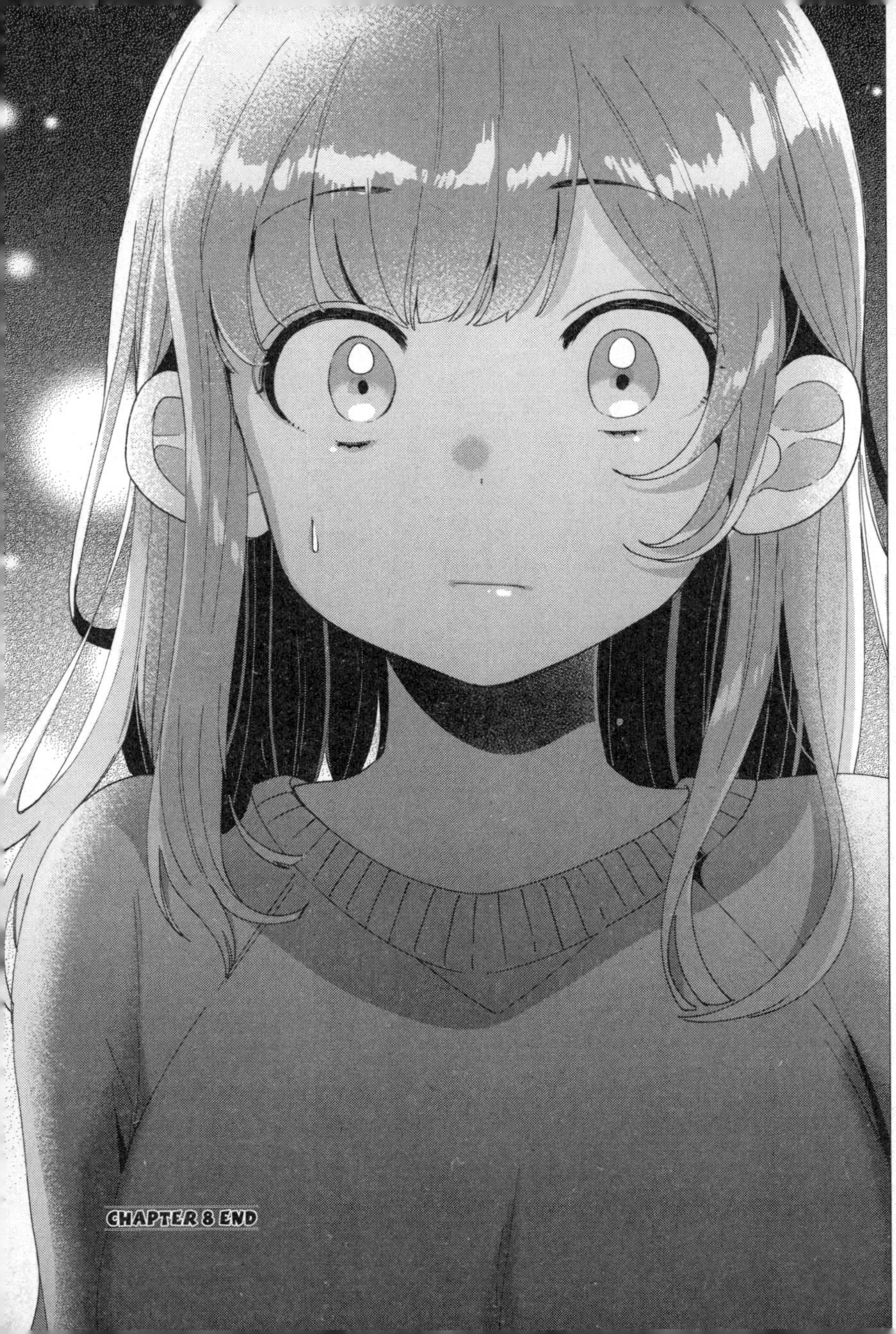
CHAPTER 8 END

HIGEHIRO
After Being Rejected,
I Shaved and Took
in a High School Runaway

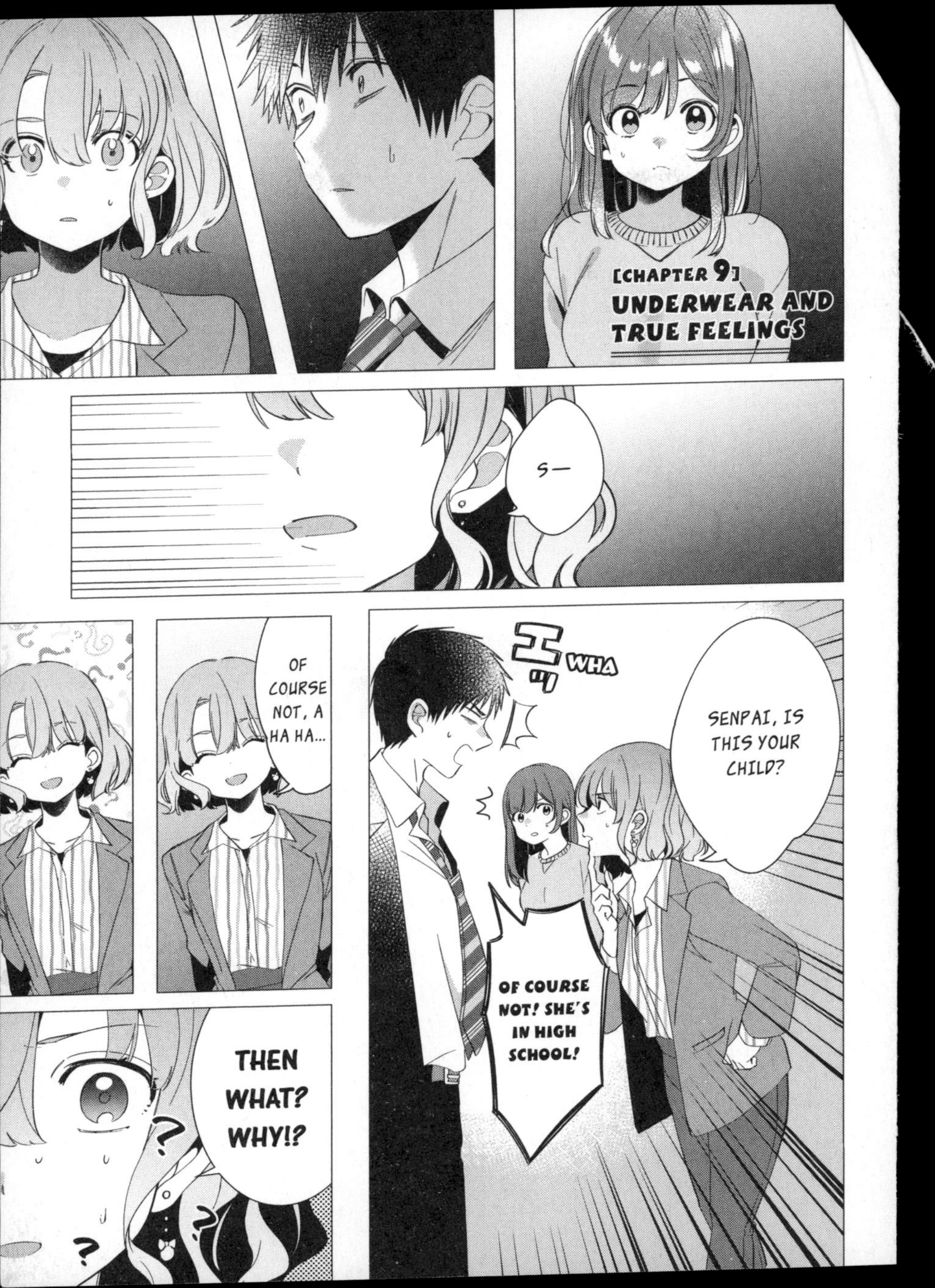
[CHAPTER 9]
UNDERWEAR AND TRUE FEELINGS
S—
SENPAI, IS THIS YOUR CHILD?
WHA
OF COURSE NOT! SHE'S IN HIGH SCHOOL!
OF COURSE NOT, A HA HA...
THEN WHAT? WHY!?

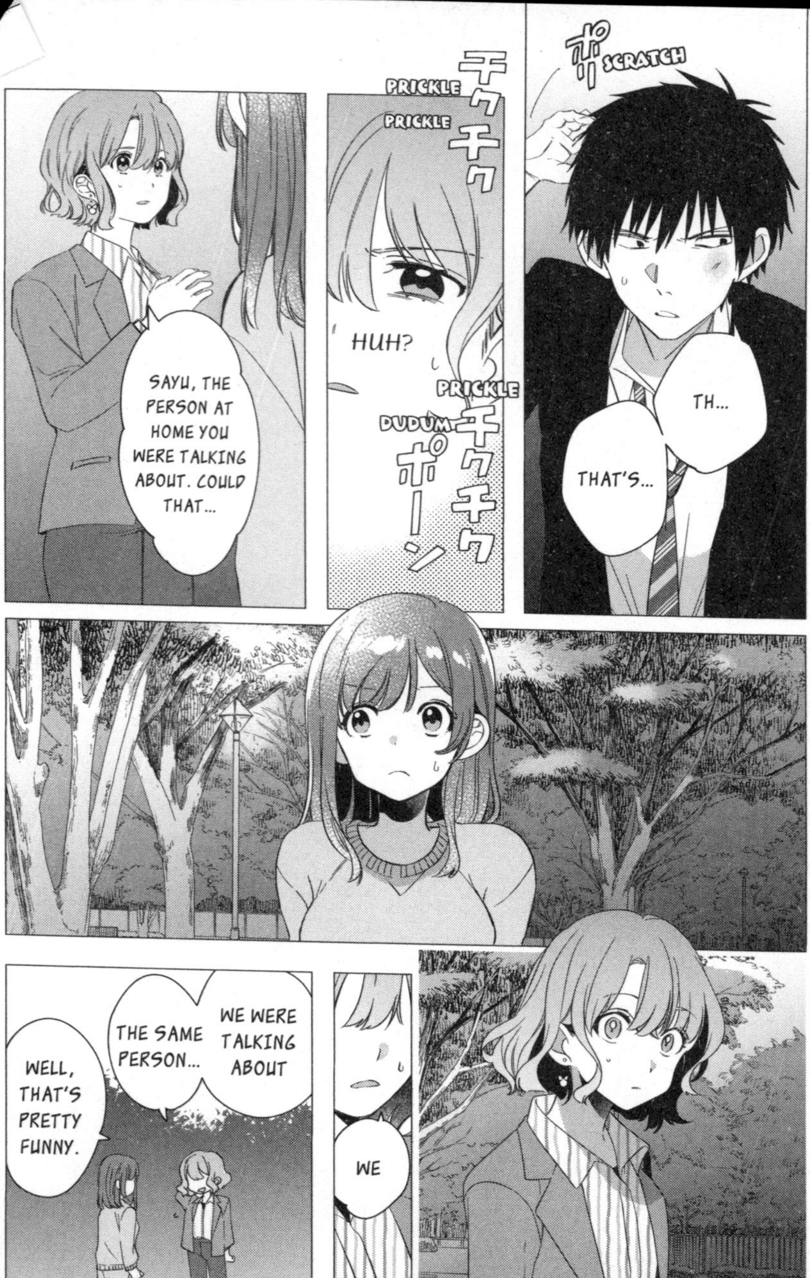

ポリ SCRATCH
TH...
THAT'S...
チクチク PRICKLE PRICKLE
HUH?
チクチク PRICKLE
ポーン DUDUM
SAYU, THE PERSON AT HOME YOU WERE TALKING ABOUT. COULD THAT...
WE
WE WERE TALKING ABOUT
THE SAME PERSON...
WELL, THAT'S PRETTY FUNNY.

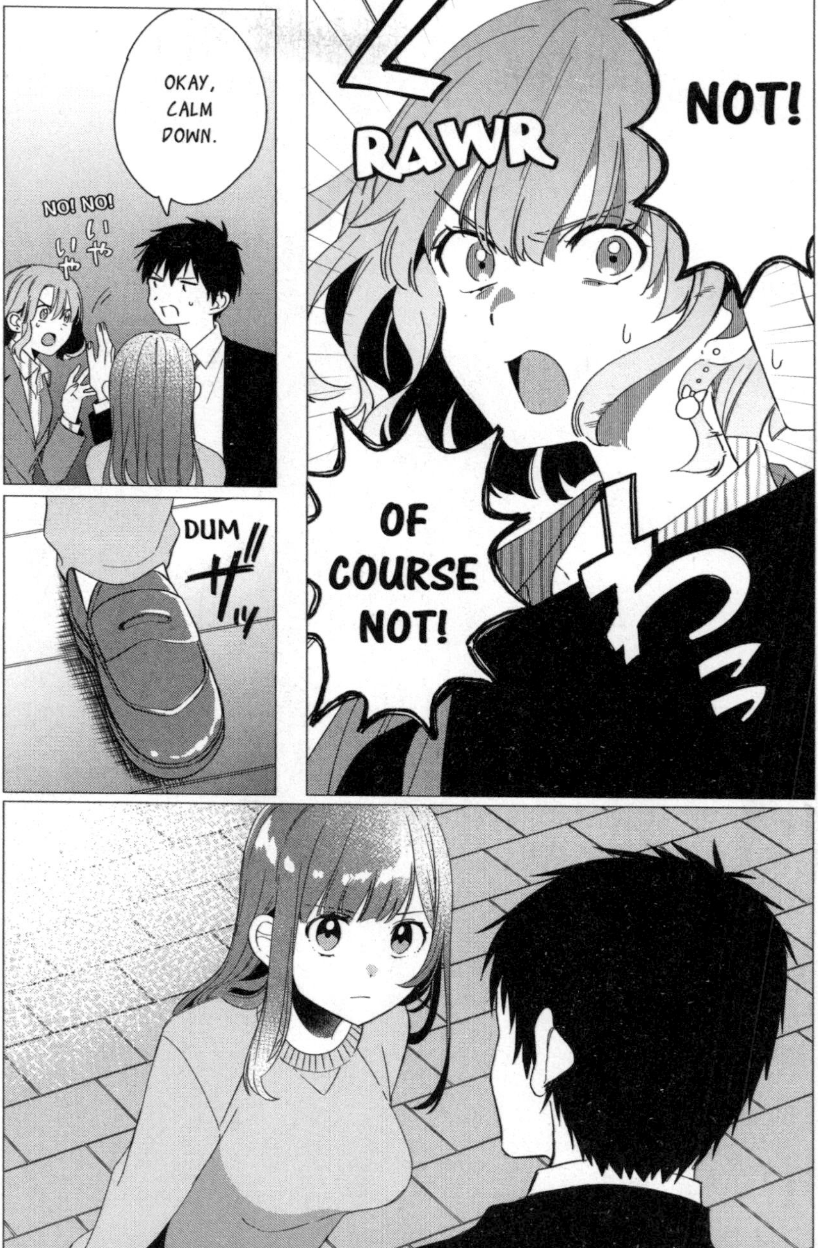
NOT!
RAWR
OF COURSE NOT!
OKAY, CALM DOWN.
NO! NO!
いや いや
DUM

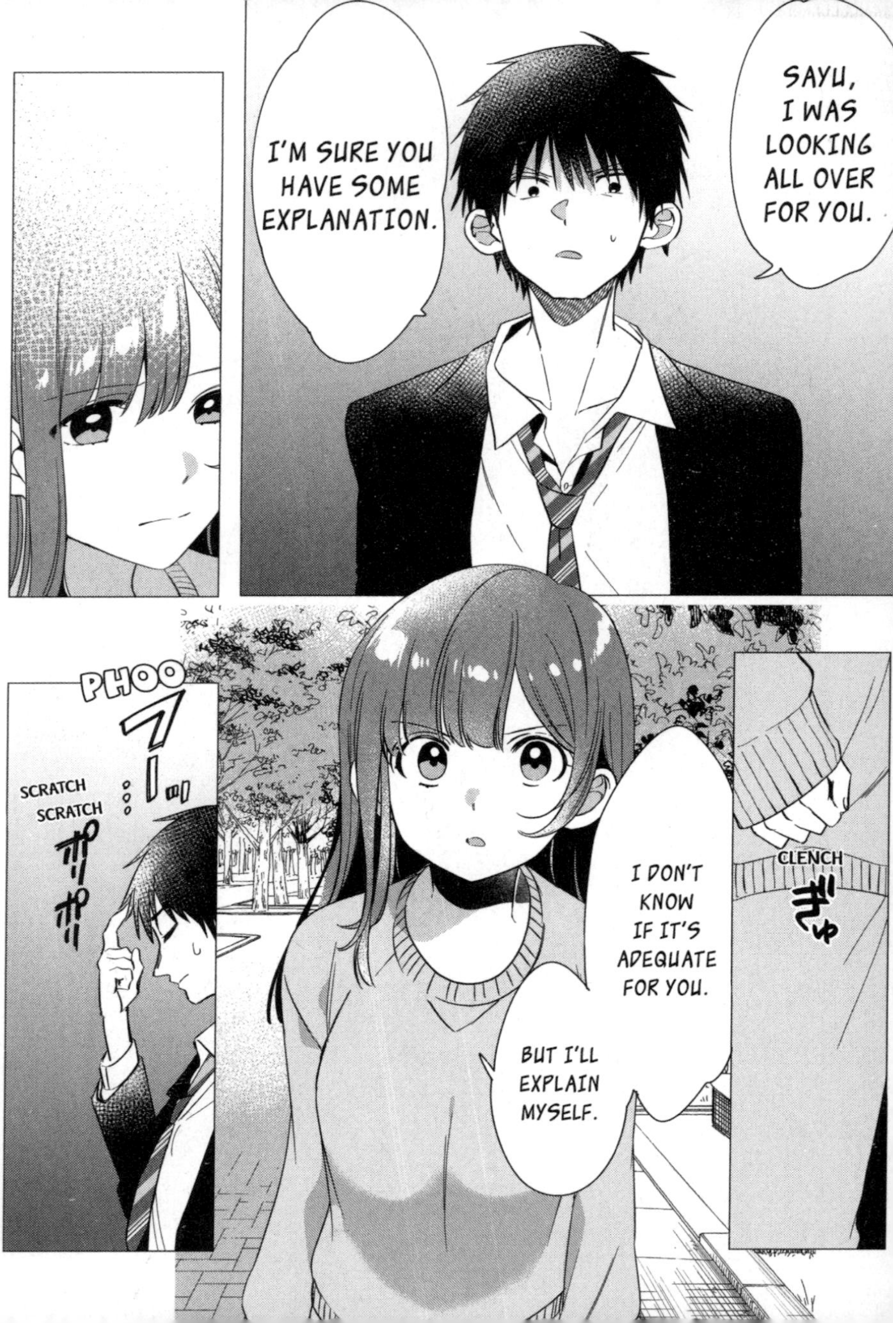
SAYU, I WAS LOOKING ALL OVER FOR YOU.
I'M SURE YOU HAVE SOME EXPLANATION.
CLENCH
ぎゅ
I DON'T KNOW IF IT'S ADEQUATE FOR YOU.
BUT I'LL EXPLAIN MYSELF.
PHOO
フーッ…
SCRATCH SCRATCH
ポリポリ

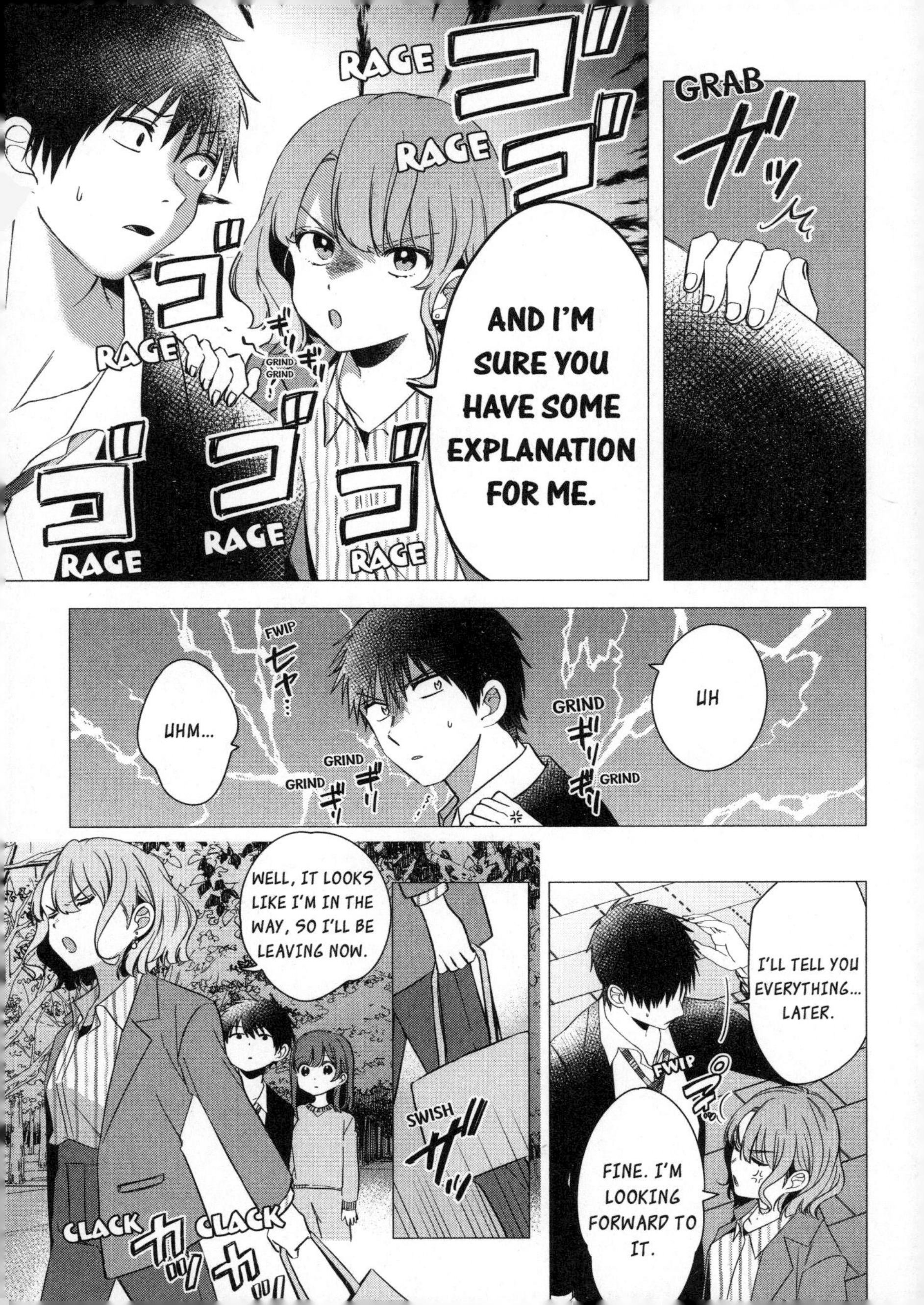
GRAB
RAGE
RAGE
AND I'M SURE YOU HAVE SOME EXPLANATION FOR ME.
RAGE
GRIND GRIND
RAGE
RAGE
RAGE
UH
GRIND
GRIND
GRIND
GRIND
FWIP
UHM...
I'LL TELL YOU EVERYTHING... LATER.
FWIP
FINE. I'M LOOKING FORWARD TO IT.
WELL, IT LOOKS LIKE I'M IN THE WAY, SO I'LL BE LEAVING NOW.
SWISH
CLACK CLACK

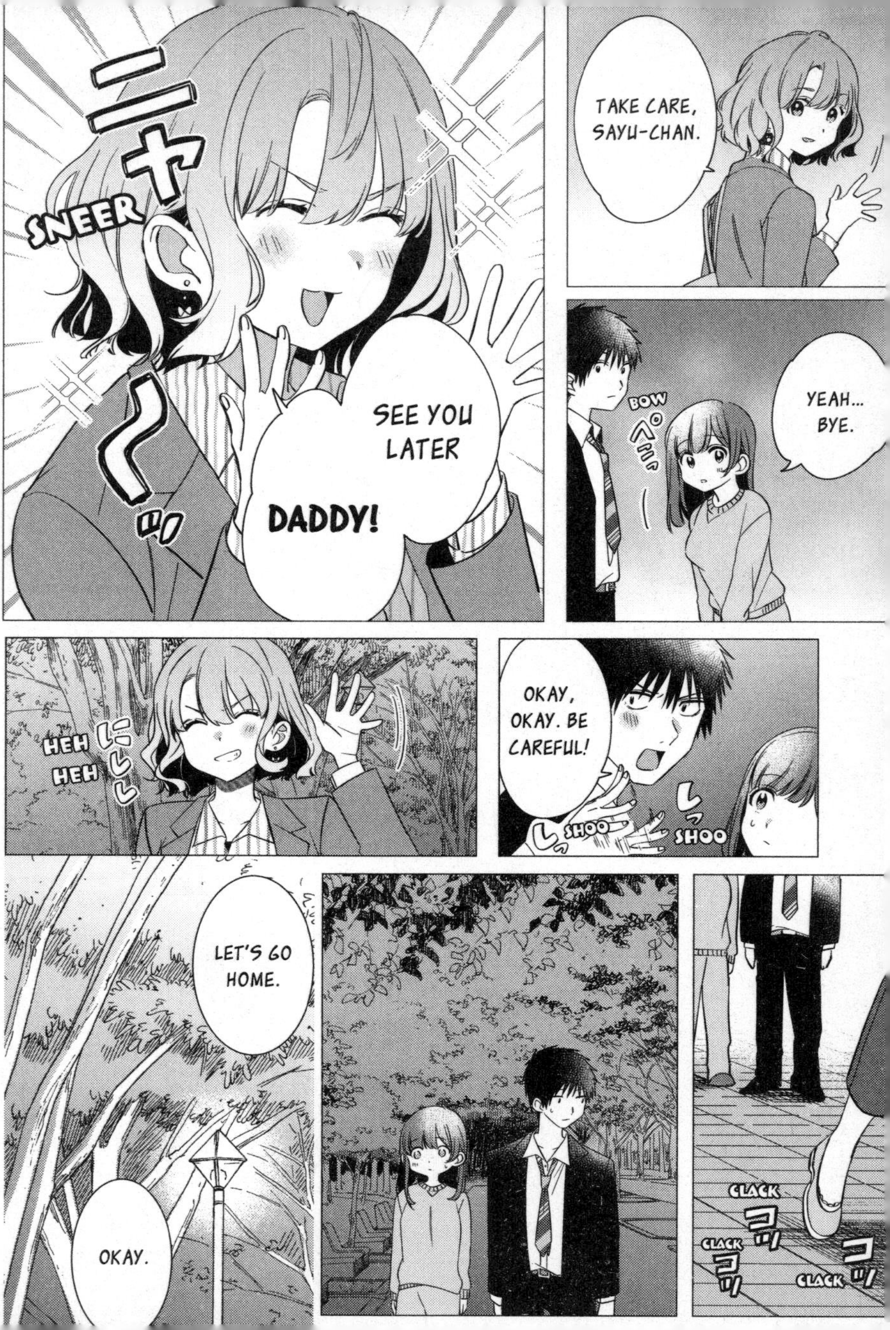
TAKE CARE, SAYU-CHAN.
BOW
YEAH... BYE.
SNEER
SEE YOU LATER DADDY!
OKAY, OKAY. BE CAREFUL!
SHOO
SHOO
HEH HEH
CLACK
CLACK
CLACK
LET'S GO HOME.
OKAY.

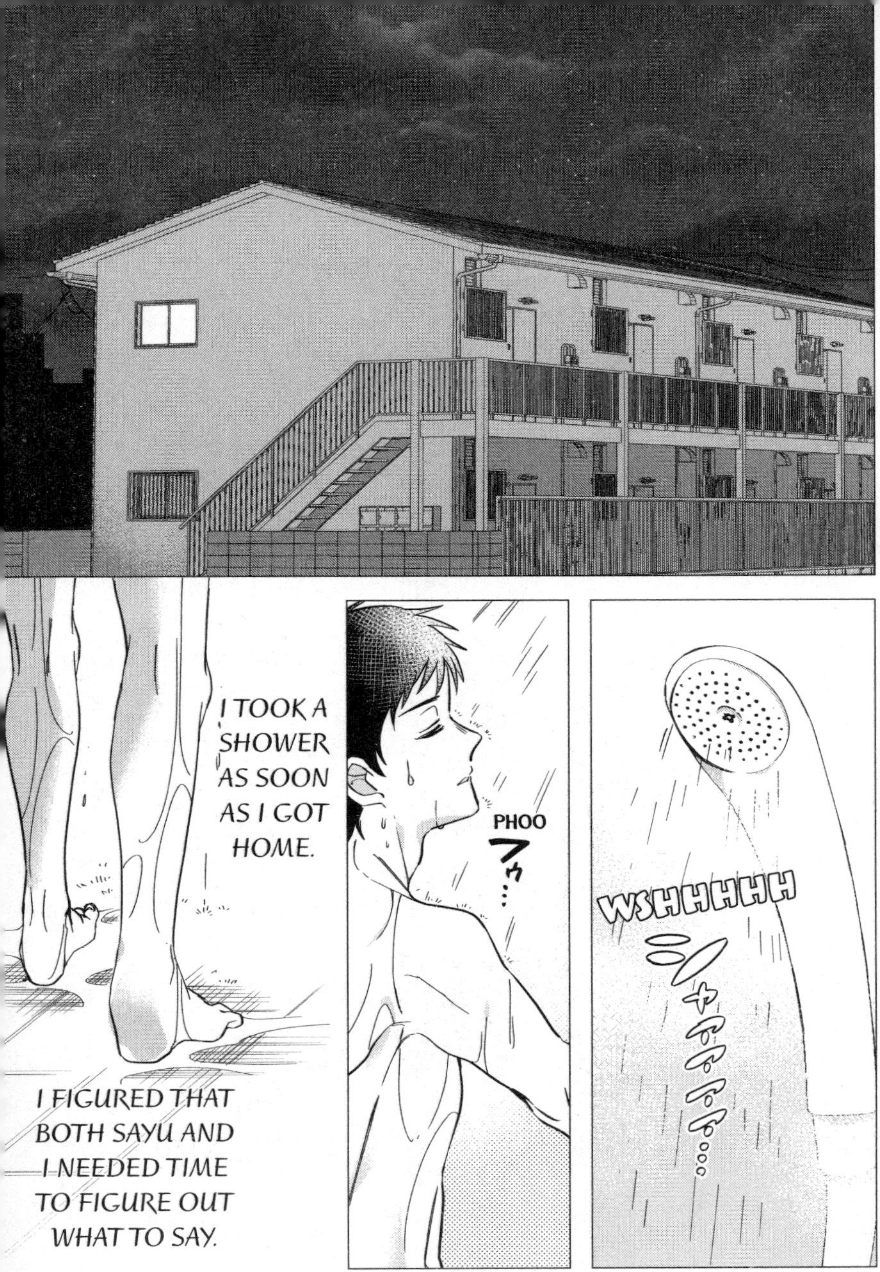
WSHHHHH
PHOO
フゥ…
I TOOK A SHOWER AS SOON AS I GOT HOME.
I FIGURED THAT BOTH SAYU AND I NEEDED TIME TO FIGURE OUT WHAT TO SAY.

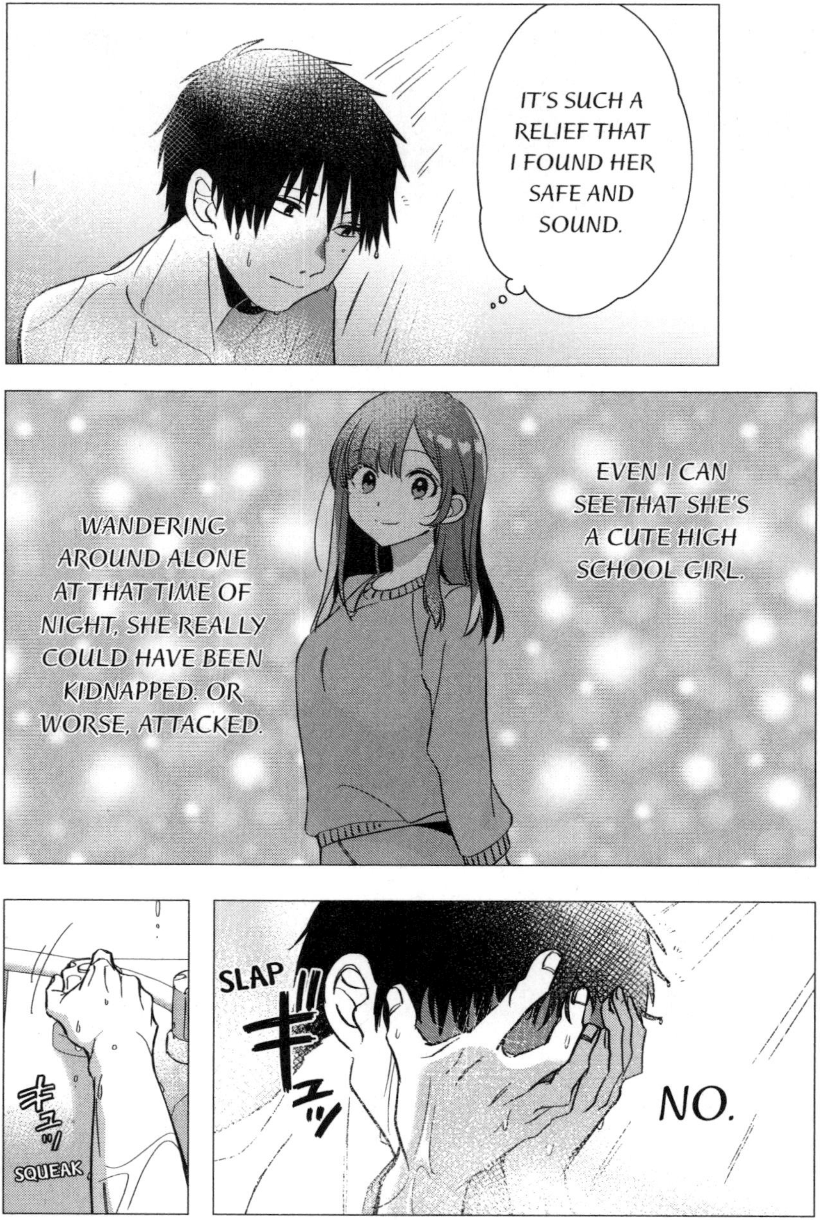
IT'S SUCH A RELIEF THAT I FOUND HER SAFE AND SOUND.
EVEN I CAN SEE THAT SHE'S A CUTE HIGH SCHOOL GIRL.
WANDERING AROUND ALONE AT THAT TIME OF NIGHT, SHE REALLY COULD HAVE BEEN KIDNAPPED. OR WORSE, ATTACKED.
SLAP
ギュッ
NO.
キュッ
SQUEAK

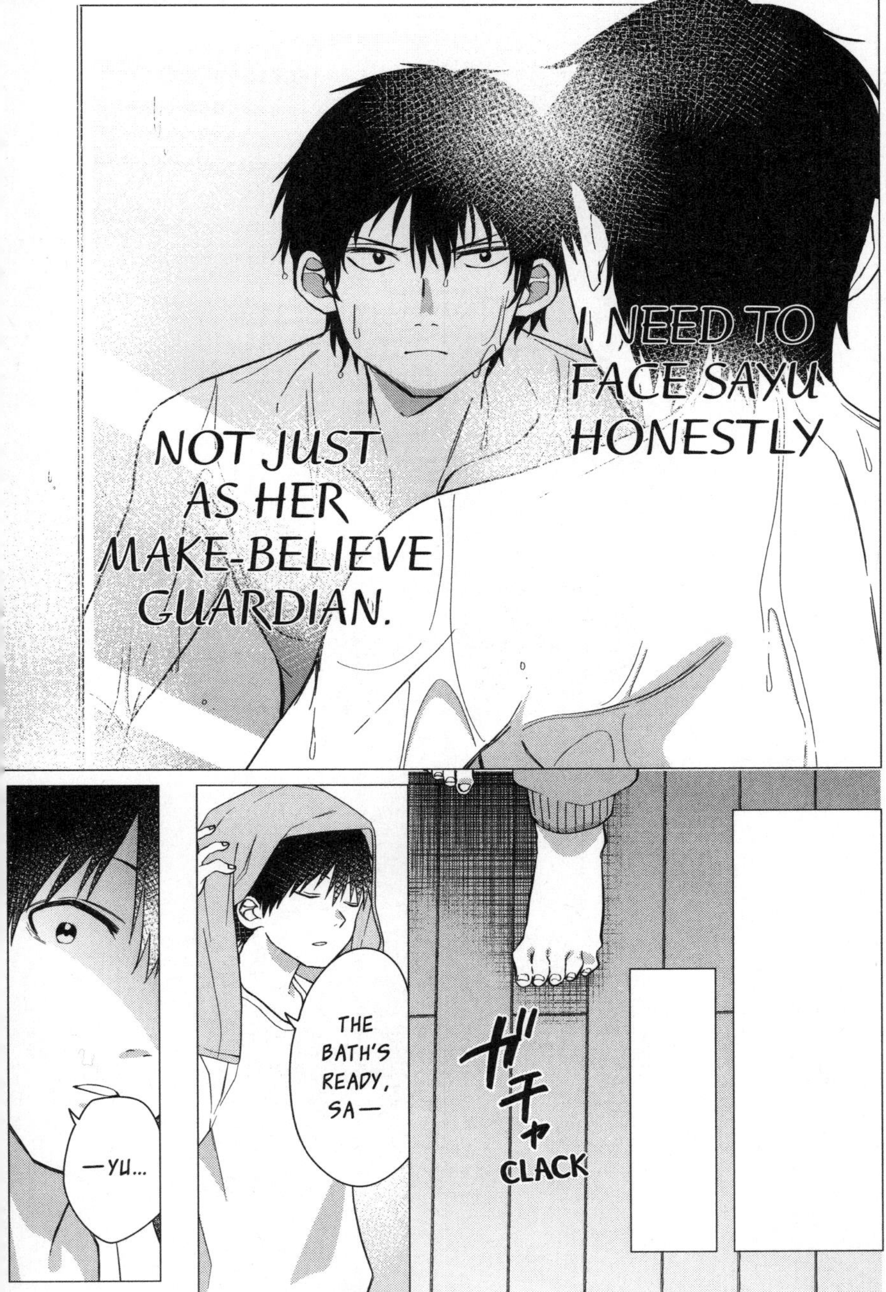
I NEED TO FACE SAYU HONESTLY
NOT JUST AS HER MAKE-BELIEVE GUARDIAN.
ガチャ
CLACK
THE BATH'S READY, SA—
—YU...

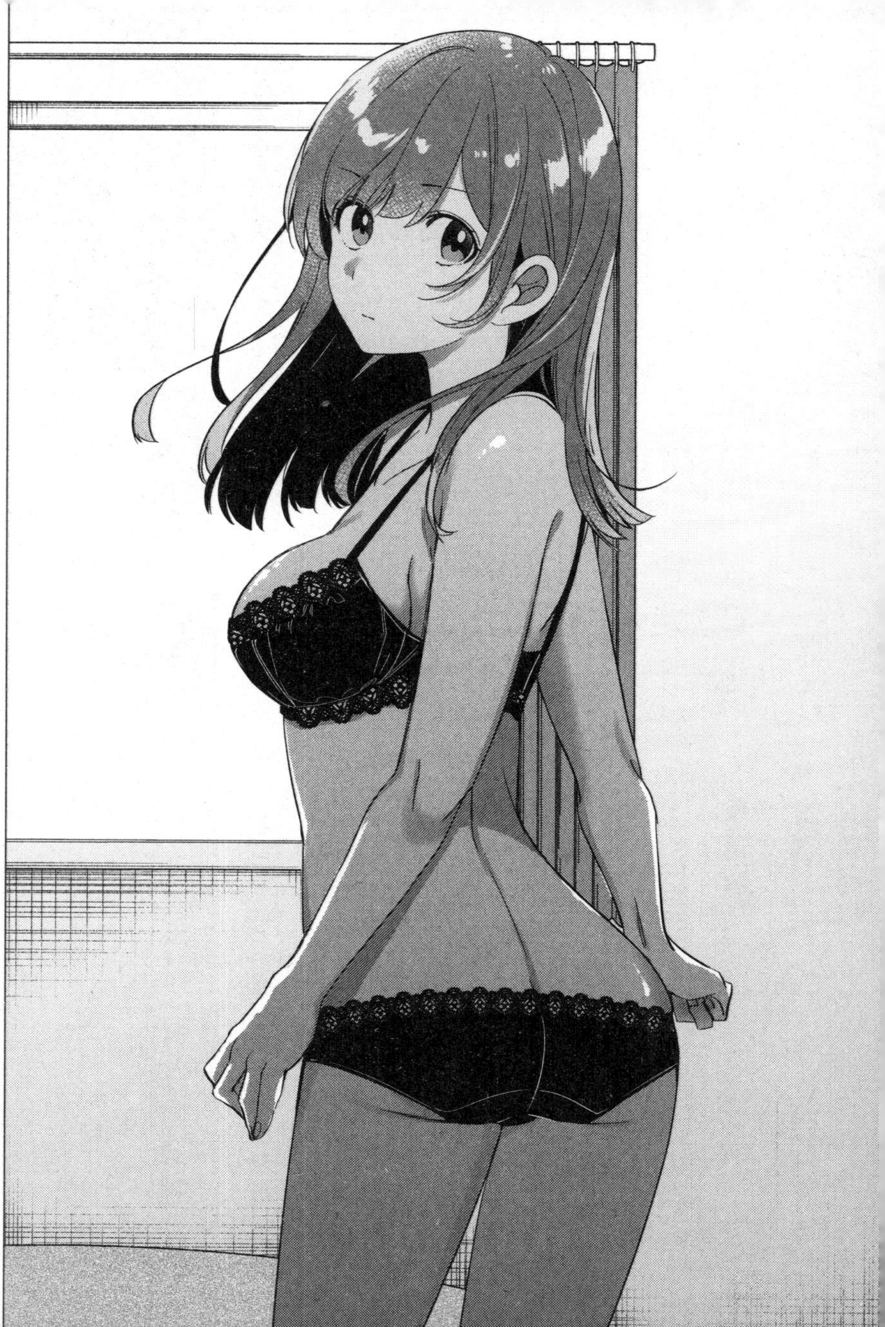

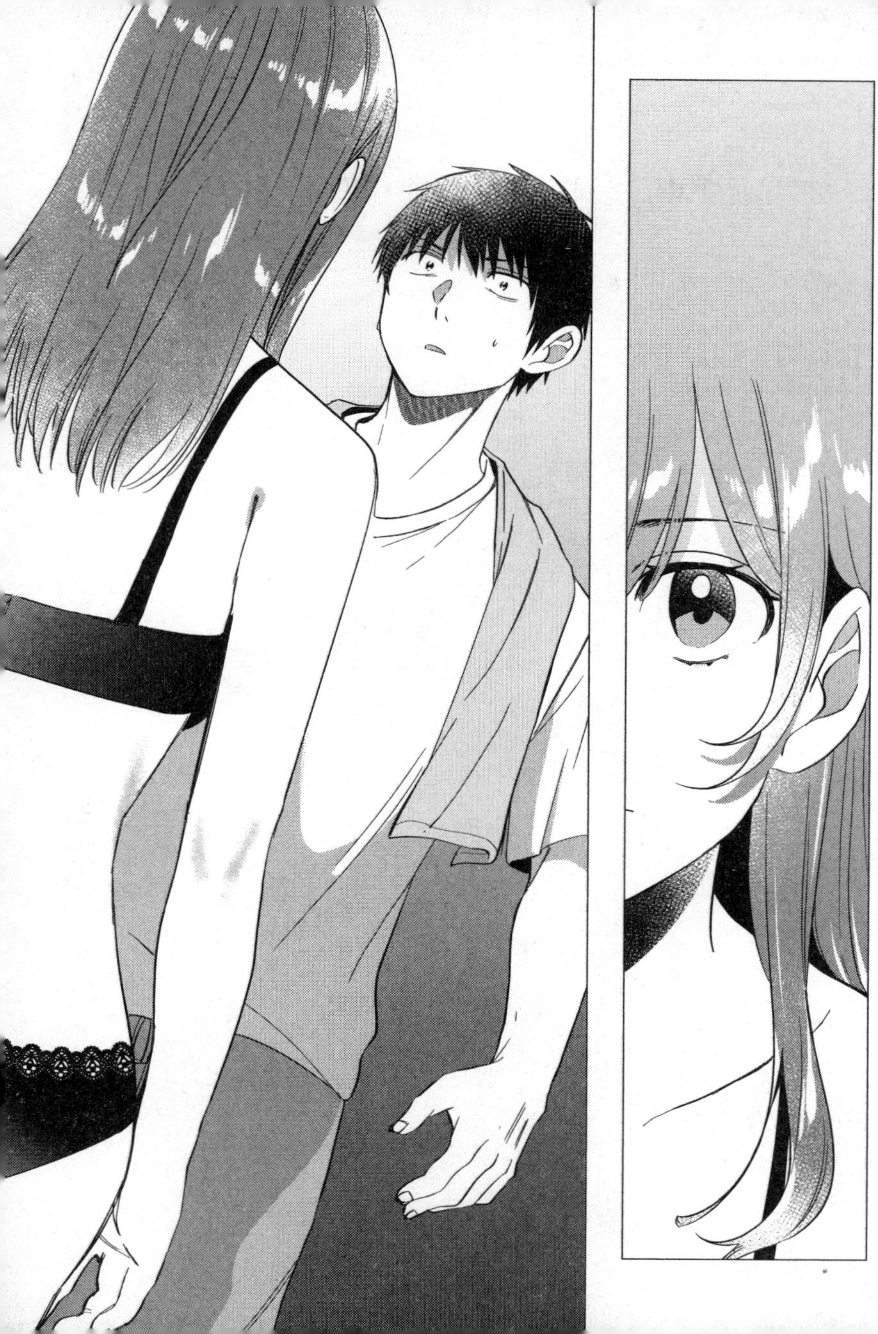

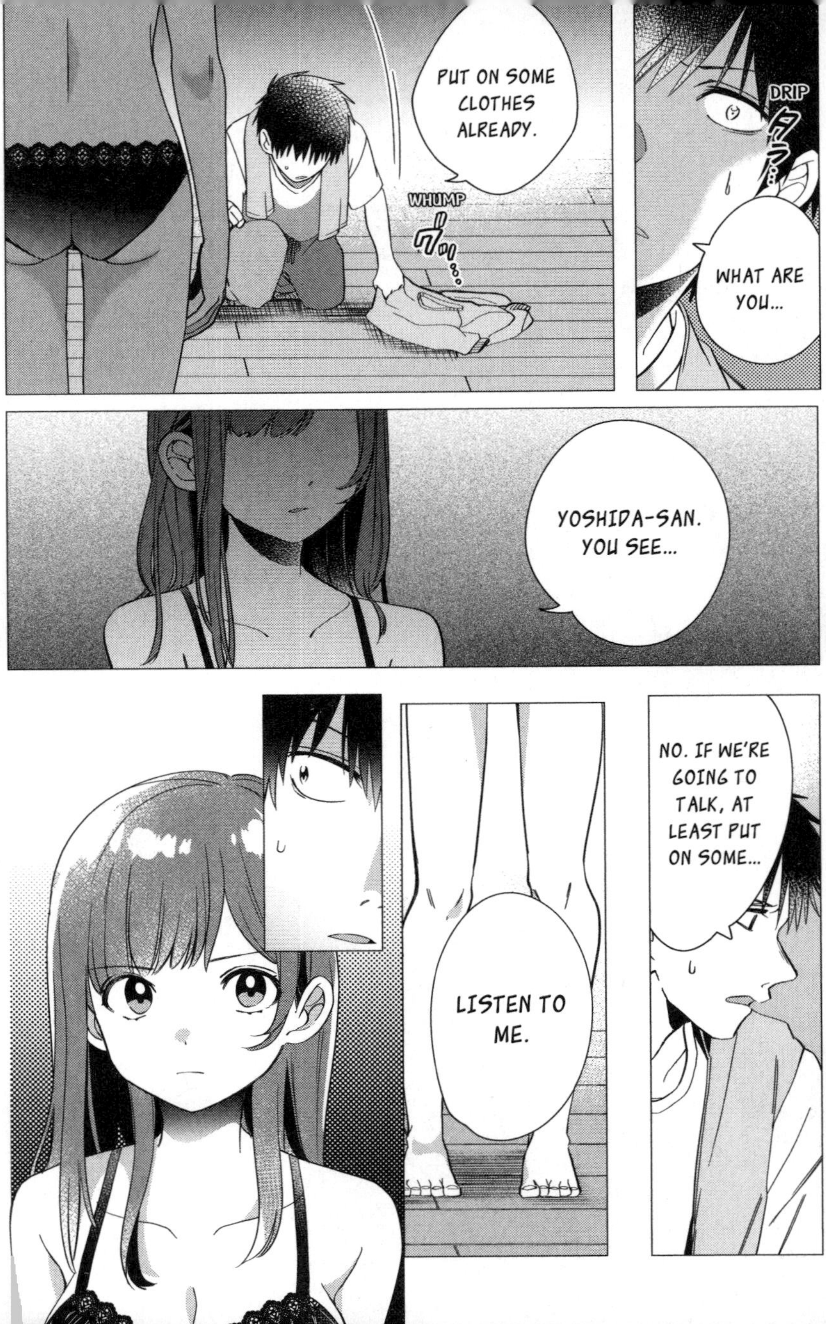
DRIP
WHAT ARE YOU...
PUT ON SOME CLOTHES ALREADY.
WHUMP
YOSHIDA-SAN. YOU SEE...
NO. IF WE'RE GOING TO TALK, AT LEAST PUT ON SOME...
LISTEN TO ME.

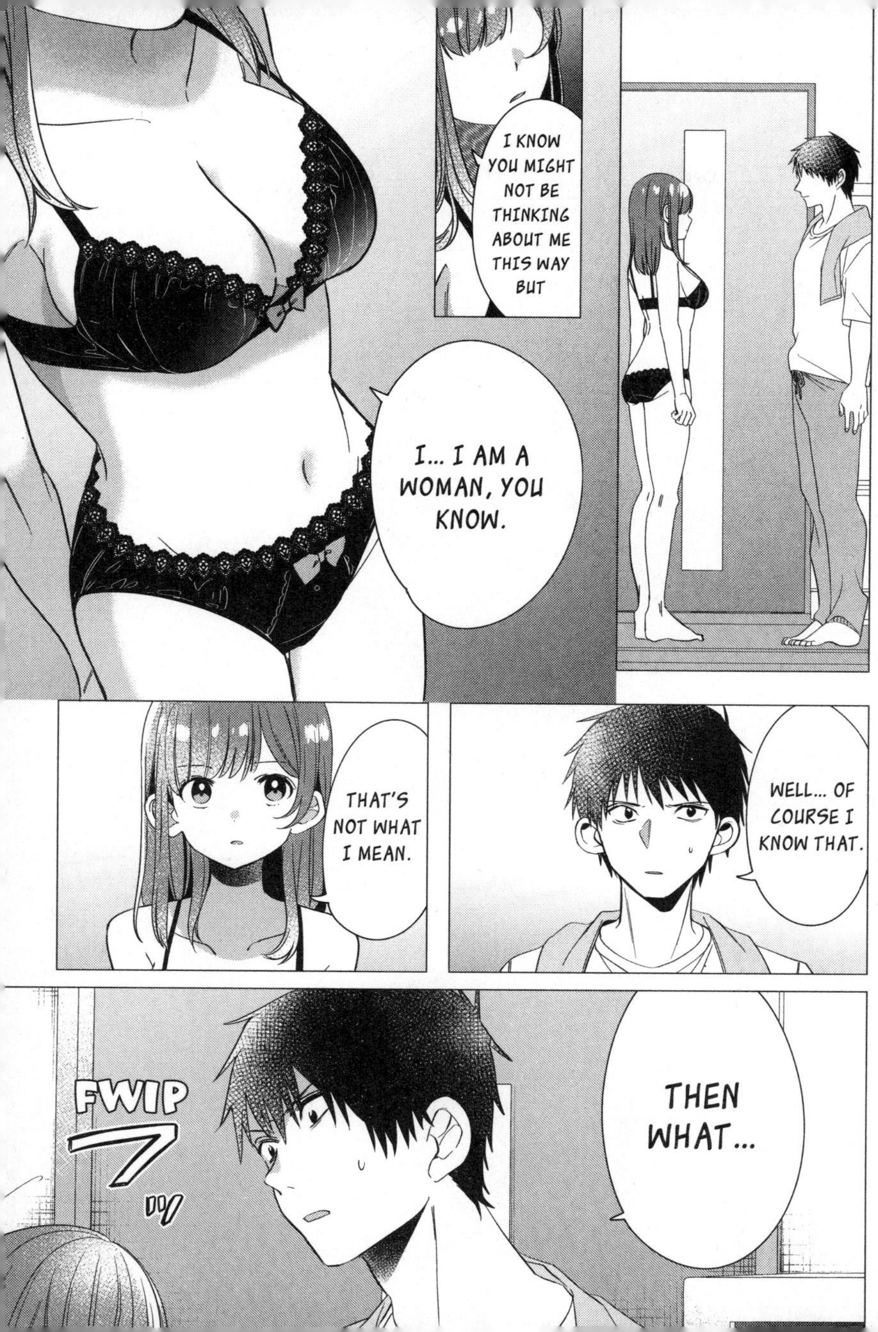
I KNOW YOU MIGHT NOT BE THINKING ABOUT ME THIS WAY BUT
I... I AM A WOMAN, YOU KNOW.
WELL... OF COURSE I KNOW THAT.
THAT'S NOT WHAT I MEAN.
THEN WHAT...
FWIP

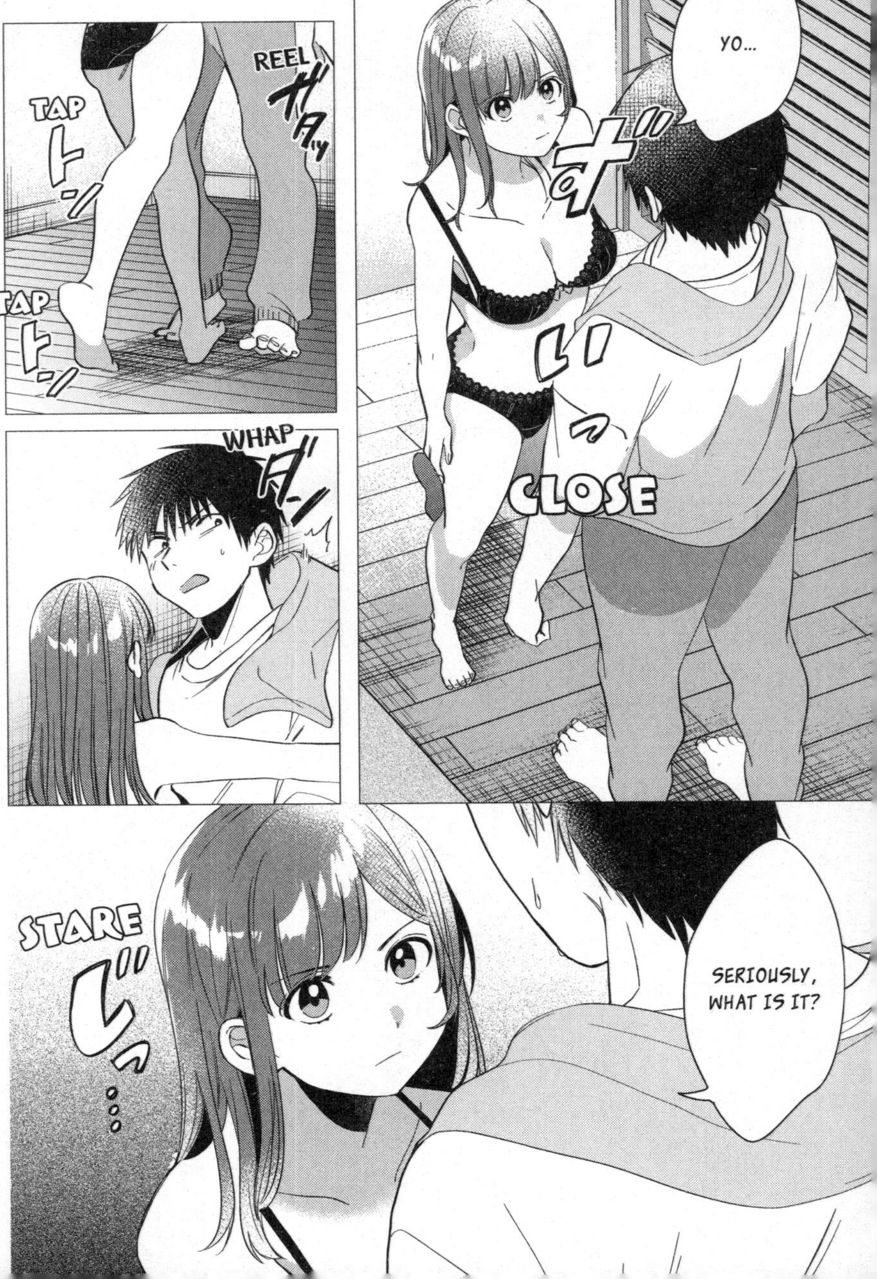
YO...
CLOSE
REEL
TAP
TAP
WHAP
SERIOUSLY, WHAT IS IT?
STARE

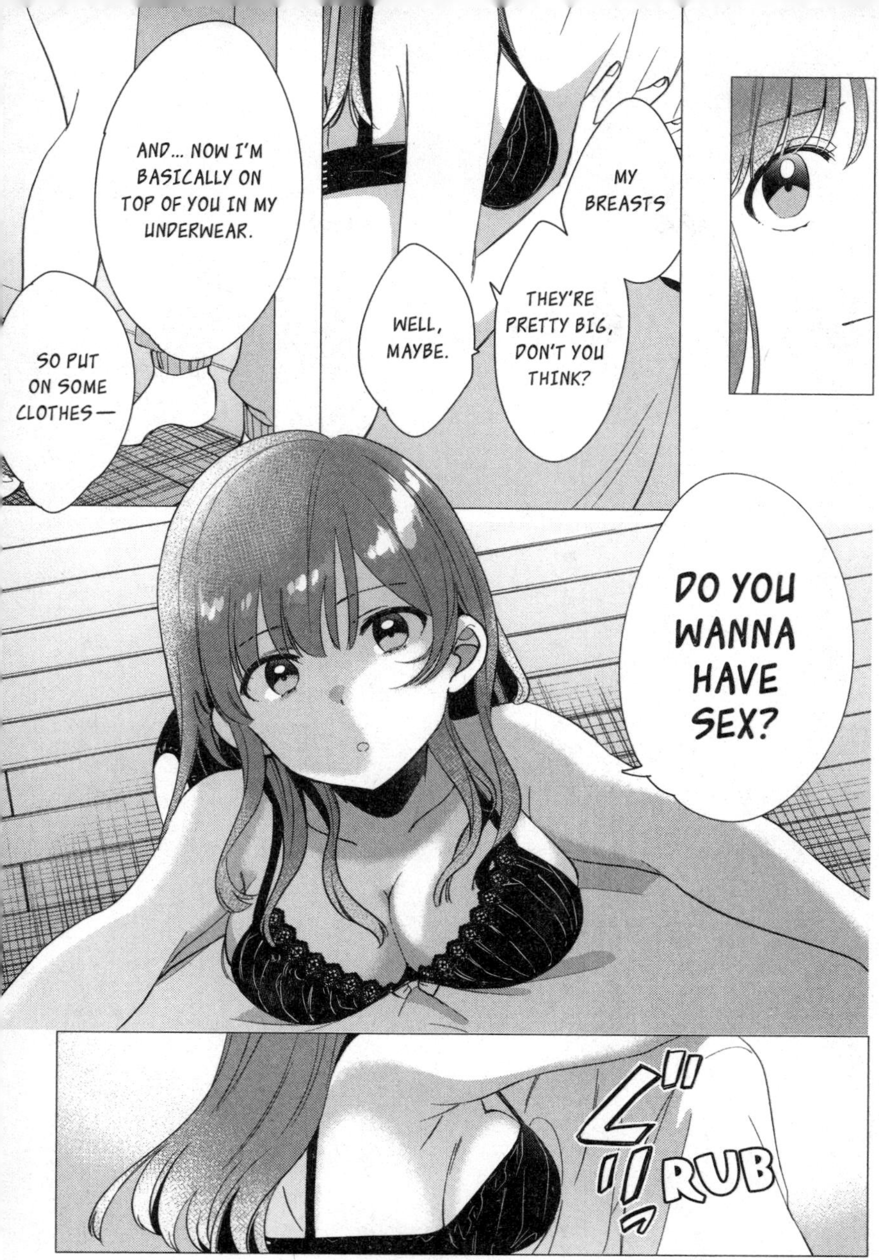
MY BREASTS
THEY'RE PRETTY BIG, DON'T YOU THINK?
WELL, MAYBE.
AND... NOW I'M BASICALLY ON TOP OF YOU IN MY UNDERWEAR.
SO PUT ON SOME CLOTHES—
DO YOU WANNA HAVE SEX?
RUB

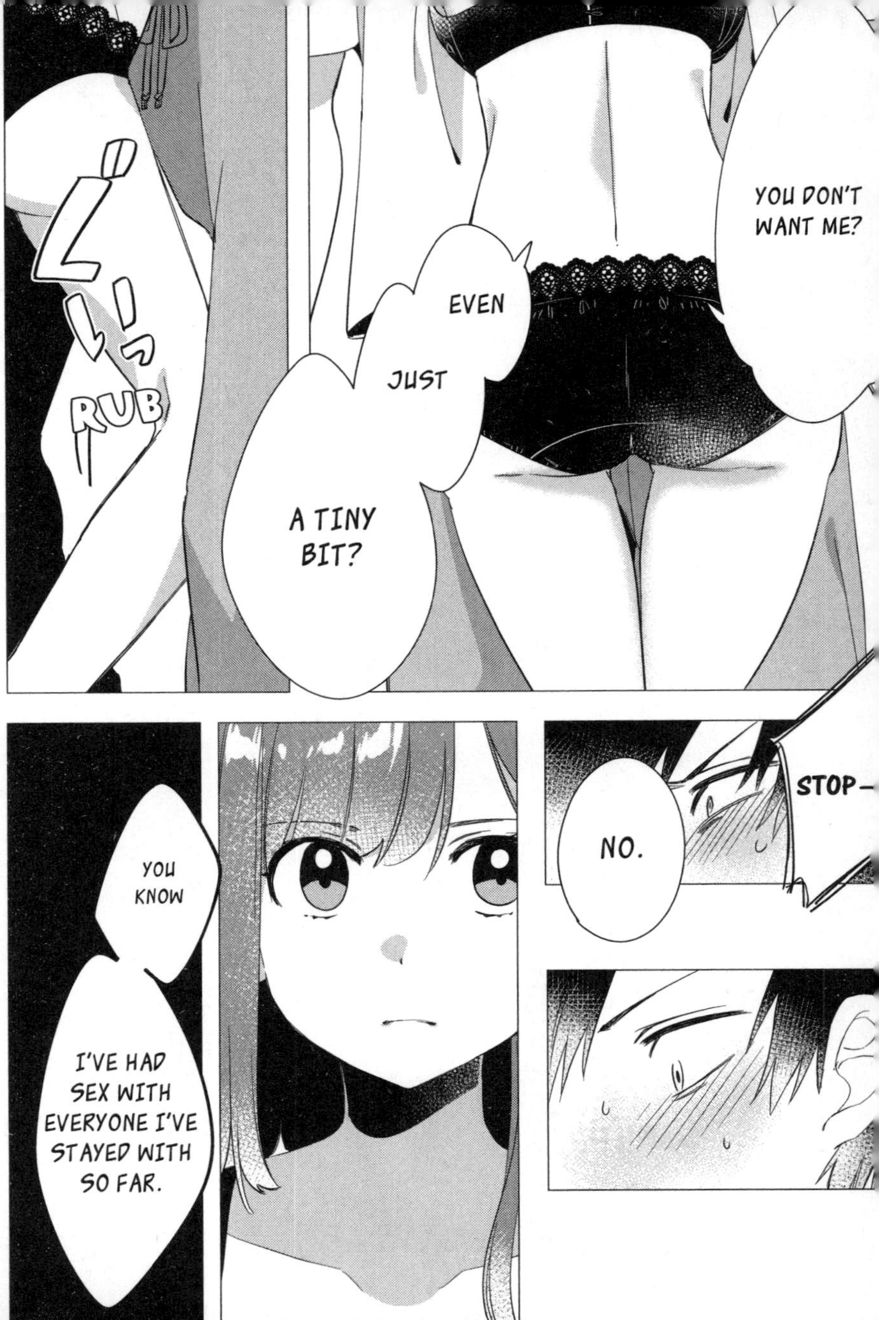
YOU DON'T WANT ME?
EVEN JUST A TINY BIT?
RUB
STOP—
NO.
YOU KNOW
I'VE HAD SEX WITH EVERYONE I'VE STAYED WITH SO FAR.

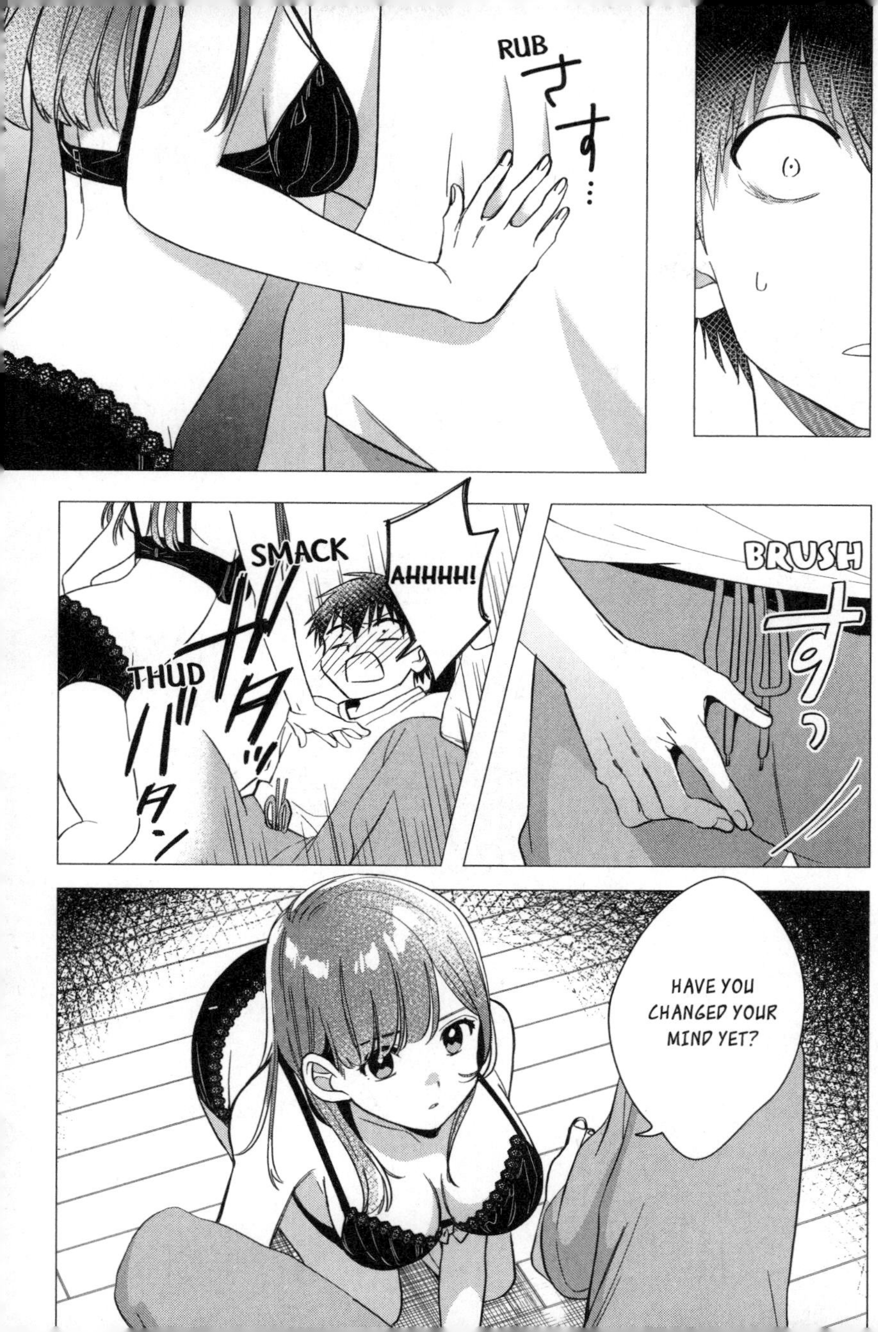
RUB
さす…
BRUSH
すっ
AHHHH!
SMACK
THUD
HAVE YOU CHANGED YOUR MIND YET?

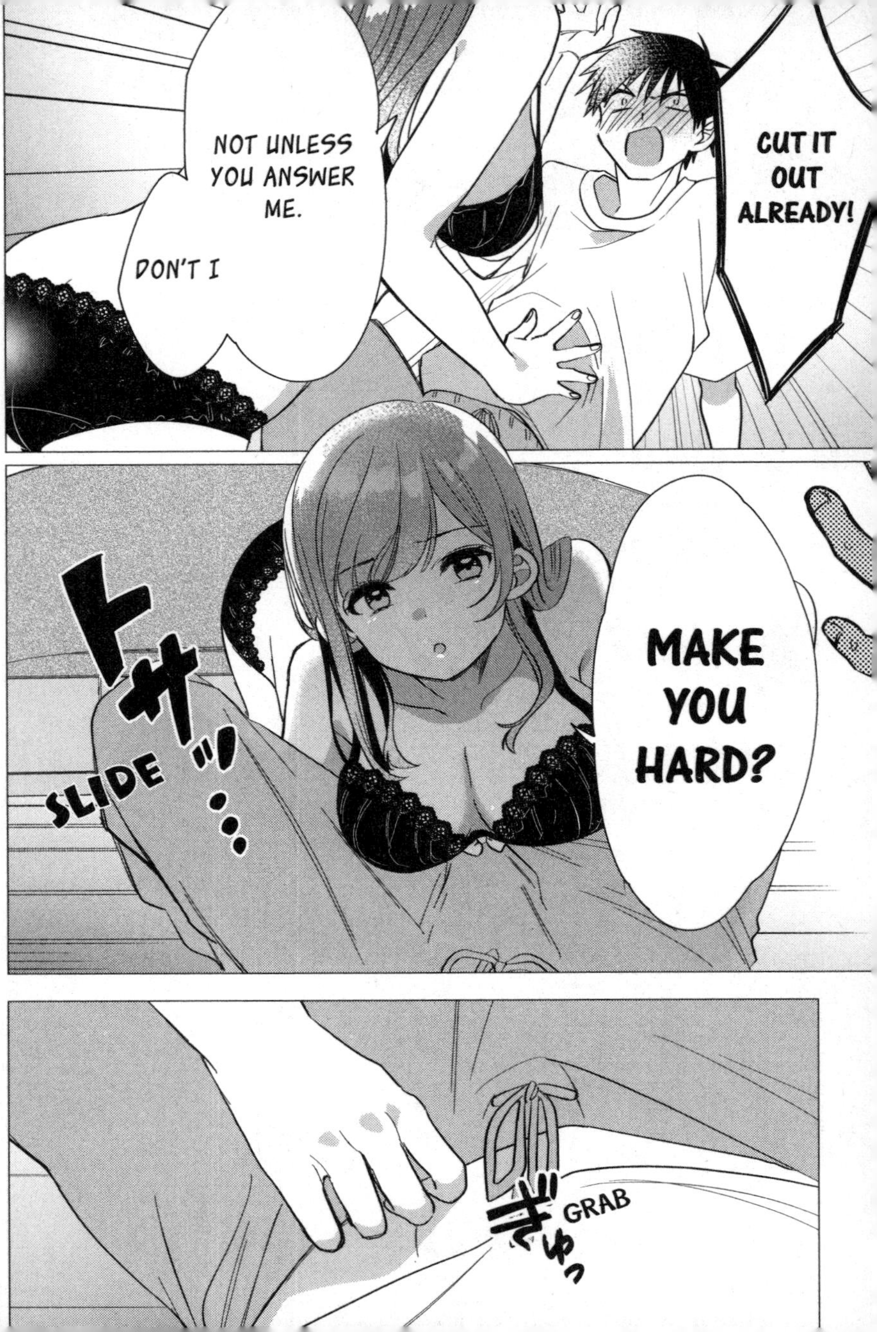
CUT IT OUT ALREADY!
NOT UNLESS YOU ANSWER ME.
DON'T I
MAKE YOU HARD?
SLIDE...
GRAB

 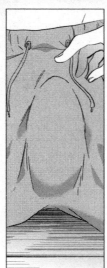 

FLUSH

IN THIS SITUATION, THERE'S NOT A MAN ALIVE WHO WOULDN'T BE.

YEAH, YOU DO.

STAGGER

WHY ARE YOU ACTING ALL EMBARRASSED? GET OUT OF HERE. AND GIVE ME SOME SPACE.

S-SORRY...

FLUSTER

O-OKAY.

FLUSTER

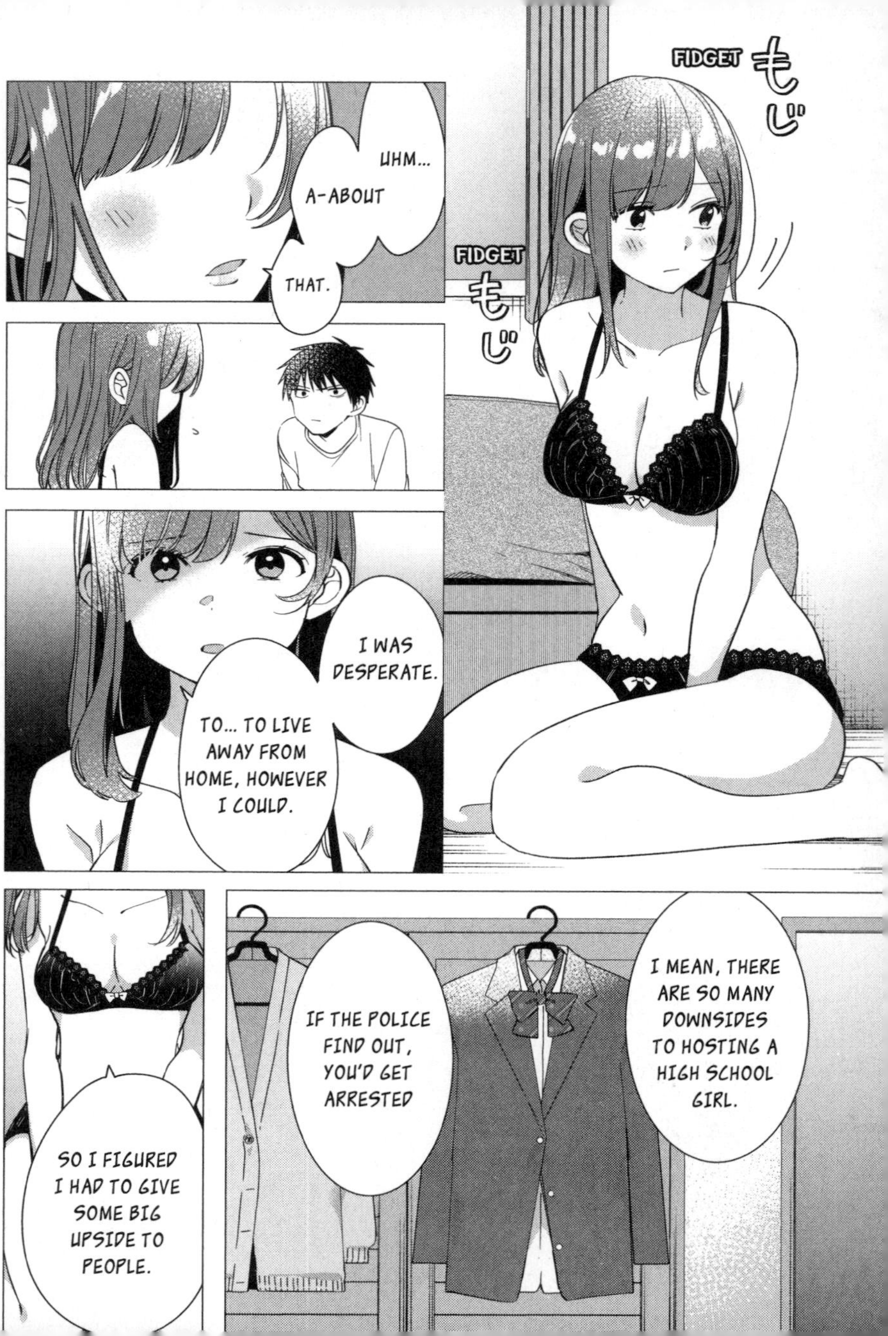
FIDGET もじ
FIDGET もじ
UHM... A-ABOUT THAT.
I WAS DESPERATE.
TO... TO LIVE AWAY FROM HOME, HOWEVER I COULD.
I MEAN, THERE ARE SO MANY DOWNSIDES TO HOSTING A HIGH SCHOOL GIRL.
IF THE POLICE FIND OUT, YOU'D GET ARRESTED
SO I FIGURED I HAD TO GIVE SOME BIG UPSIDE TO PEOPLE.

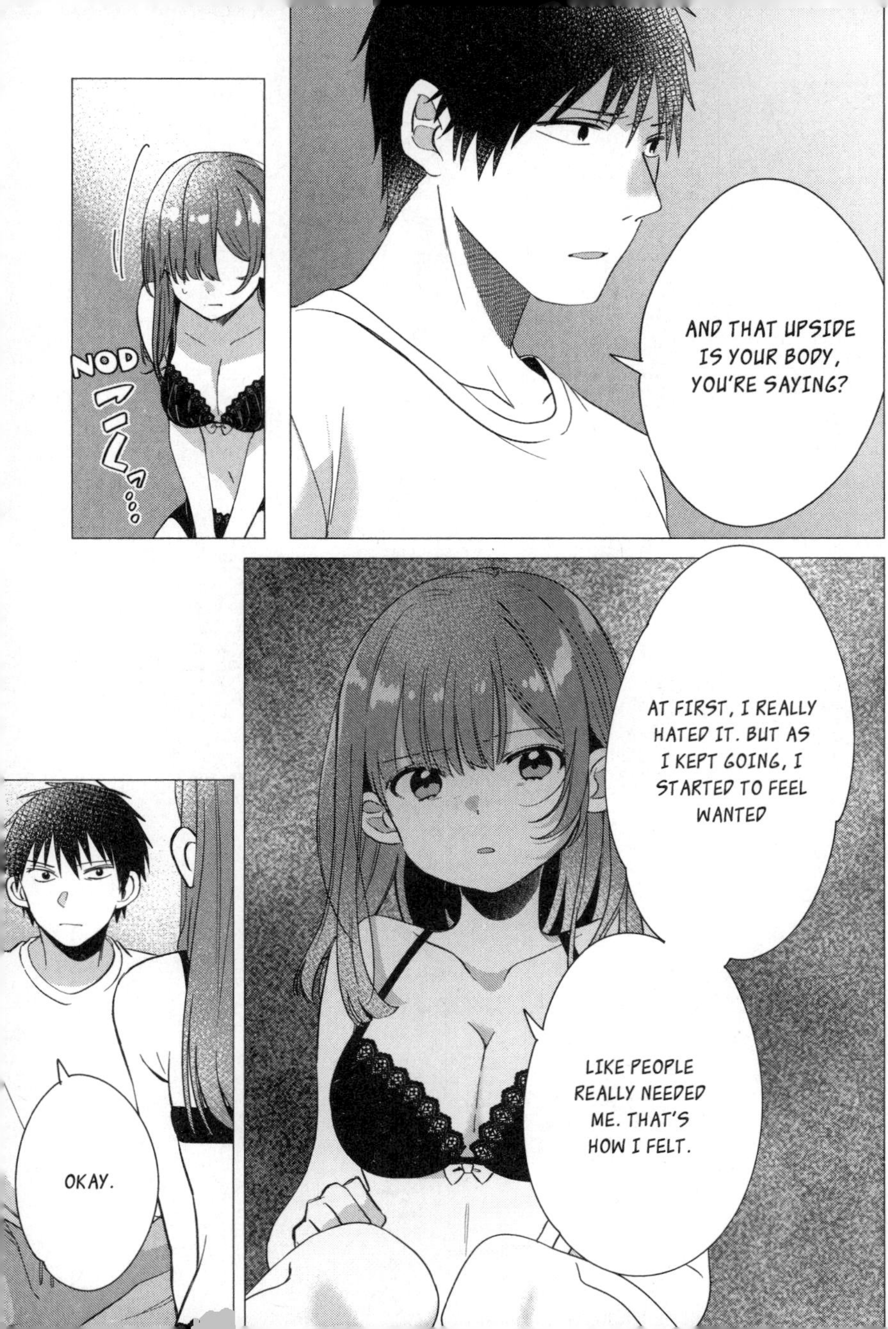
AND THAT UPSIDE IS YOUR BODY, YOU'RE SAYING?
NOD
AT FIRST, I REALLY HATED IT. BUT AS I KEPT GOING, I STARTED TO FEEL WANTED
LIKE PEOPLE REALLY NEEDED ME. THAT'S HOW I FELT.
OKAY.

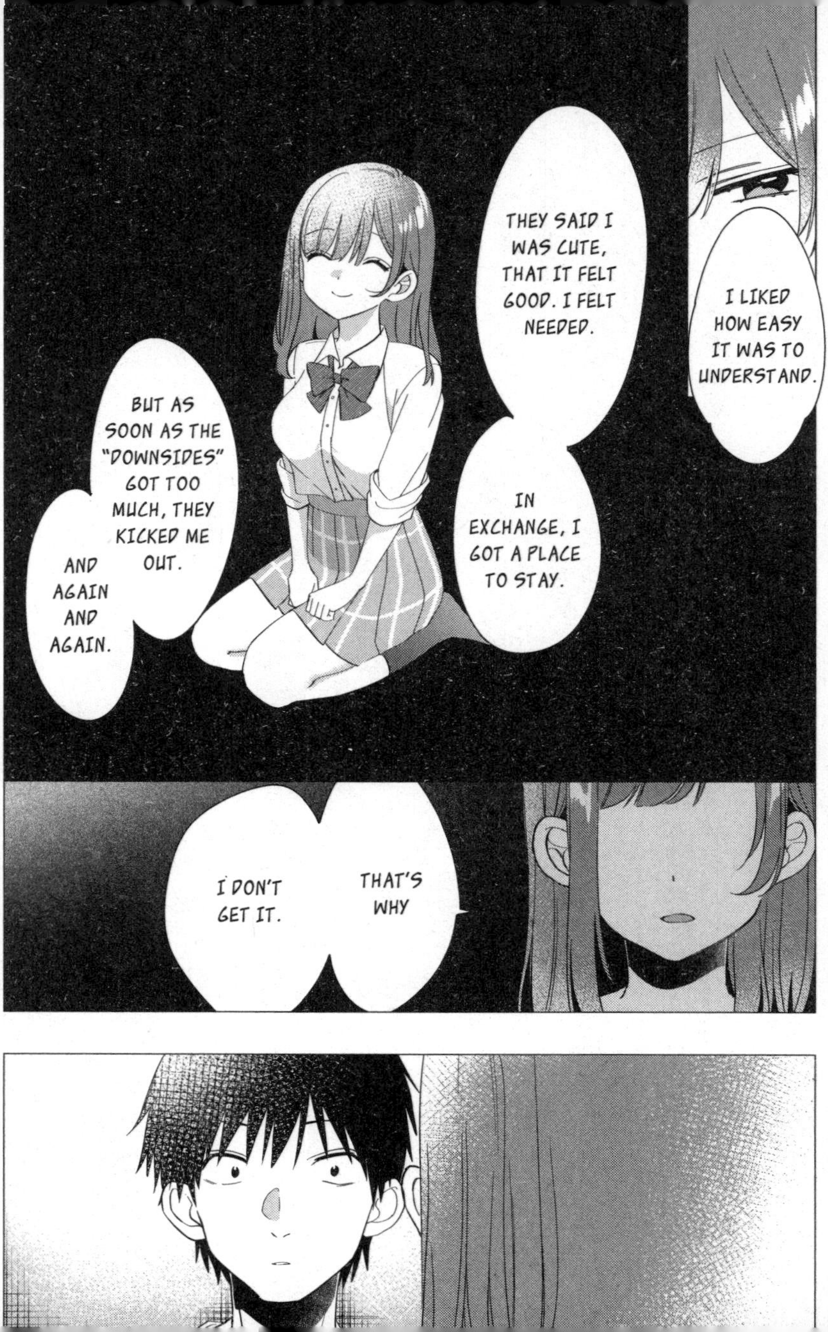
I LIKED HOW EASY IT WAS TO UNDERSTAND.
THEY SAID I WAS CUTE, THAT IT FELT GOOD. I FELT NEEDED.
IN EXCHANGE, I GOT A PLACE TO STAY.
BUT AS SOON AS THE "DOWNSIDES" GOT TOO MUCH, THEY KICKED ME OUT.
AND AGAIN AND AGAIN.
THAT'S WHY
I DON'T GET IT.

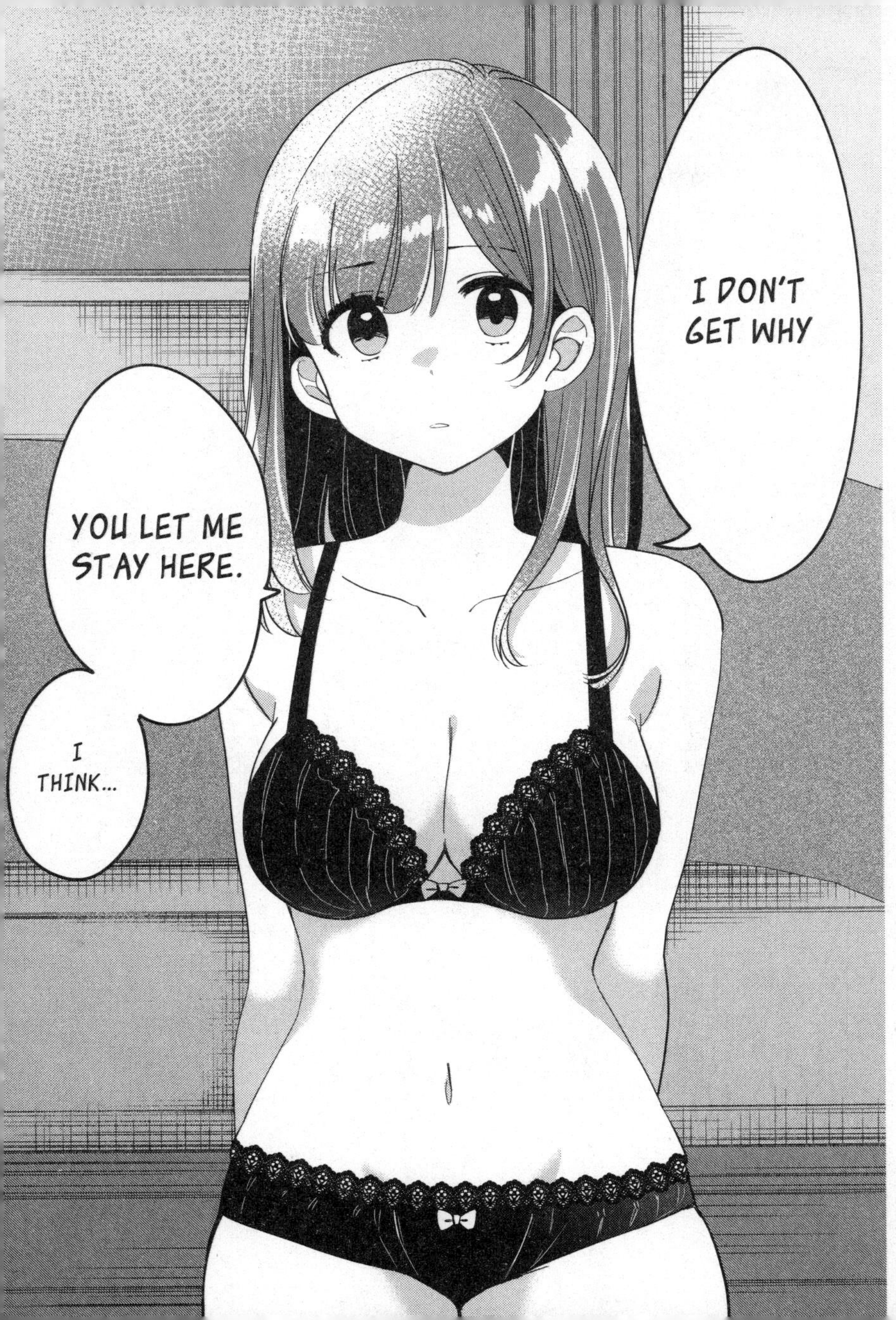
I DON'T GET WHY
YOU LET ME STAY HERE.
I THINK...

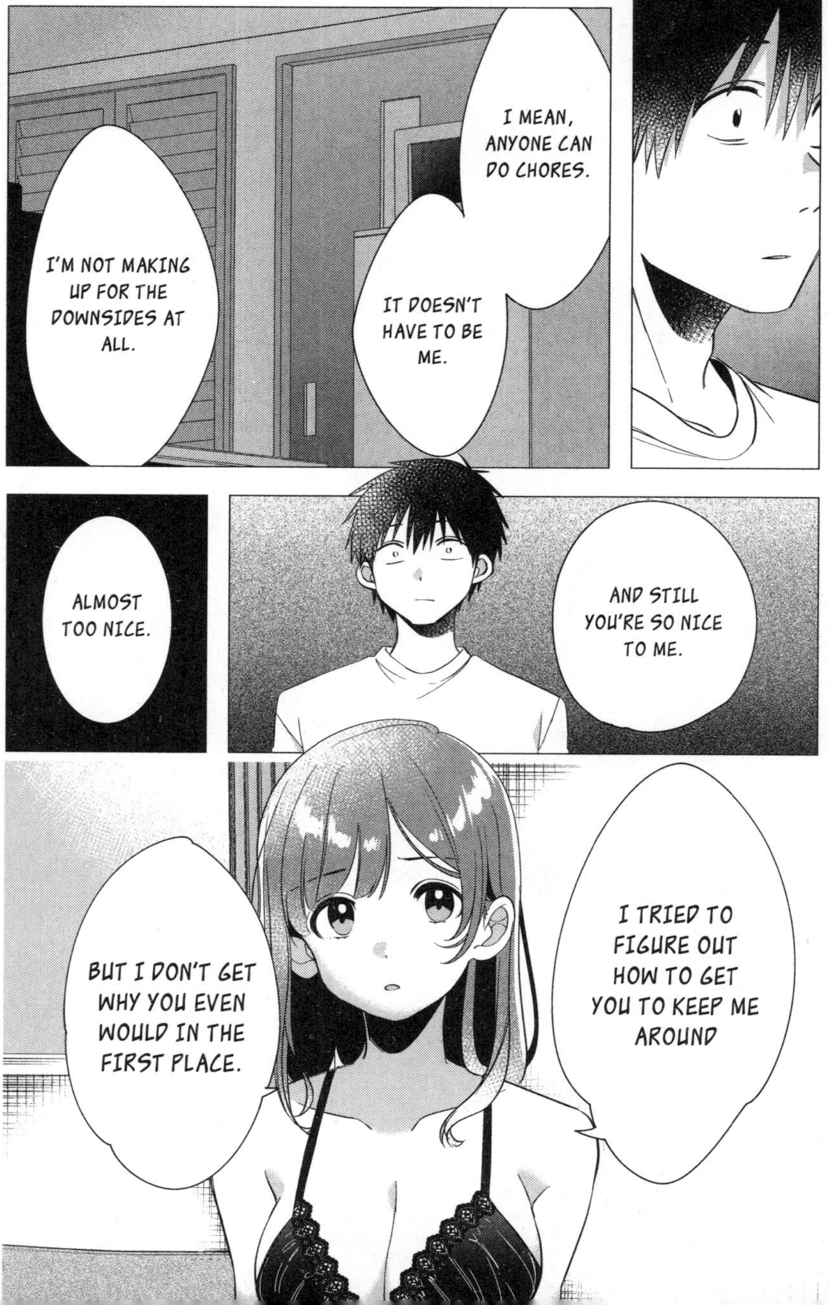

I MEAN, ANYONE CAN DO CHORES.
IT DOESN'T HAVE TO BE ME.
I'M NOT MAKING UP FOR THE DOWNSIDES AT ALL.
AND STILL YOU'RE SO NICE TO ME.
ALMOST TOO NICE.
I TRIED TO FIGURE OUT HOW TO GET YOU TO KEEP ME AROUND
BUT I DON'T GET WHY YOU EVEN WOULD IN THE FIRST PLACE.

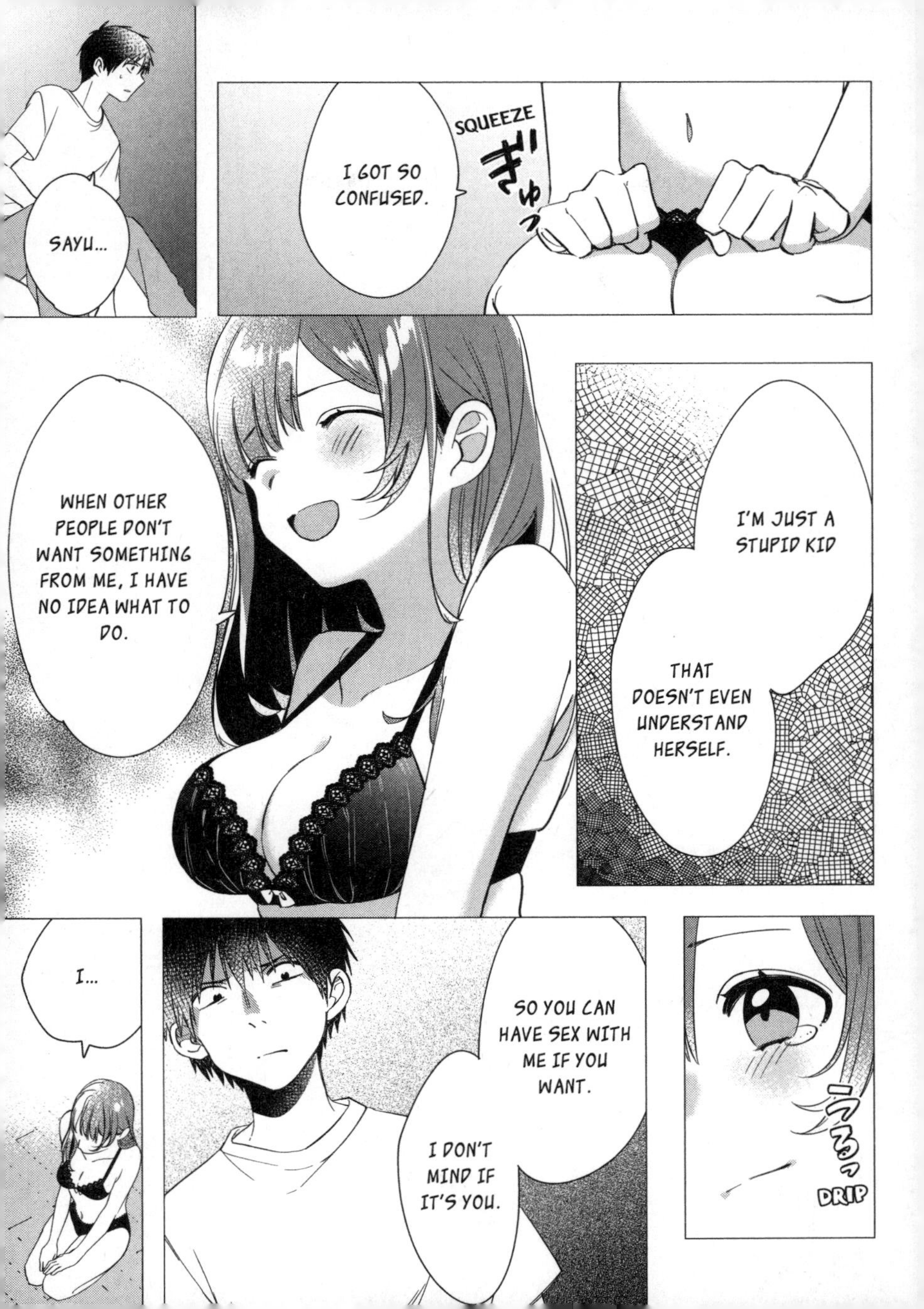
SQUEEZE
ぎゅっ
I GOT SO CONFUSED.
SAYU...
I'M JUST A STUPID KID
THAT DOESN'T EVEN UNDERSTAND HERSELF.
WHEN OTHER PEOPLE DON'T WANT SOMETHING FROM ME, I HAVE NO IDEA WHAT TO DO.
うるっ
DRIP
SO YOU CAN HAVE SEX WITH ME IF YOU WANT.
I DON'T MIND IF IT'S YOU.
I...

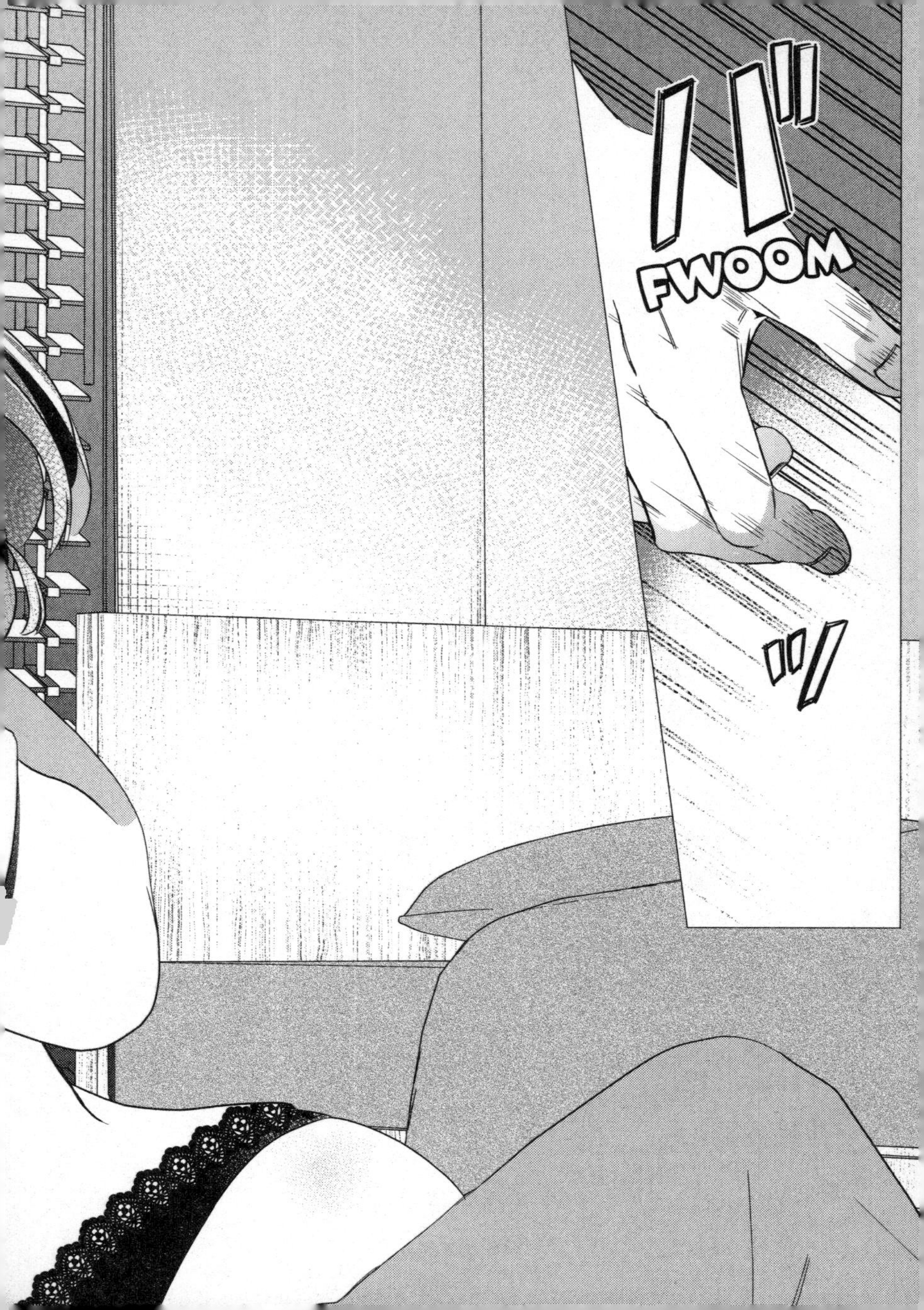
FWOOM

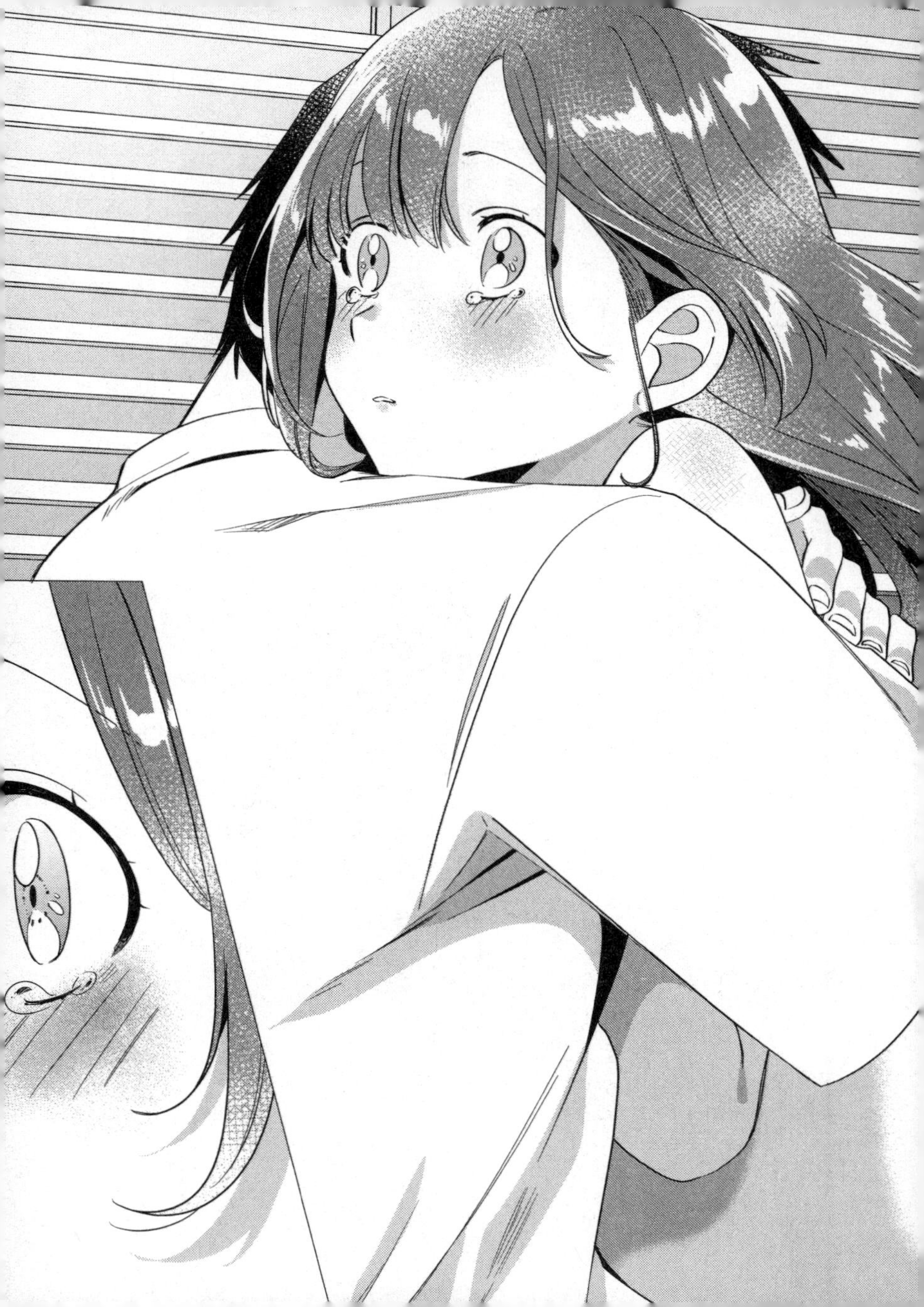

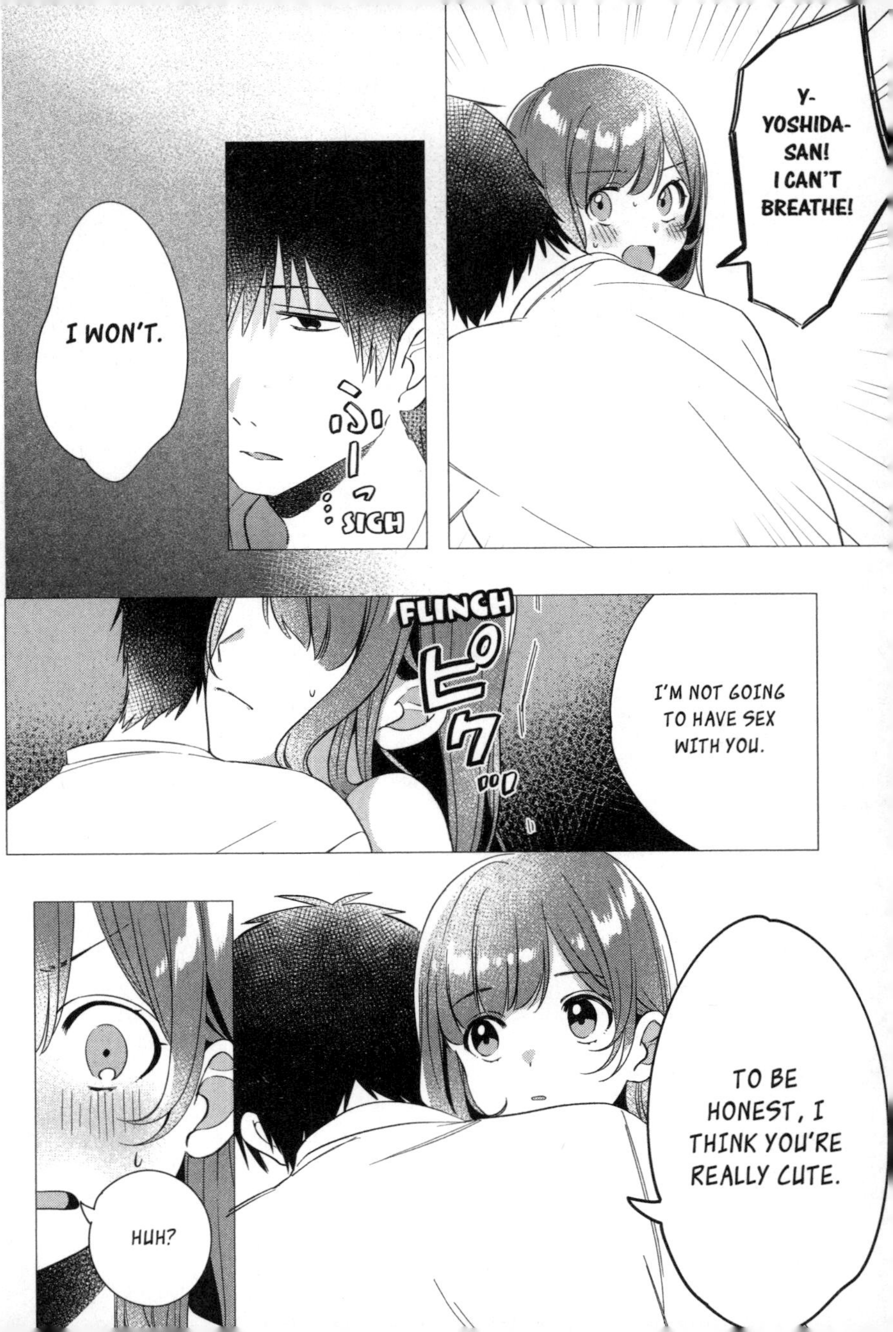
Y-YOSHIDA-SAN! I CAN'T BREATHE!
SIGH
I WON'T.
I'M NOT GOING TO HAVE SEX WITH YOU.
FLINCH
TO BE HONEST, I THINK YOU'RE REALLY CUTE.
HUH?

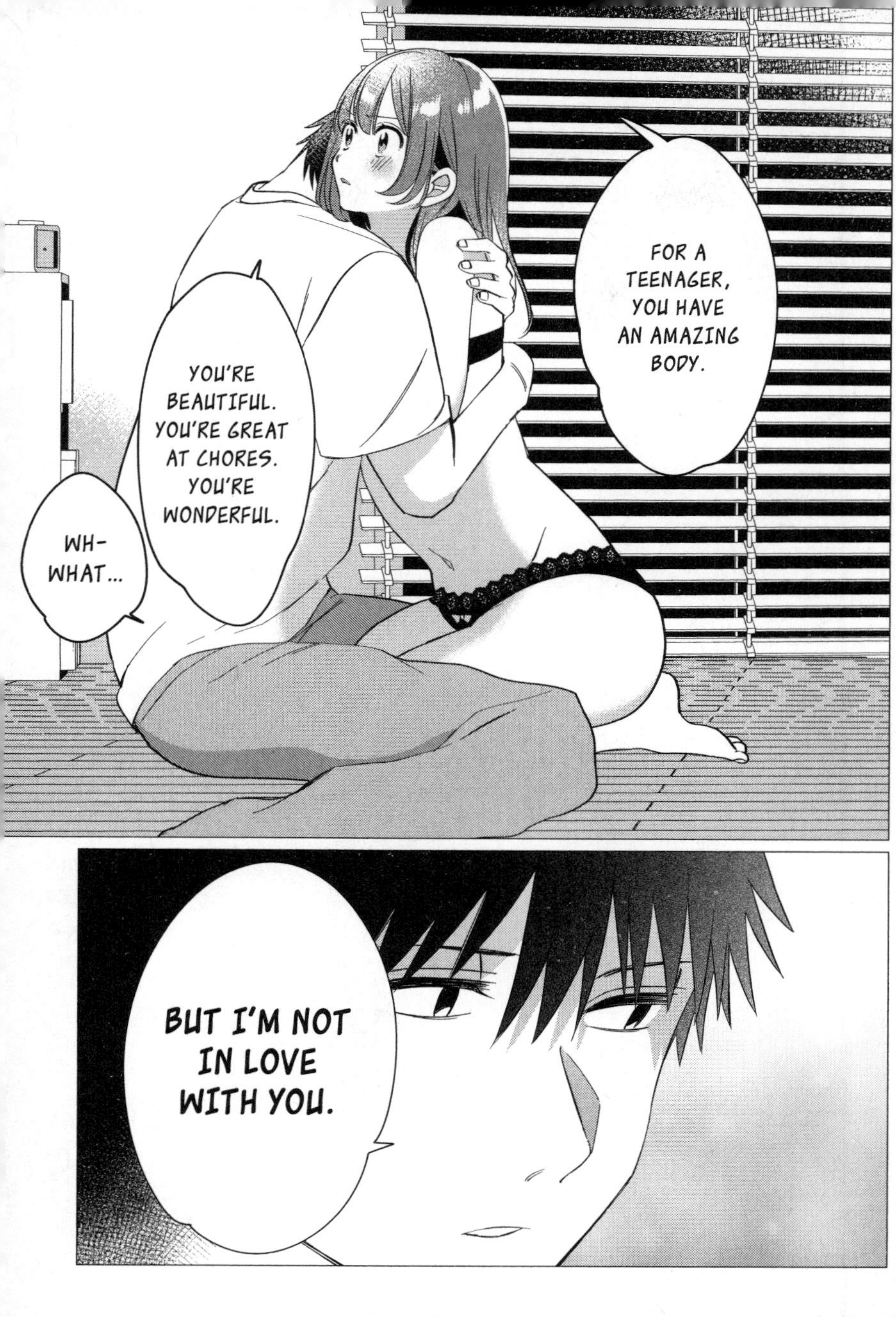
FOR A TEENAGER, YOU HAVE AN AMAZING BODY.
YOU'RE BEAUTIFUL. YOU'RE GREAT AT CHORES. YOU'RE WONDERFUL.
WH- WHAT...
BUT I'M NOT IN LOVE WITH YOU.

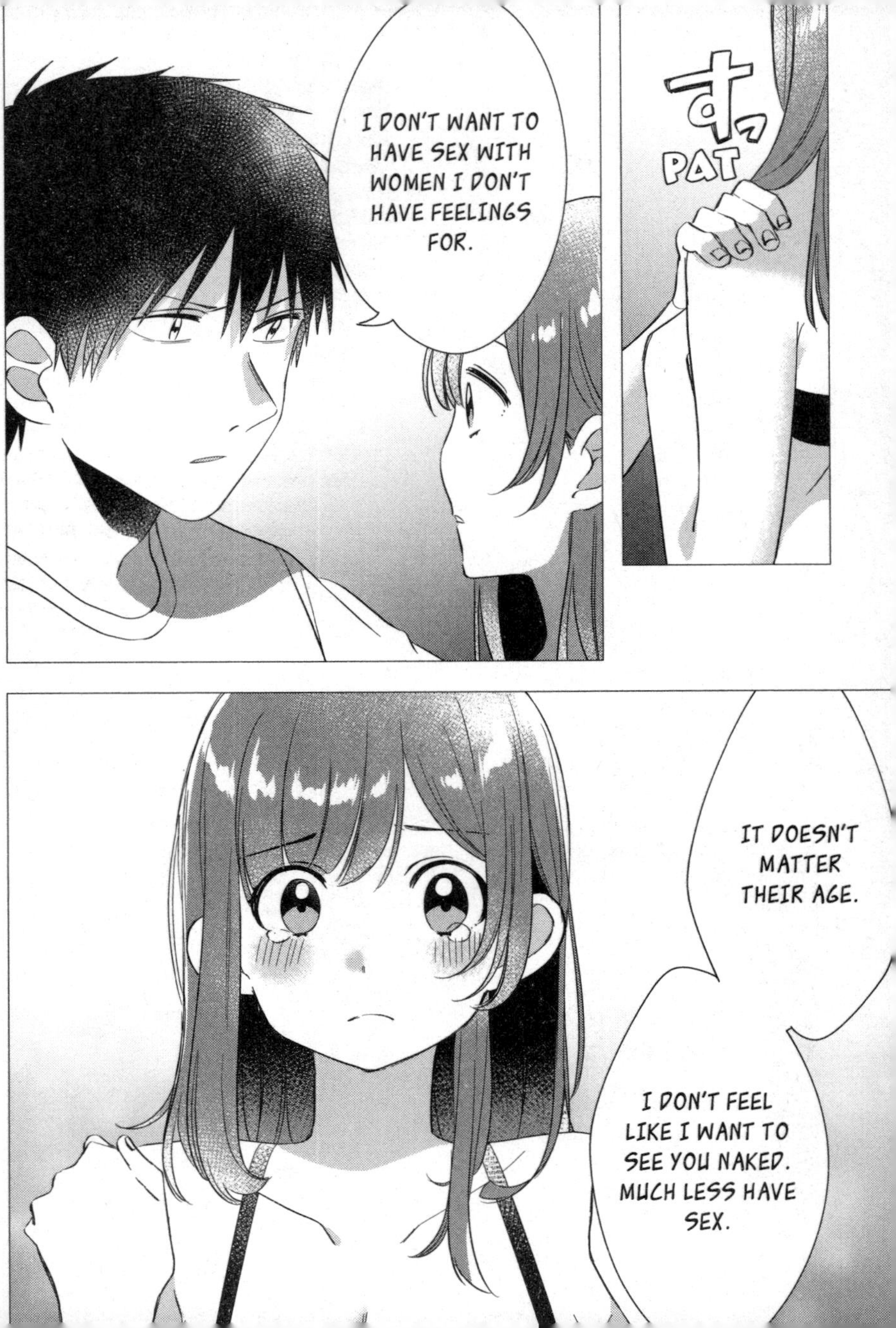
すっ
PAT
I DON'T WANT TO HAVE SEX WITH WOMEN I DON'T HAVE FEELINGS FOR.
IT DOESN'T MATTER THEIR AGE.
I DON'T FEEL LIKE I WANT TO SEE YOU NAKED. MUCH LESS HAVE SEX.

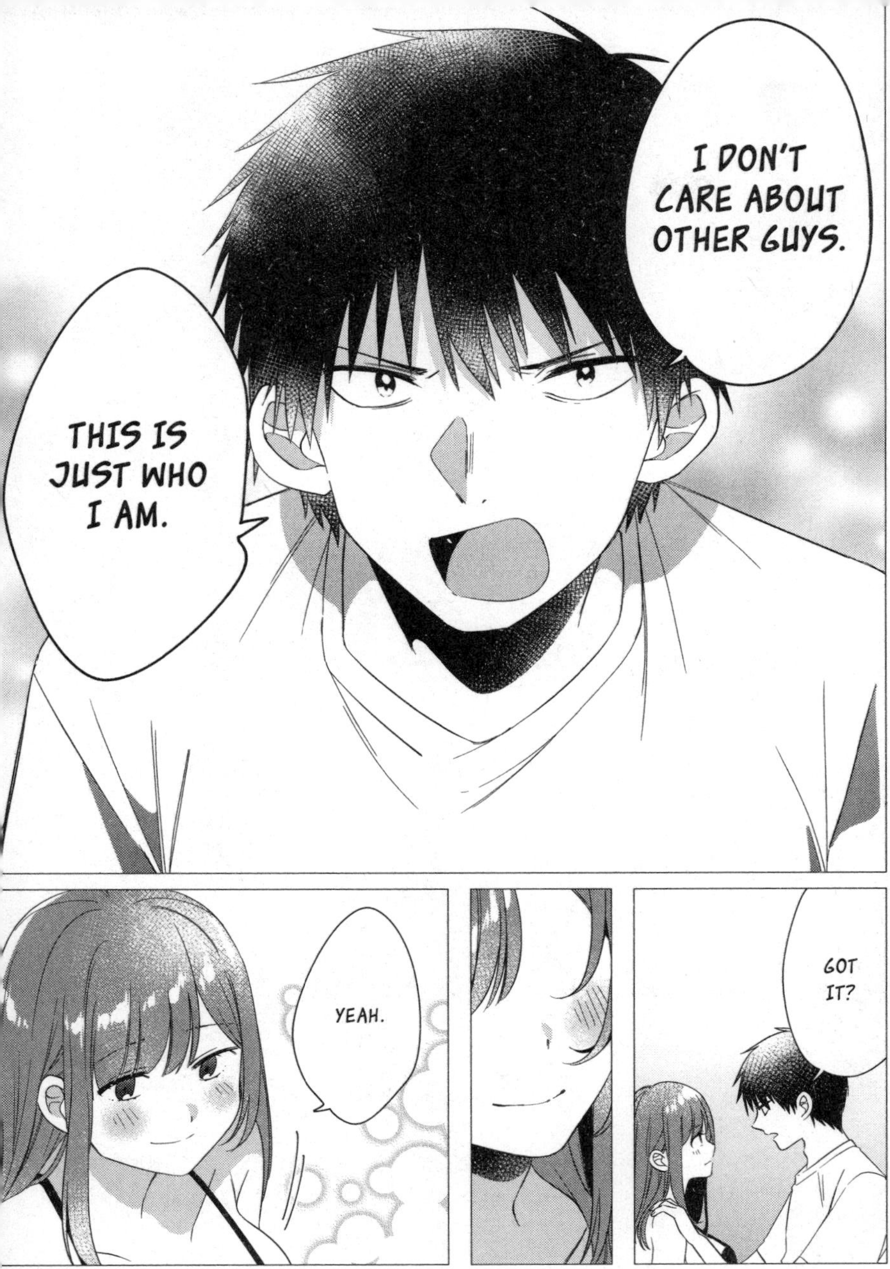
I DON'T CARE ABOUT OTHER GUYS.
THIS IS JUST WHO I AM.
GOT IT?
YEAH.

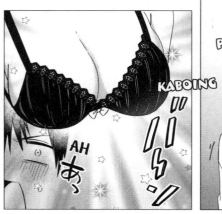

KABOING

AH

PHOO

PUSH

AH! YES!

C'MON, GET DRESSED ALREADY!

UP UNTIL NOW

PAH

HOME WAS JUST A PLACE FOR ME TO EAT, TAKE A BATH

AND GO TO SLEEP.

FFT

FFT

YOU SAID THAT YOU CAN'T DO ANYTHING FOR ME, BUT THAT'S NOT TRUE.

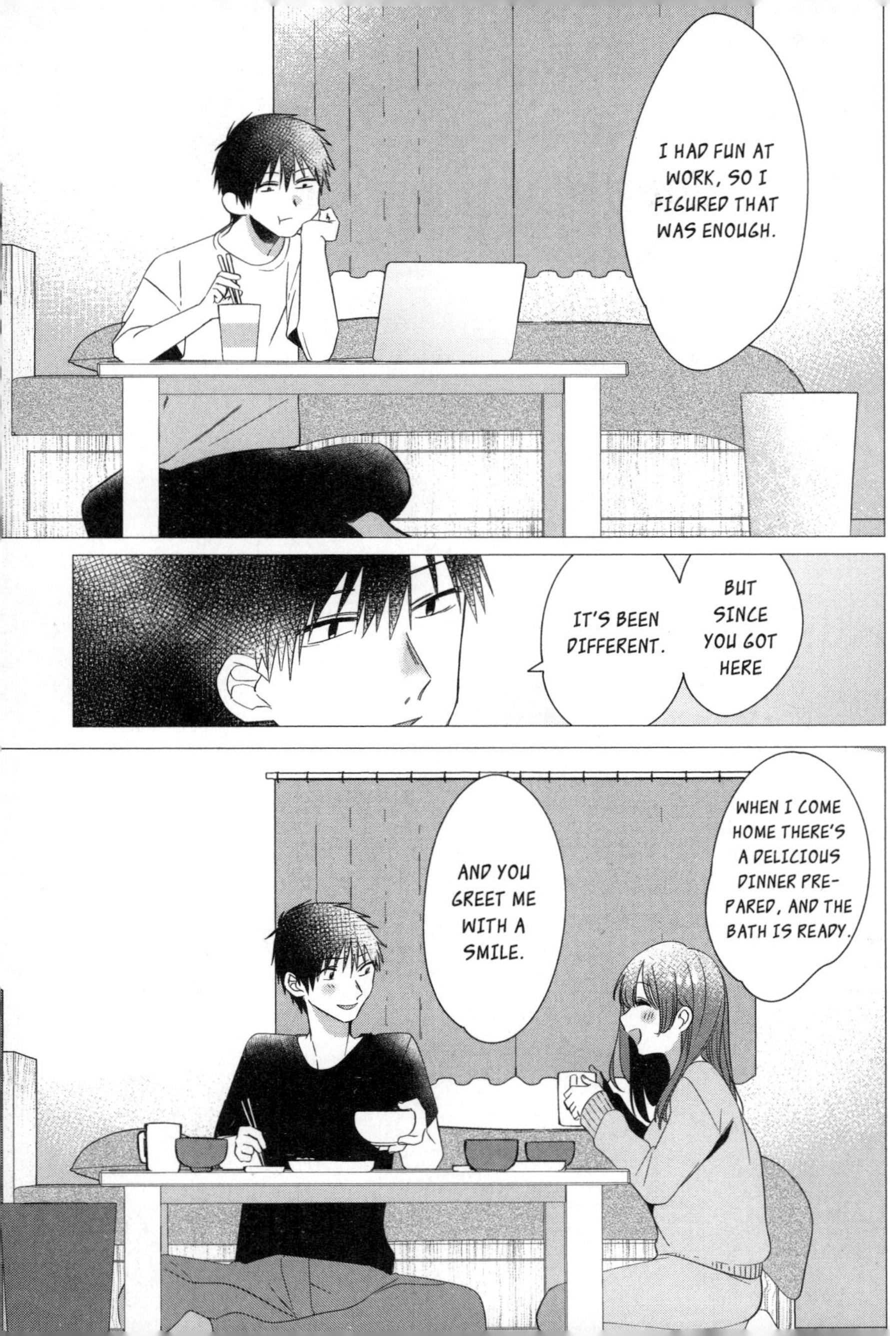
I HAD FUN AT WORK, SO I FIGURED THAT WAS ENOUGH.
BUT SINCE YOU GOT HERE
IT'S BEEN DIFFERENT.
WHEN I COME HOME THERE'S A DELICIOUS DINNER PRE-PARED, AND THE BATH IS READY.
AND YOU GREET ME WITH A SMILE.

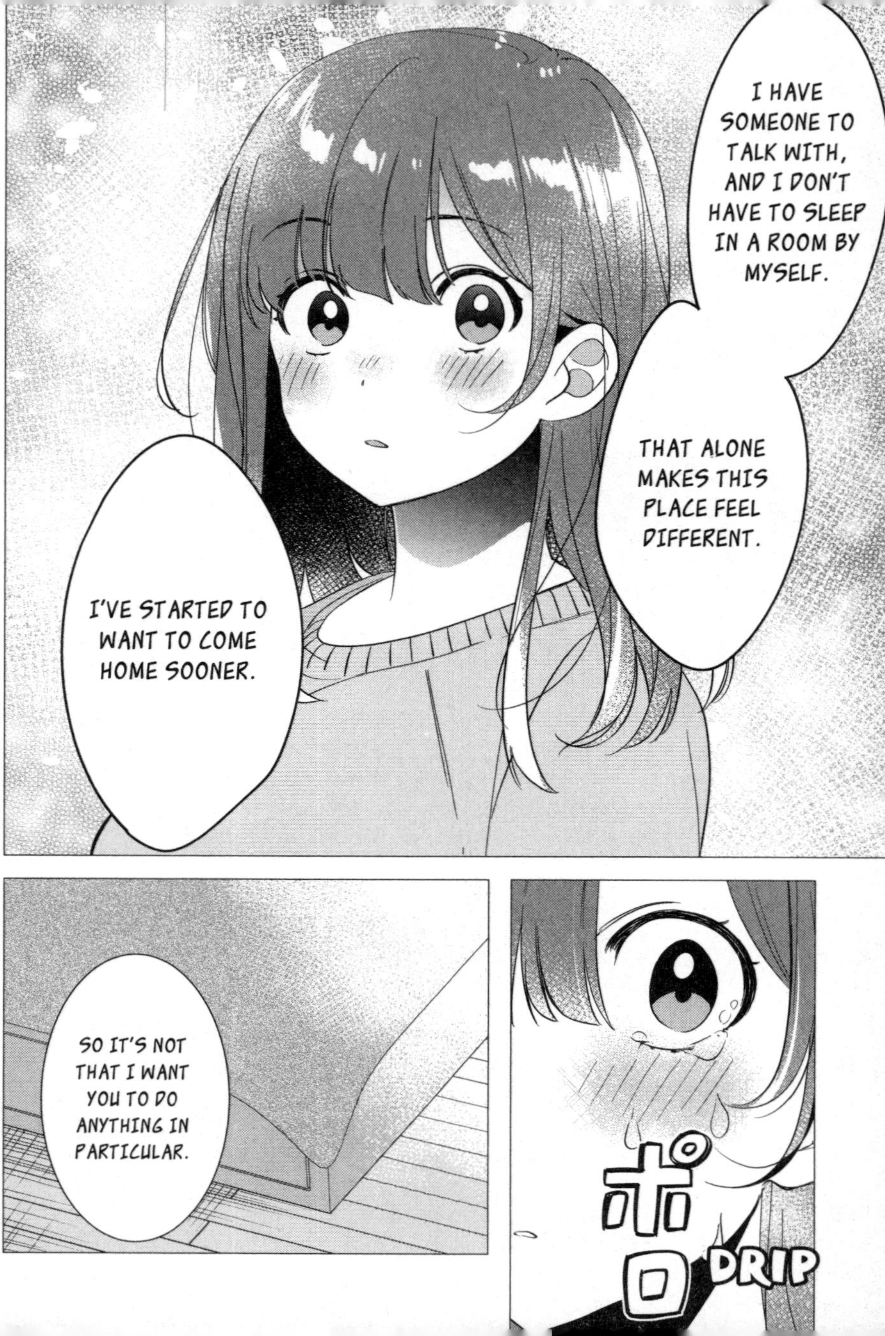
I HAVE SOMEONE TO TALK WITH, AND I DON'T HAVE TO SLEEP IN A ROOM BY MYSELF.
THAT ALONE MAKES THIS PLACE FEEL DIFFERENT.
I'VE STARTED TO WANT TO COME HOME SOONER.
ポロ
DRIP
SO IT'S NOT THAT I WANT YOU TO DO ANYTHING IN PARTICULAR.

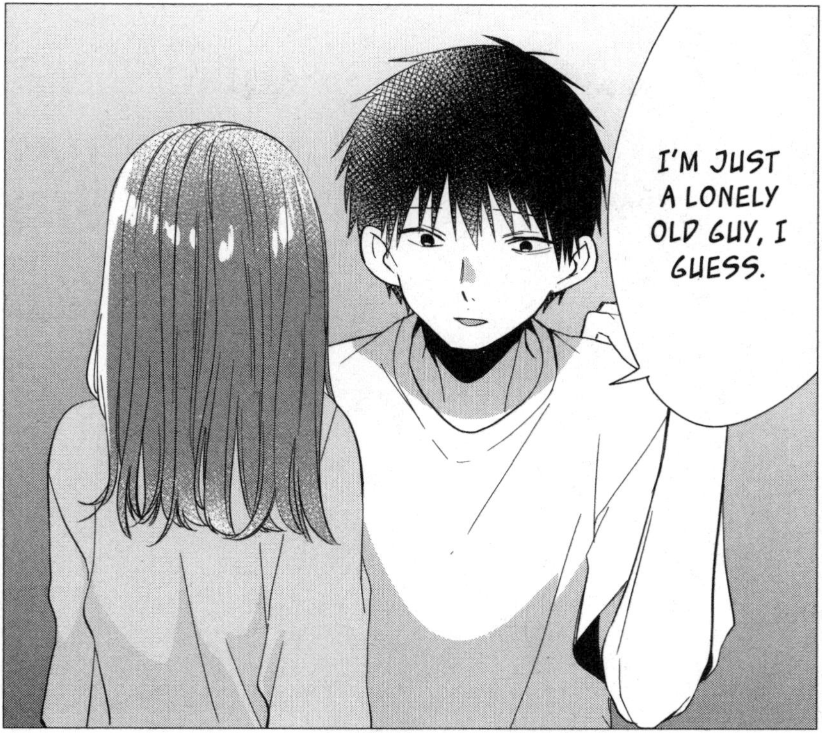
I'M JUST A LONELY OLD GUY, I GUESS.
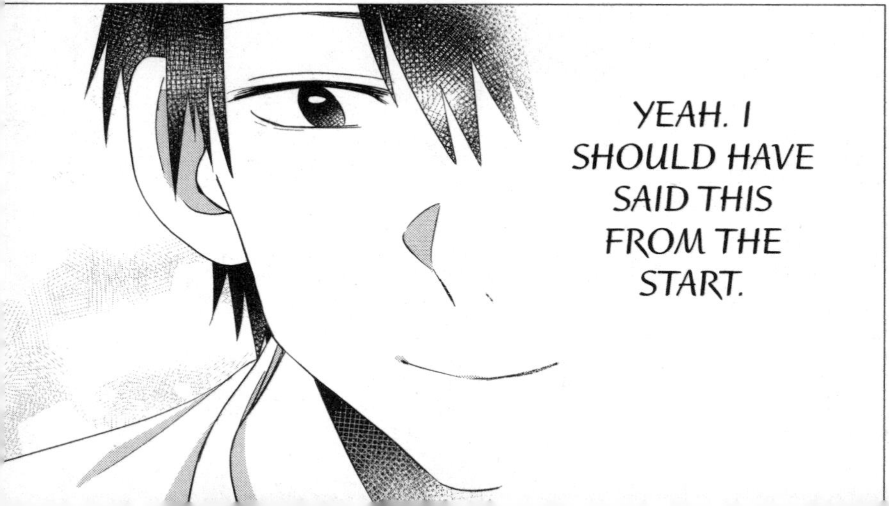
YEAH. I SHOULD HAVE SAID THIS FROM THE START.

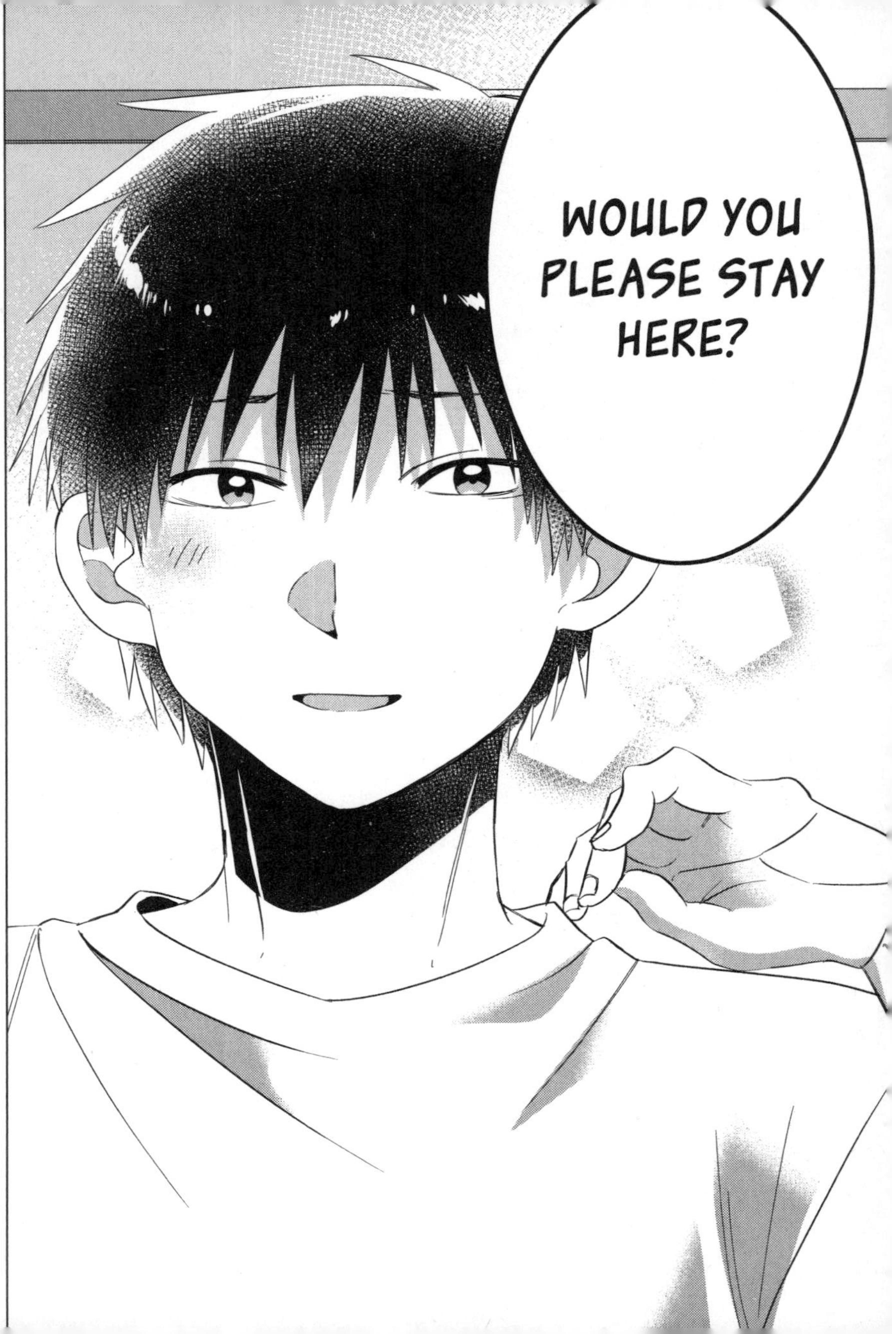
WOULD YOU PLEASE STAY HERE?

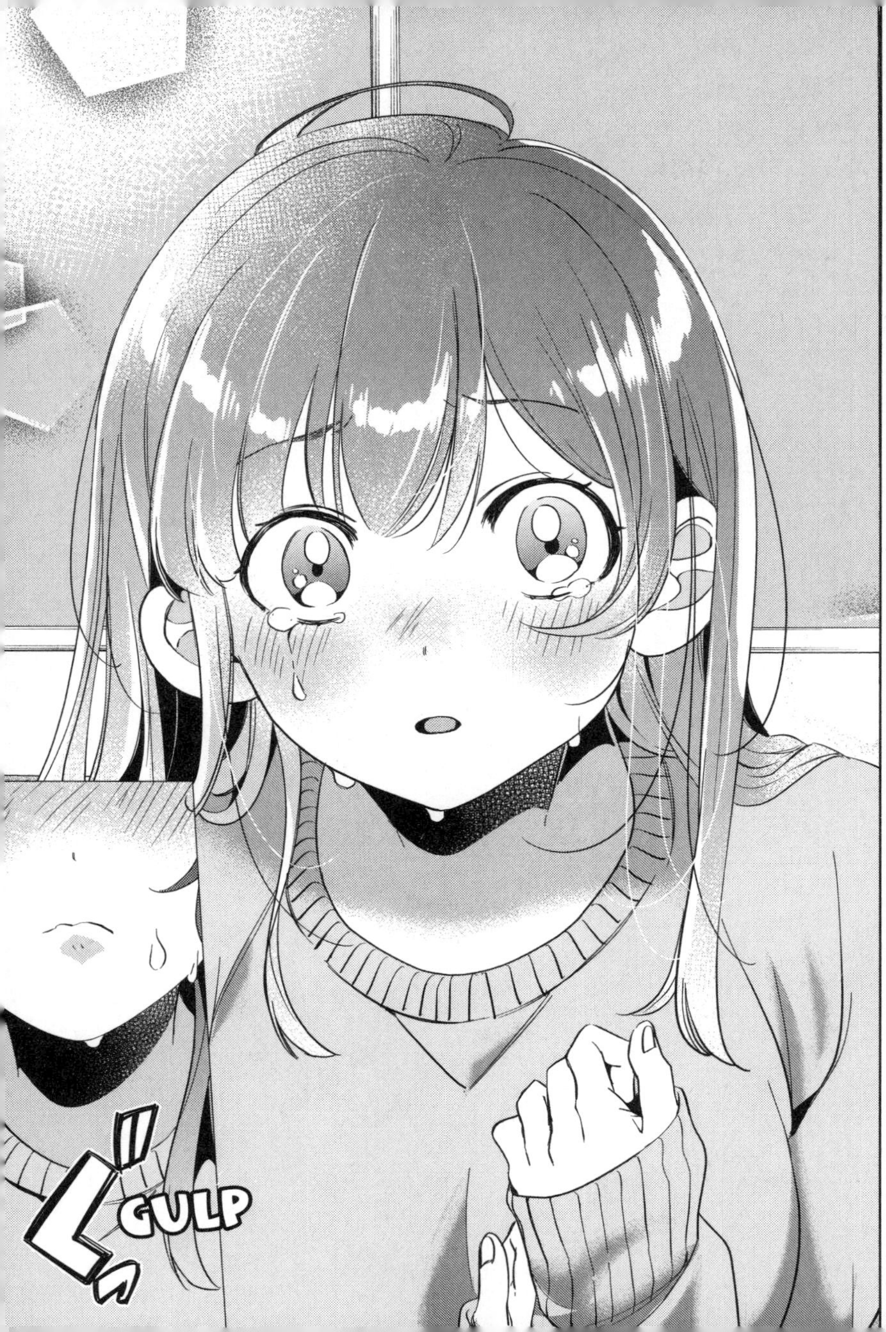
GULP

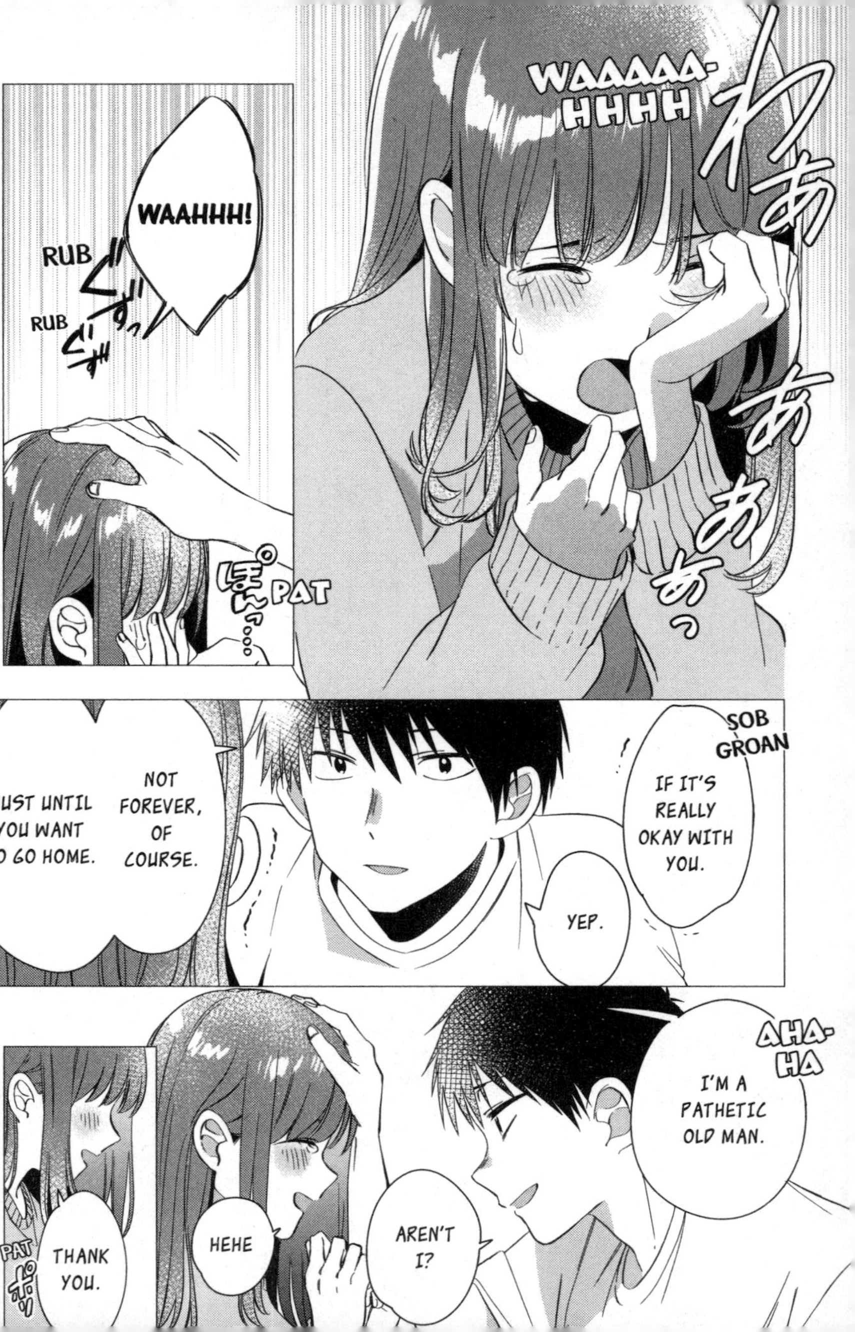
WAAAAA-HHHH
WAAHHH!
RUB
RUB
PAT
SOB
GROAN
IF IT'S REALLY OKAY WITH YOU.
YEP.
NOT FOREVER, OF COURSE.
JUST UNTIL YOU WANT TO GO HOME.
AHA-HA
I'M A PATHETIC OLD MAN.
AREN'T I?
HEHE
THANK YOU.
PAT

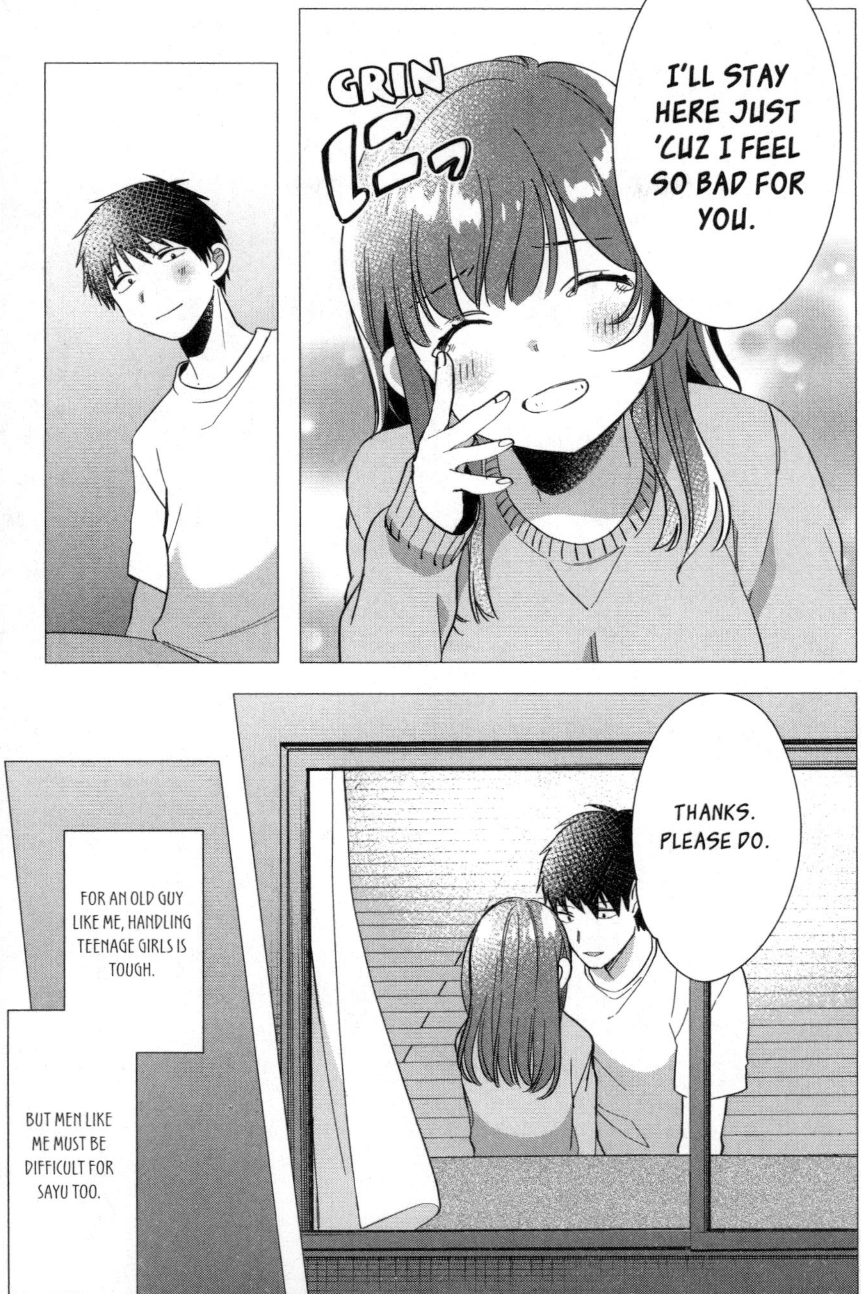
GRIN
I'LL STAY HERE JUST 'CUZ I FEEL SO BAD FOR YOU.
THANKS. PLEASE DO.
FOR AN OLD GUY LIKE ME, HANDLING TEENAGE GIRLS IS TOUGH.
BUT MEN LIKE ME MUST BE DIFFICULT FOR SAYU TOO.

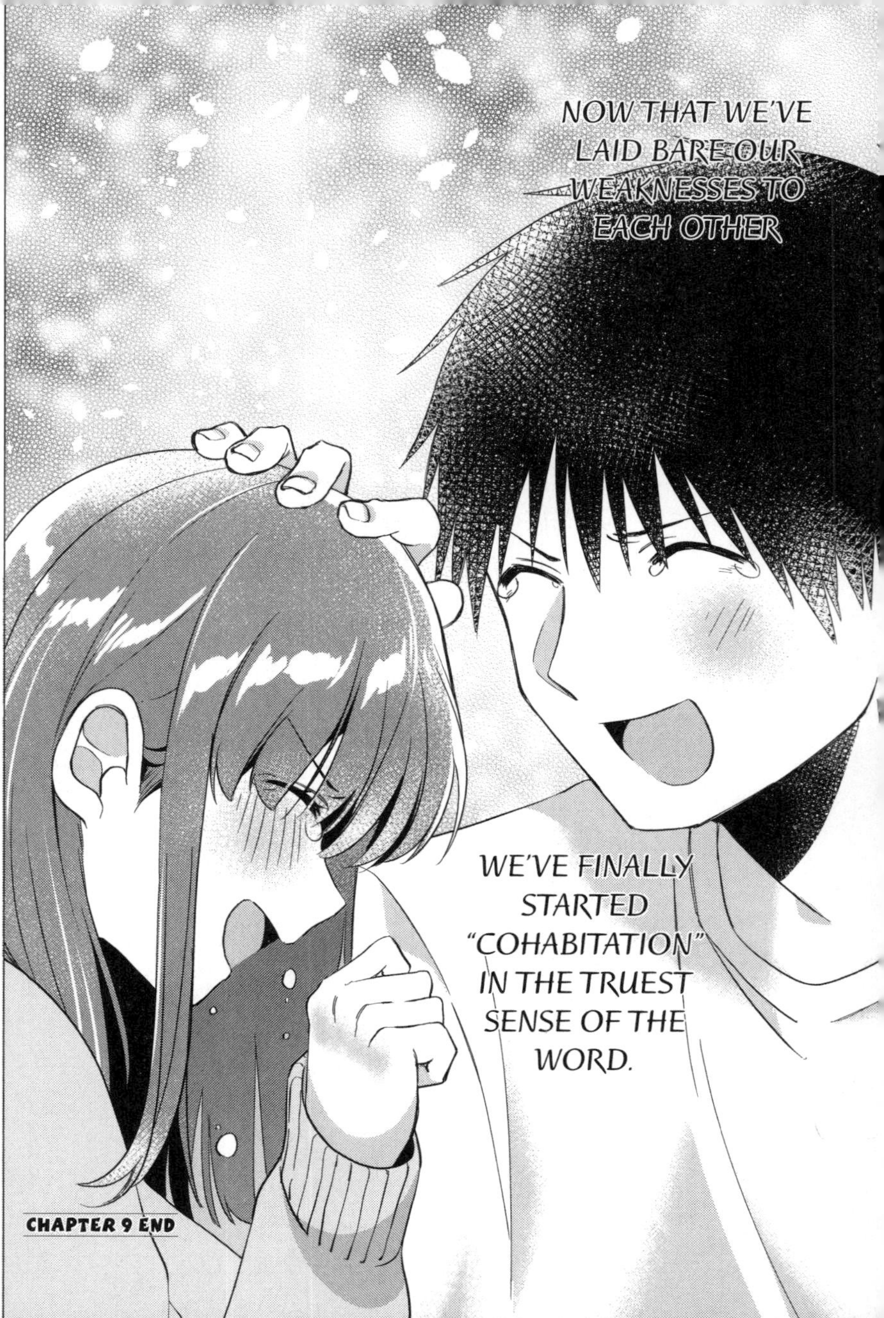
NOW THAT WE'VE LAID BARE OUR WEAKNESSES TO EACH OTHER
WE'VE FINALLY STARTED "COHABITATION" IN THE TRUEST SENSE OF THE WORD.
CHAPTER 9 END

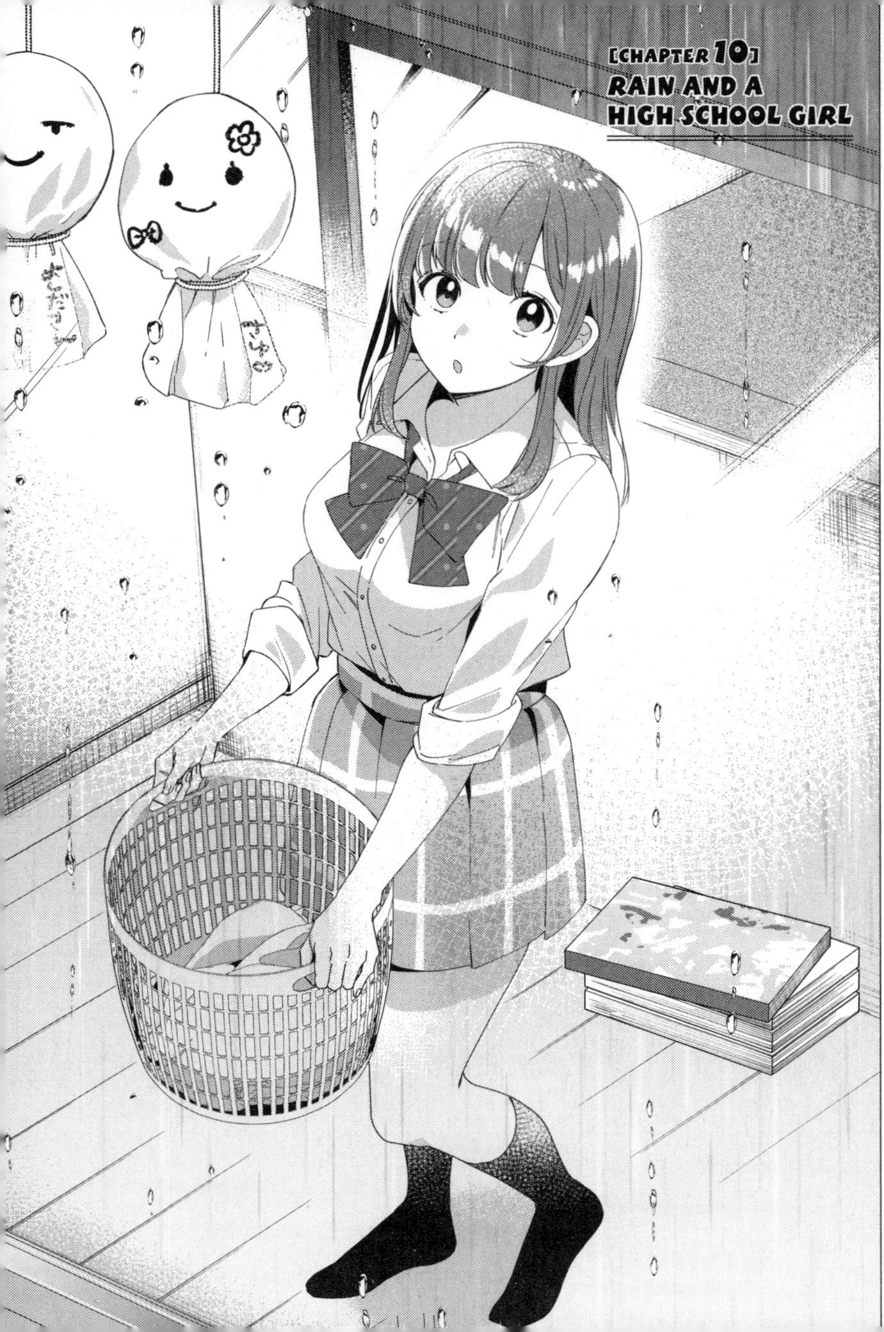
[CHAPTER 10]
RAIN AND A HIGH SCHOOL GIRL

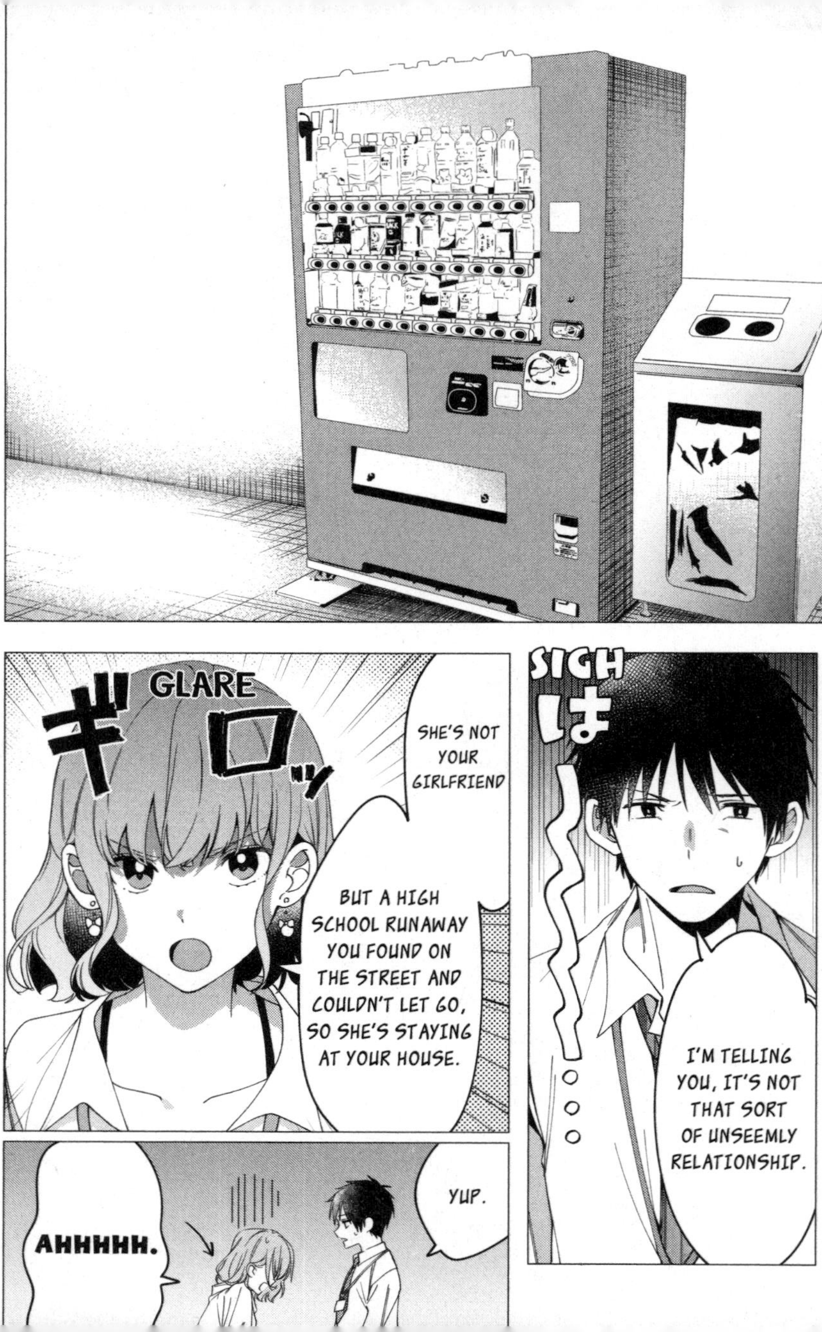
SIGH
は
I'M TELLING YOU, IT'S NOT THAT SORT OF UNSEEMLY RELATIONSHIP.
GLARE
ギロッ
SHE'S NOT YOUR GIRLFRIEND
BUT A HIGH SCHOOL RUNAWAY YOU FOUND ON THE STREET AND COULDN'T LET GO, SO SHE'S STAYING AT YOUR HOUSE.
YUP.
AHHHHH.

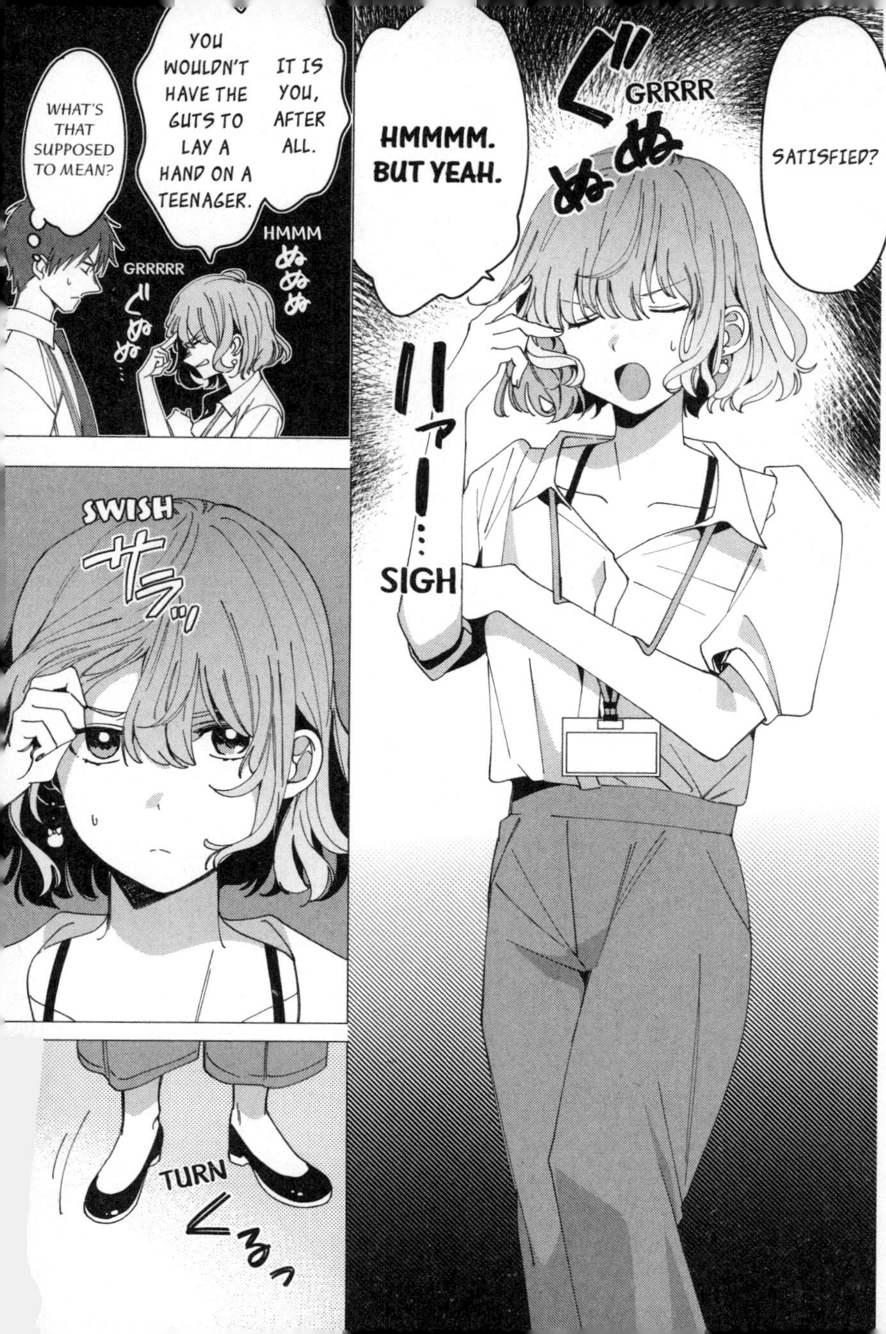
SATISFIED?
GRRRR
ぐぬぬ
HMMMM. BUT YEAH.
SIGH
YOU WOULDN'T HAVE THE GUTS TO LAY A HAND ON A TEENAGER.
IT IS YOU, AFTER ALL.
HMMM
ぬぬぬぬ
GRRRRR
ぐぬぬ…
WHAT'S THAT SUPPOSED TO MEAN?
SWISH
サラッ
TURN
くるっ

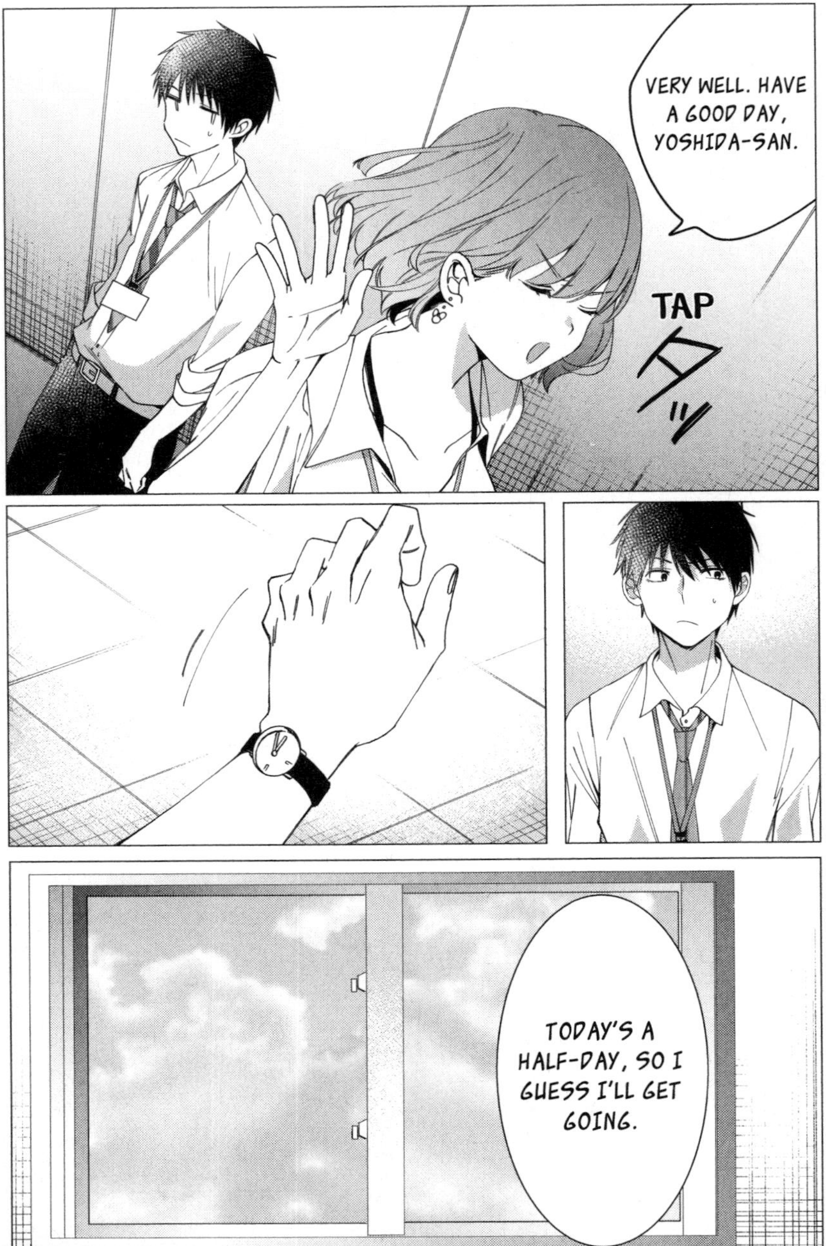
VERY WELL. HAVE A GOOD DAY, YOSHIDA-SAN.
TAP
タッ
TODAY'S A HALF-DAY, SO I GUESS I'LL GET GOING.

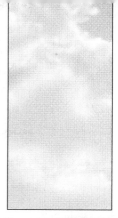

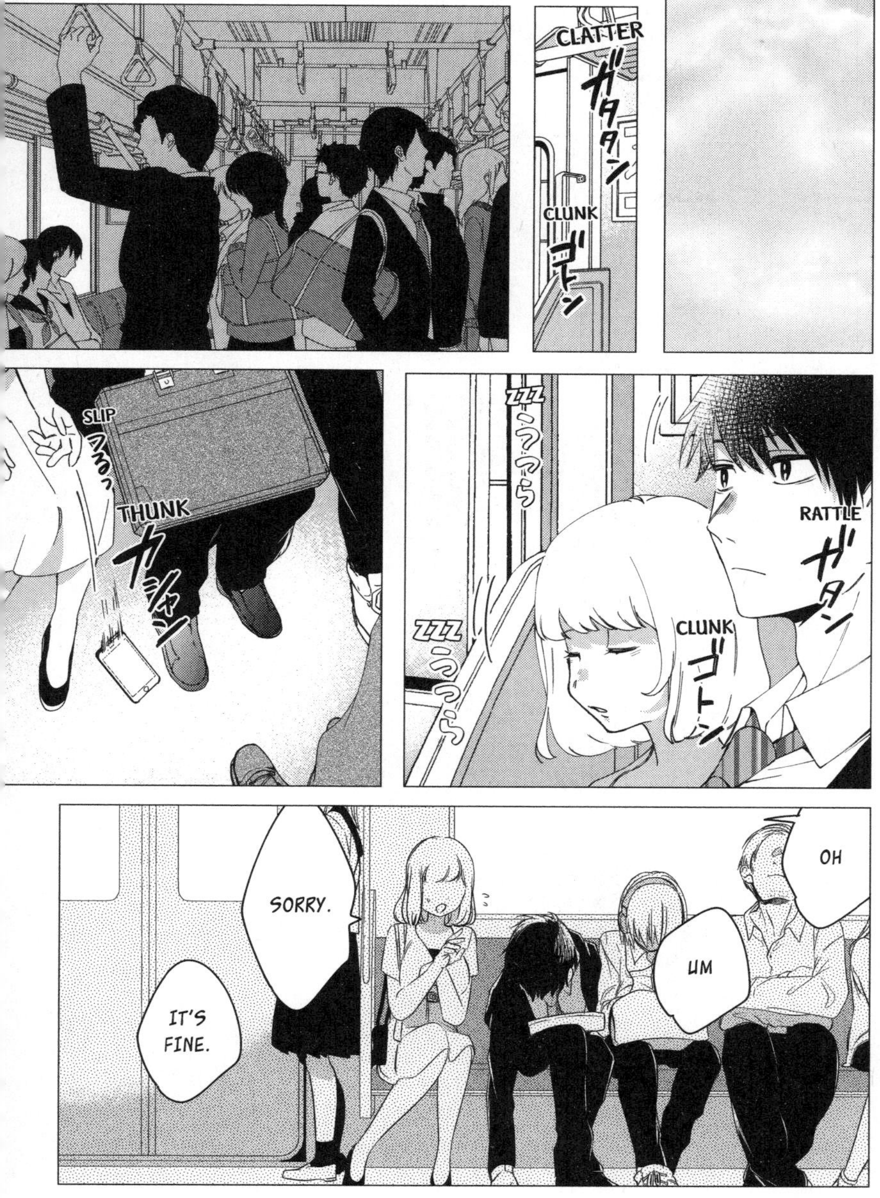
CLATTER
ガタタン
CLUNK
ゴトン
ZZZ
うつら
RATTLE
ガタン
CLUNK
ゴトン
ZZZ
うつら
SLIP
つるっ
THUNK
ガシャン
OH
UM
SORRY.
IT'S FINE.

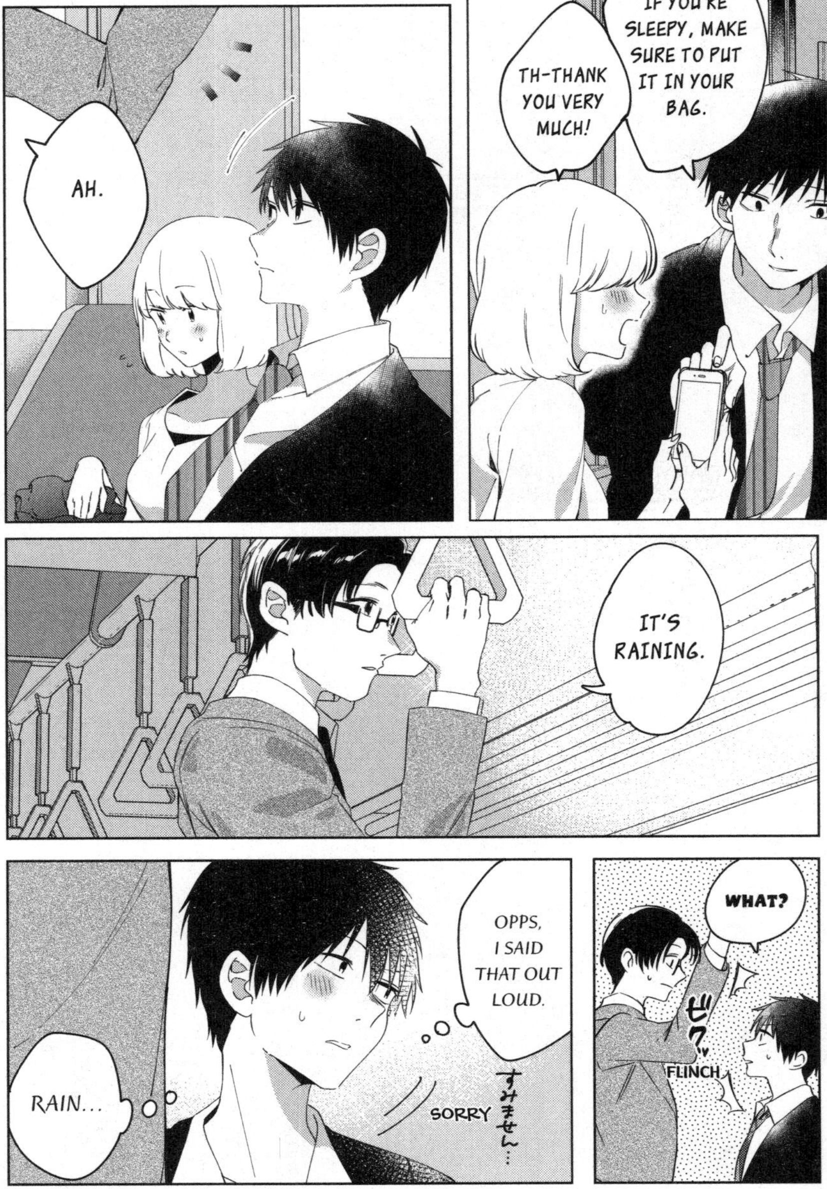
IF YOU'RE SLEEPY, MAKE SURE TO PUT IT IN YOUR BAG.
TH-THANK YOU VERY MUCH!
AH.
IT'S RAINING.
WHAT?
ビクッ
FLINCH
OPPS, I SAID THAT OUT LOUD.
すみません…
SORRY
RAIN...

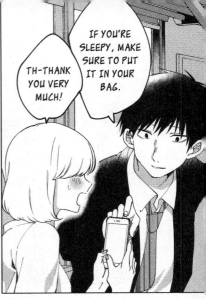

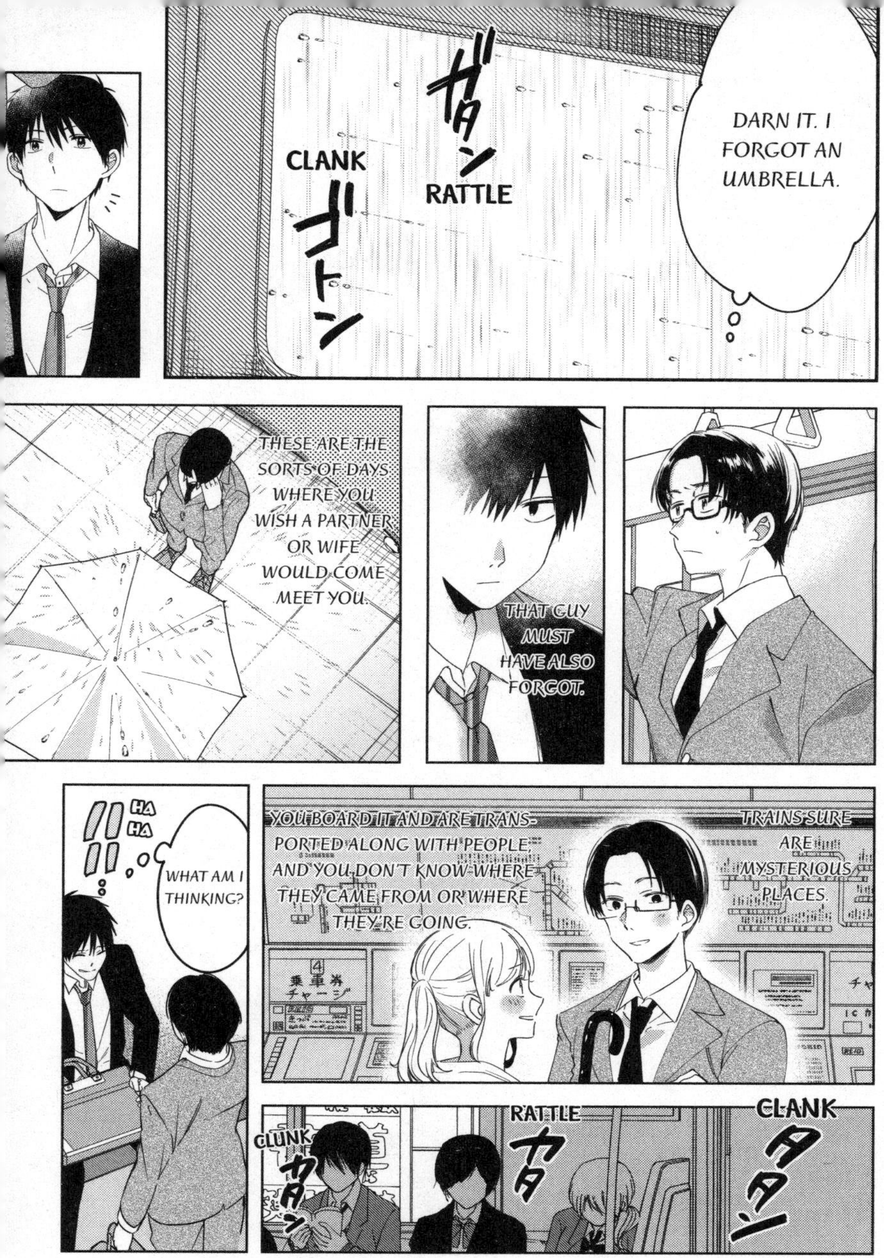
DARN IT. I FORGOT AN UMBRELLA.
ガタン
CLANK
RATTLE
ゴトン
THAT GUY MUST HAVE ALSO FORGOT.
THESE ARE THE SORTS OF DAYS WHERE YOU WISH A PARTNER OR WIFE WOULD COME MEET YOU.
TRAINS SURE ARE MYSTERIOUS PLACES.
YOU BOARD IT AND ARE TRANS-PORTED ALONG WITH PEOPLE, AND YOU DON'T KNOW WHERE THEY CAME FROM OR WHERE THEY'RE GOING.
乗車券
チャージ
CLANK
タタン
RATTLE
カタ
CLUNK
カタン
ハハ
HA HA
WHAT AM I THINKING?

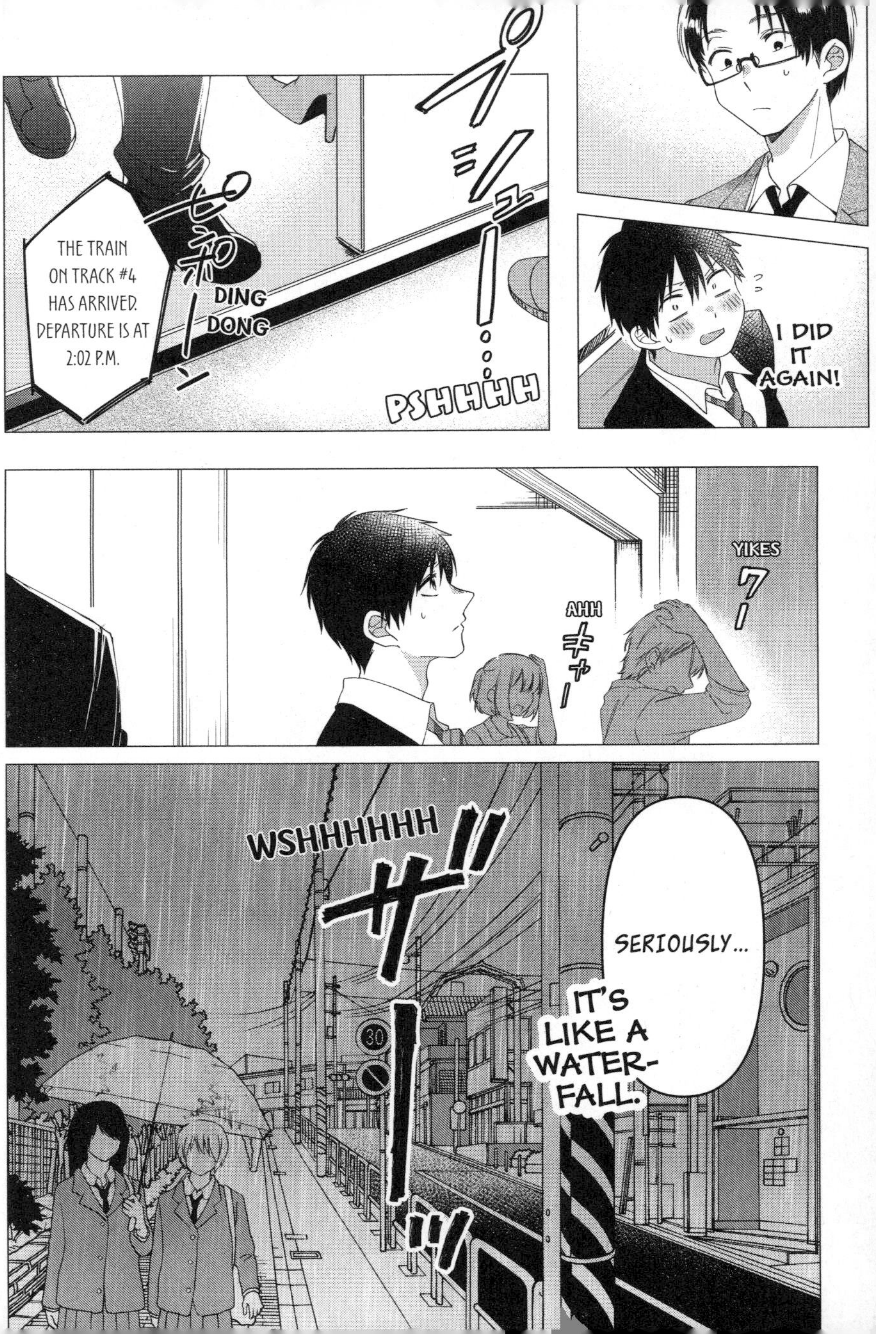
I DID IT AGAIN!
PSHHHH
DING DONG
THE TRAIN ON TRACK #4 HAS ARRIVED. DEPARTURE IS AT 2:02 P.M.
YIKES
AHH
WSHHHHHH
SERIOUSLY...
IT'S LIKE A WATERFALL.

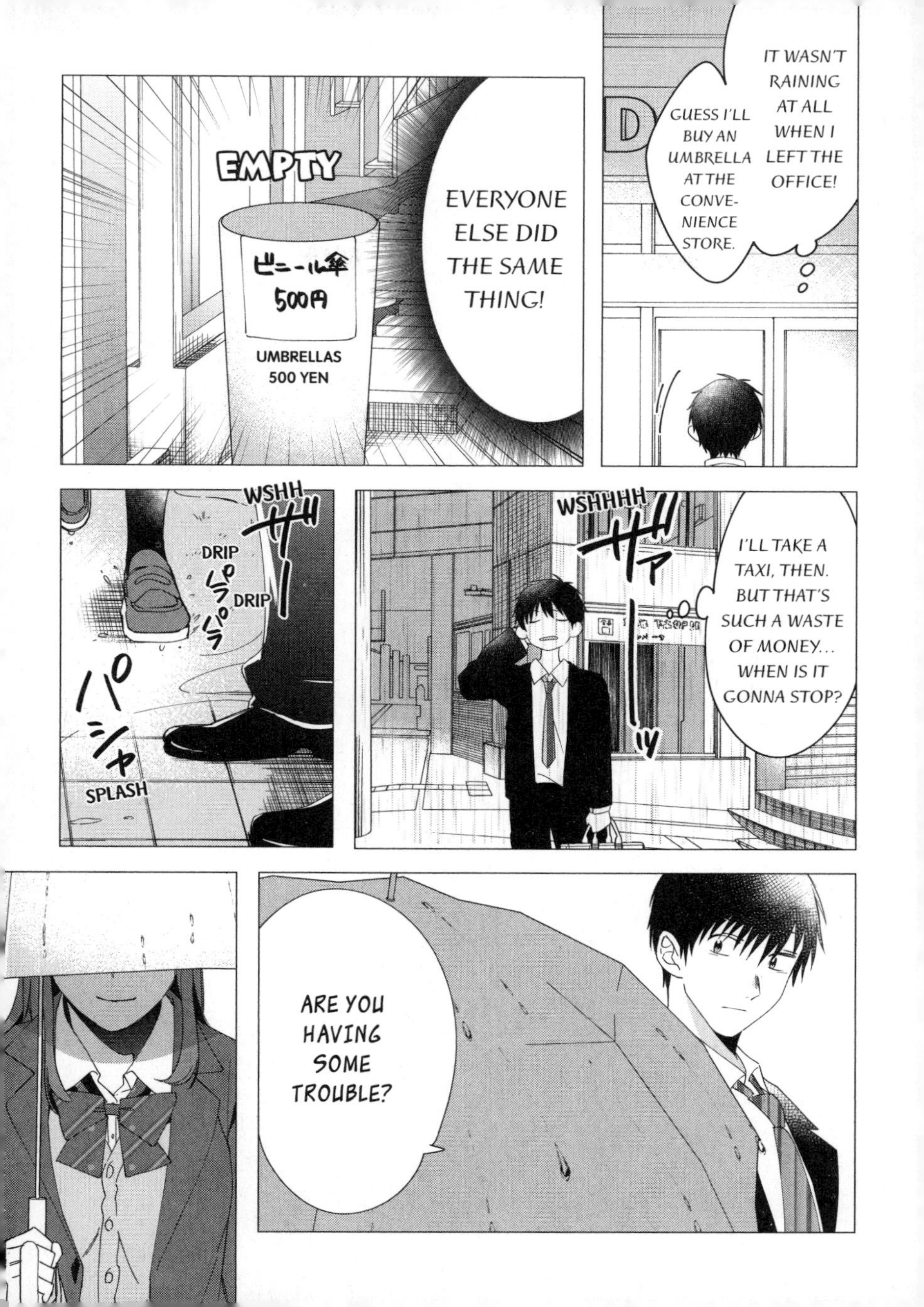

IT WASN'T RAINING AT ALL WHEN I LEFT THE OFFICE!
GUESS I'LL BUY AN UMBRELLA AT THE CONVE-NIENCE STORE.
EMPTY
ビニール傘 500円
UMBRELLAS 500 YEN
EVERYONE ELSE DID THE SAME THING!
WSHHHH
ザァー
I'LL TAKE A TAXI, THEN. BUT THAT'S SUCH A WASTE OF MONEY... WHEN IS IT GONNA STOP?
WSHH
ザー
DRIP
パラパラ
DRIP
パシャ
SPLASH
ARE YOU HAVING SOME TROUBLE?

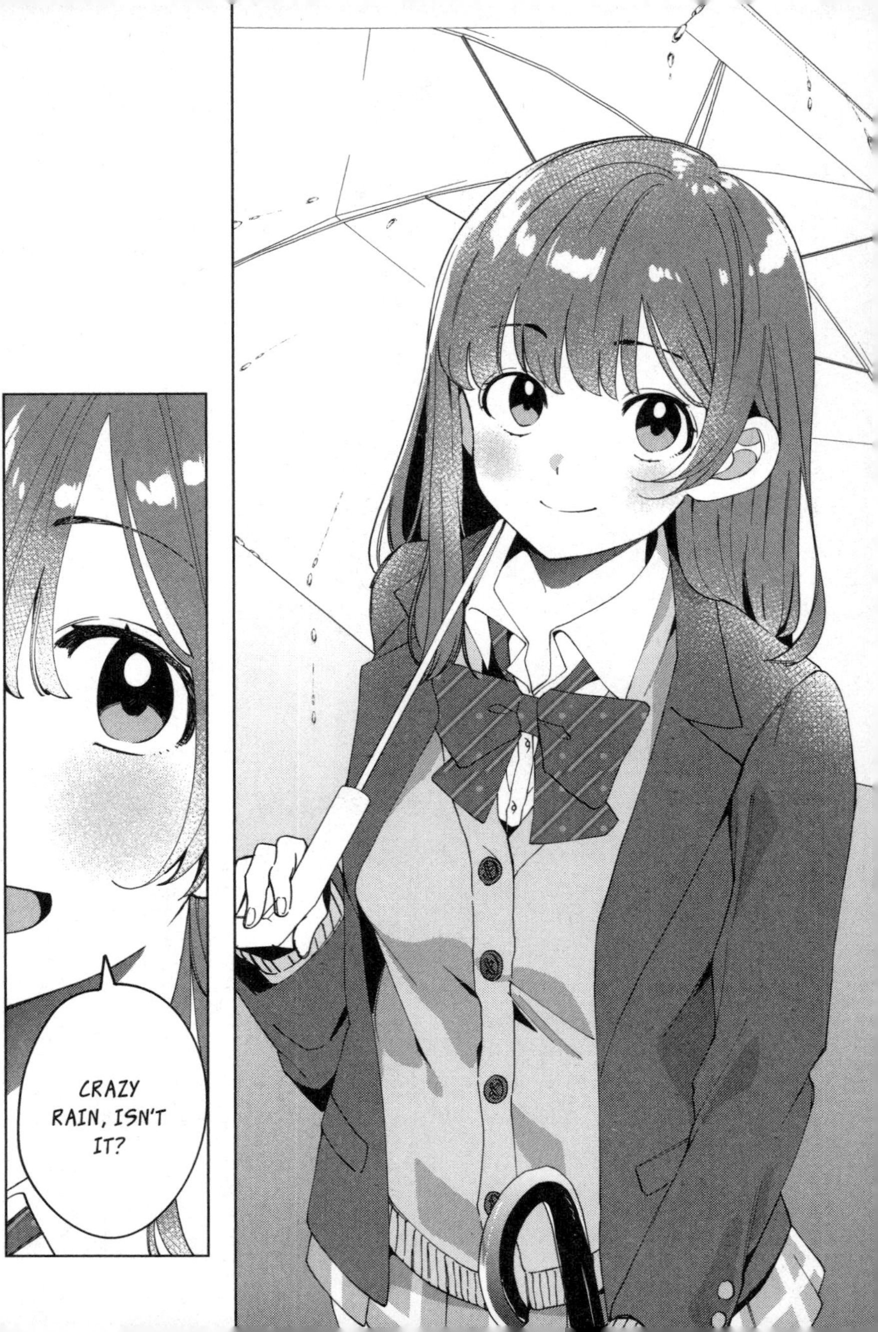
CRAZY RAIN, ISN'T IT?

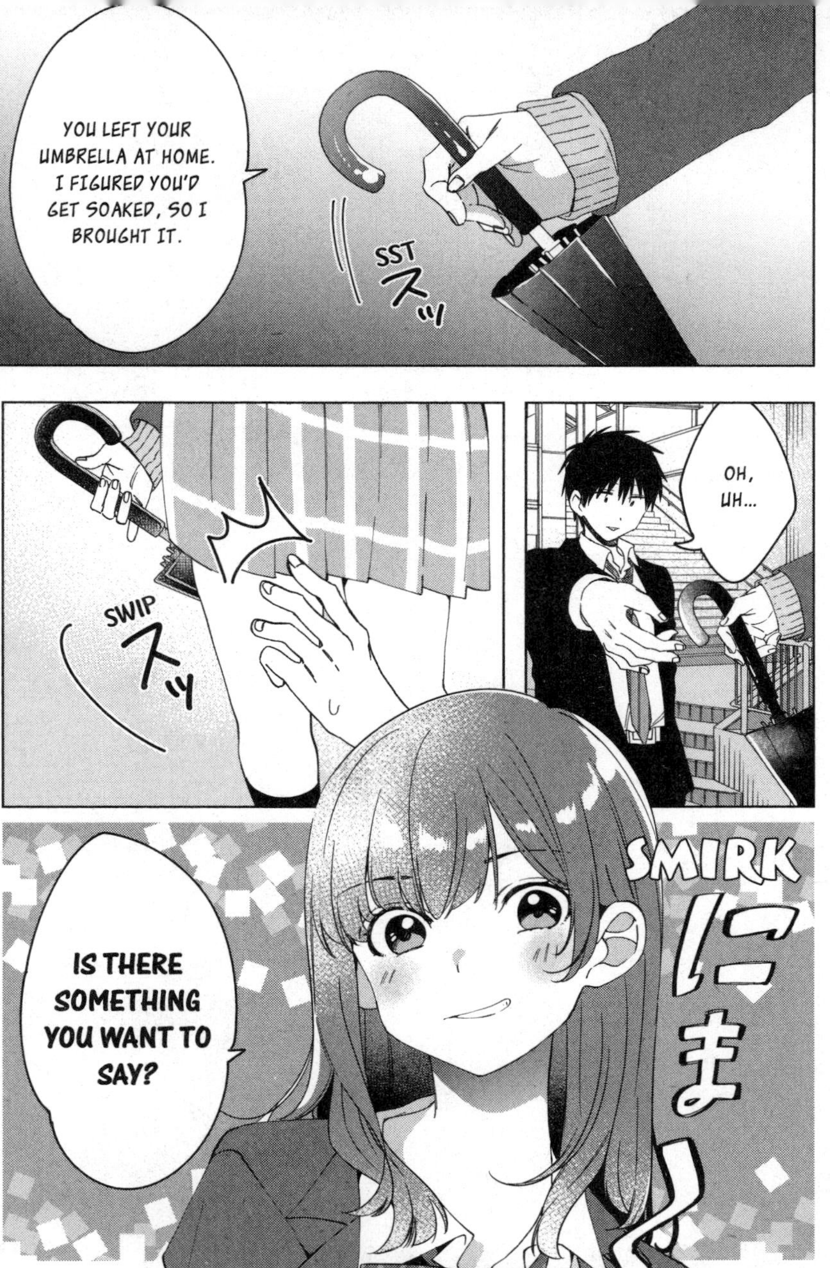
YOU LEFT YOUR UMBRELLA AT HOME. I FIGURED YOU'D GET SOAKED, SO I BROUGHT IT.
SST
スッ
OH, UH...
SWIP
スッ
SMIRK
にま
IS THERE SOMETHING YOU WANT TO SAY?

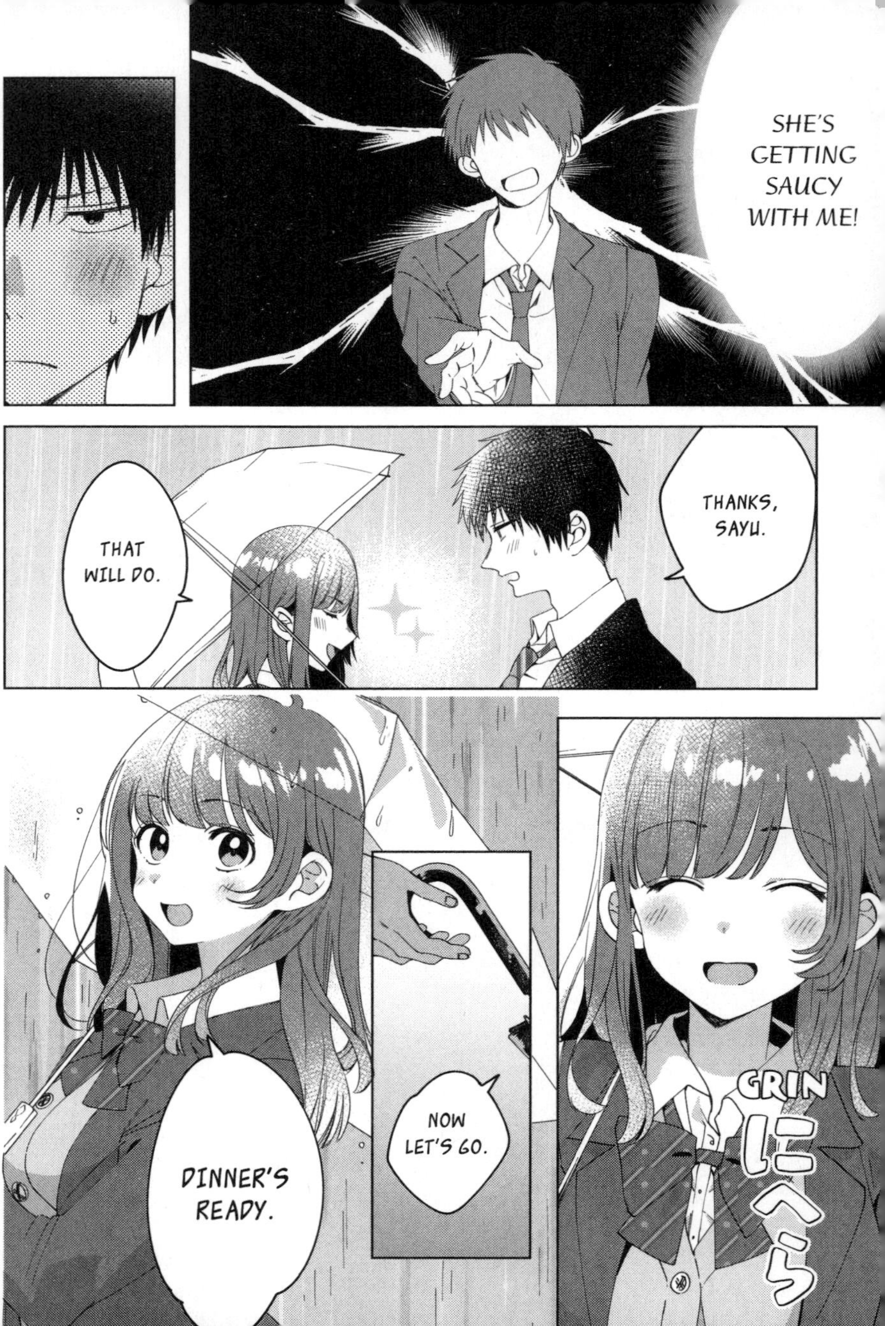
SHE'S GETTING SAUCY WITH ME!
THANKS, SAYU.
THAT WILL DO.
GRIN
にへら
NOW LET'S GO.
DINNER'S READY.

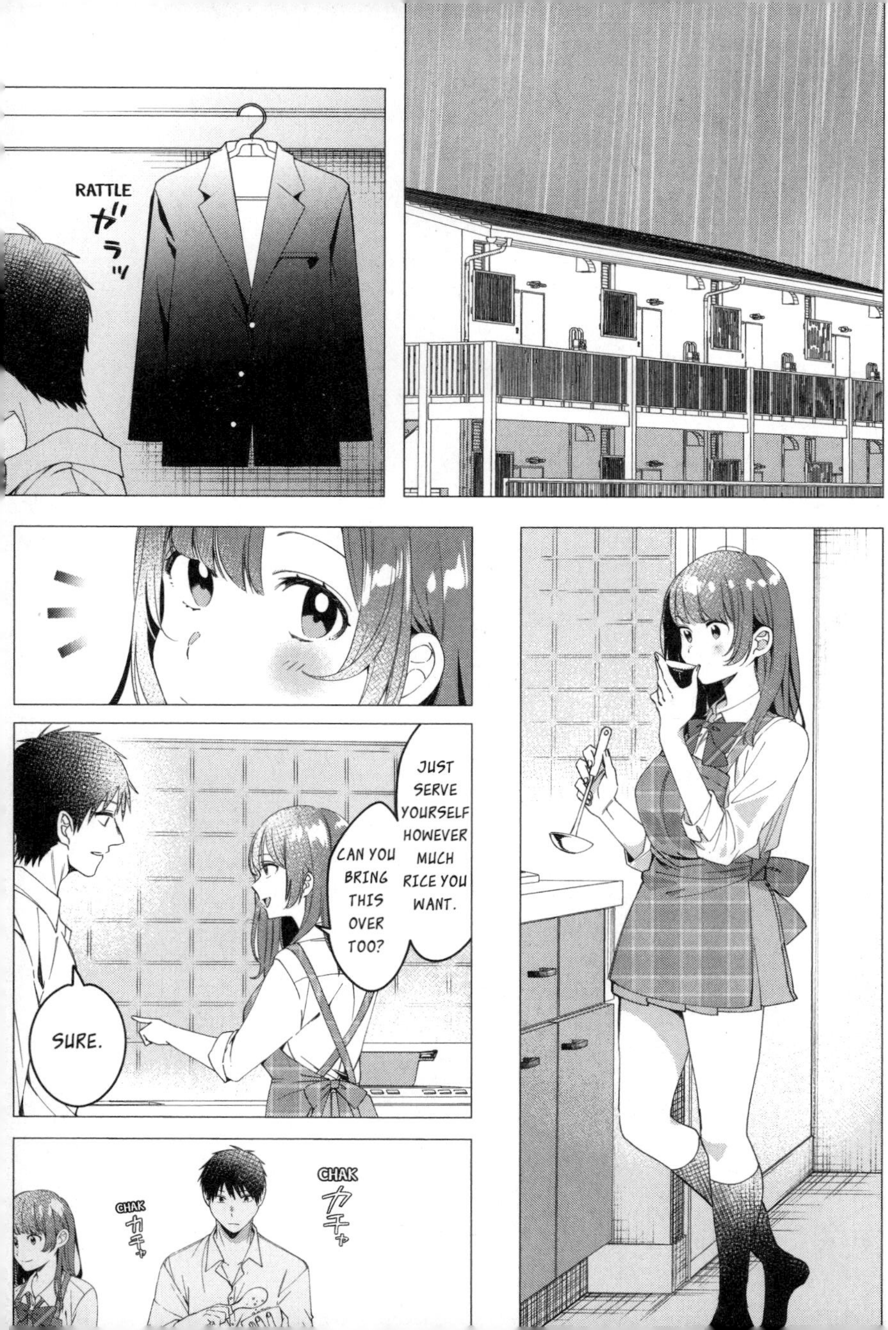
RATTLE
ガラッ
JUST SERVE YOURSELF HOWEVER MUCH RICE YOU WANT.
CAN YOU BRING THIS OVER TOO?
SURE.
CHAK
カチャ
CHAK
カチャ

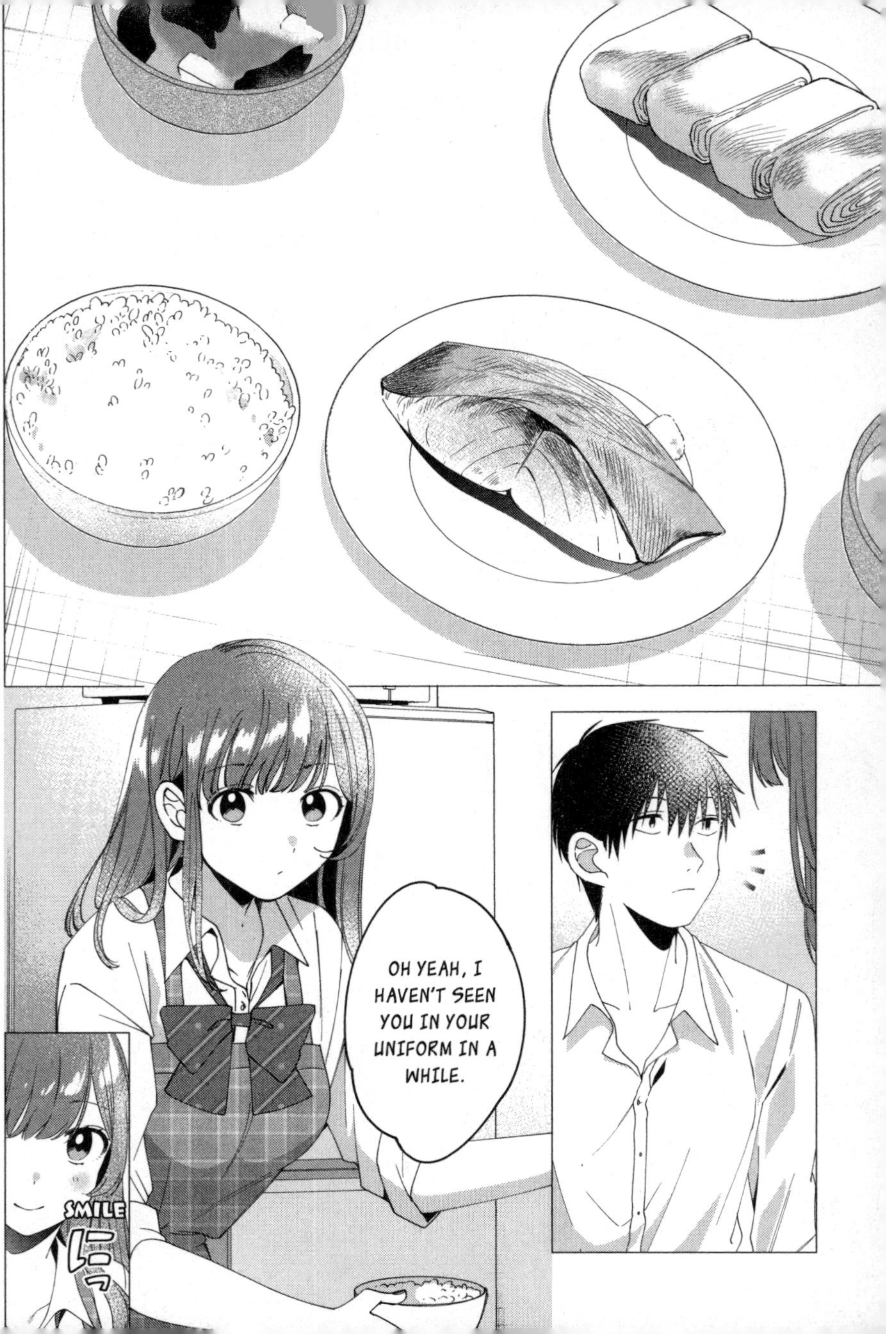
OH YEAH, I HAVEN'T SEEN YOU IN YOUR UNIFORM IN A WHILE.
SMILE

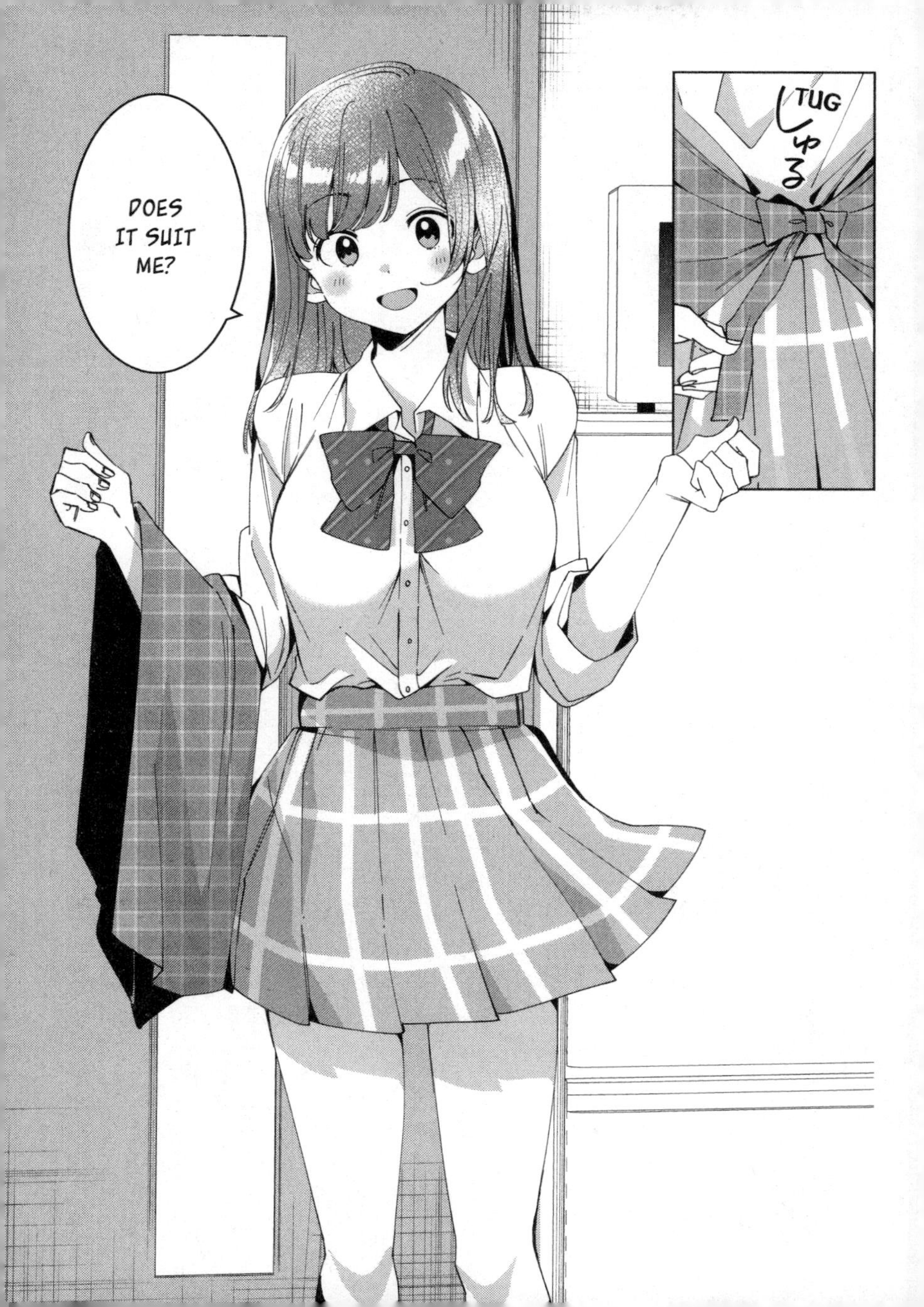
TUG
しゅる
DOES IT SUIT ME?

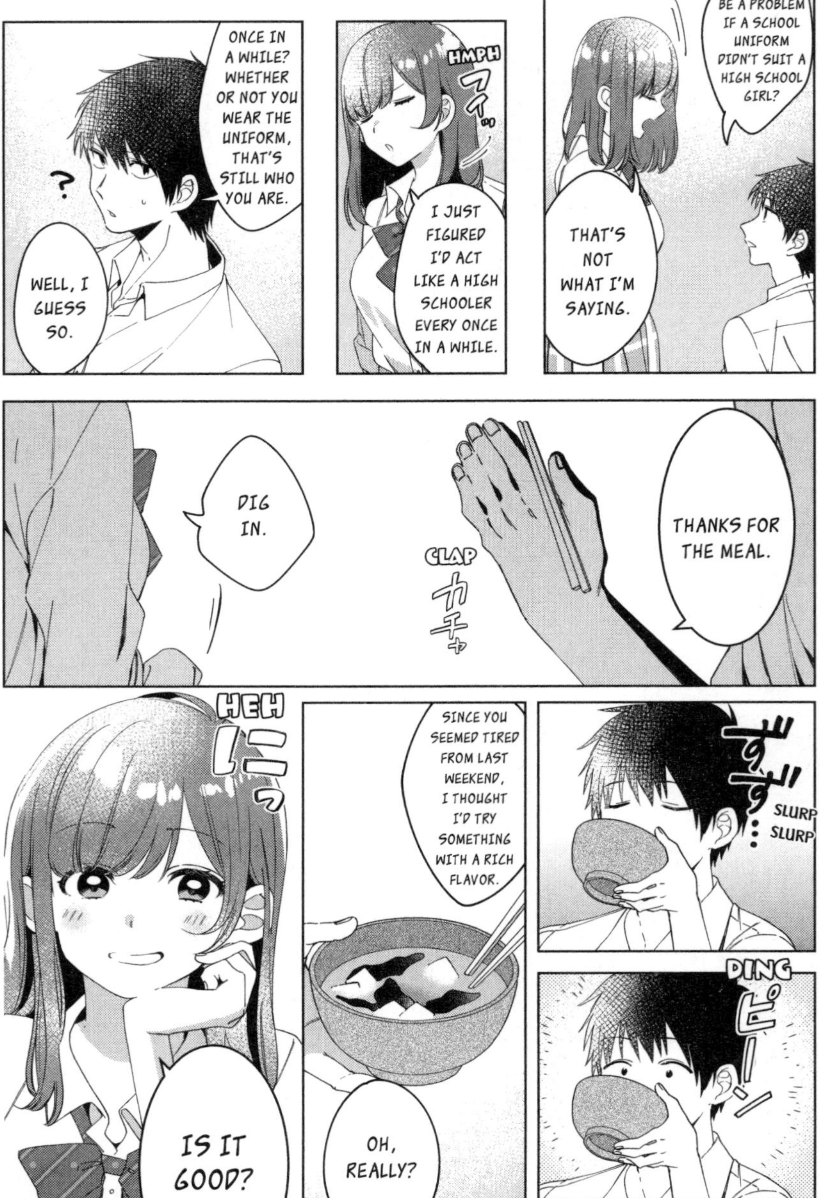
WOULDN'T IT BE A PROBLEM IF A SCHOOL UNIFORM DIDN'T SUIT A HIGH SCHOOL GIRL?
THAT'S NOT WHAT I'M SAYING.
HMPH
フイッ
I JUST FIGURED I'D ACT LIKE A HIGH SCHOOLER EVERY ONCE IN A WHILE.
ONCE IN A WHILE? WHETHER OR NOT YOU WEAR THE UNIFORM, THAT'S STILL WHO YOU ARE.
?
WELL, I GUESS SO.
THANKS FOR THE MEAL.
CLAP
カチャ
DIG IN.
ずずッ
ずッ…
SLURP SLURP
DING
ピー
SINCE YOU SEEMED TIRED FROM LAST WEEKEND, I THOUGHT I'D TRY SOMETHING WITH A RICH FLAVOR.
OH, REALLY?
HEH
にこっ
IS IT GOOD?

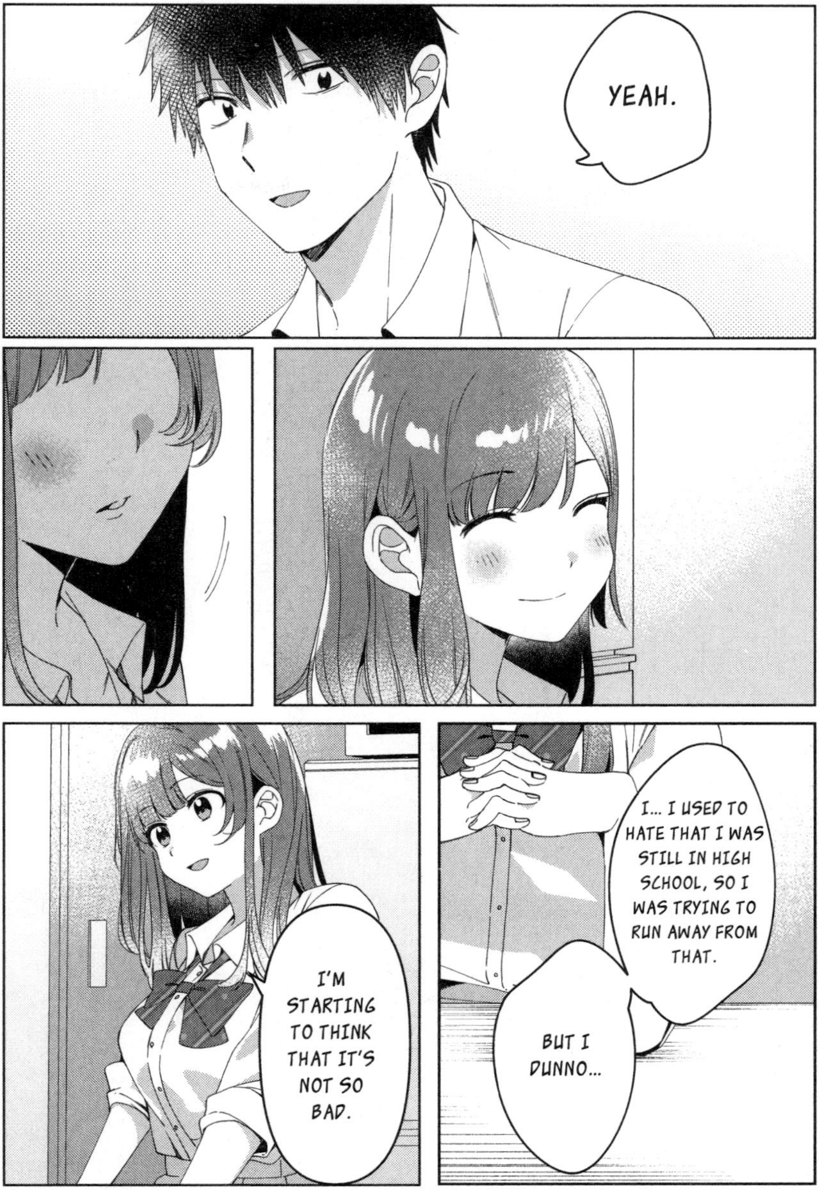
YEAH.
I... I USED TO HATE THAT I WAS STILL IN HIGH SCHOOL, SO I WAS TRYING TO RUN AWAY FROM THAT.
BUT I DUNNO...
I'M STARTING TO THINK THAT IT'S NOT SO BAD.

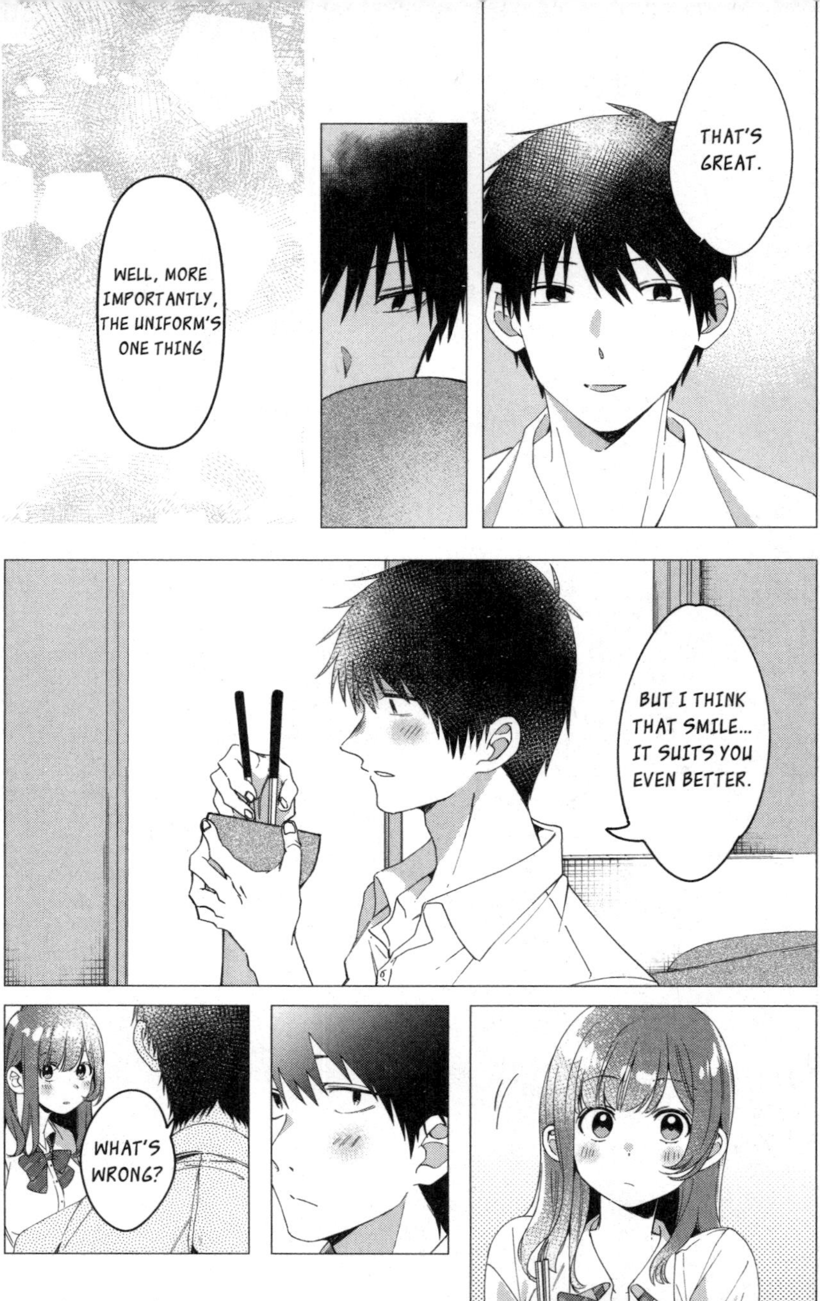
THAT'S GREAT.
WELL, MORE IMPORTANTLY, THE UNIFORM'S ONE THING
BUT I THINK THAT SMILE... IT SUITS YOU EVEN BETTER.
WHAT'S WRONG?

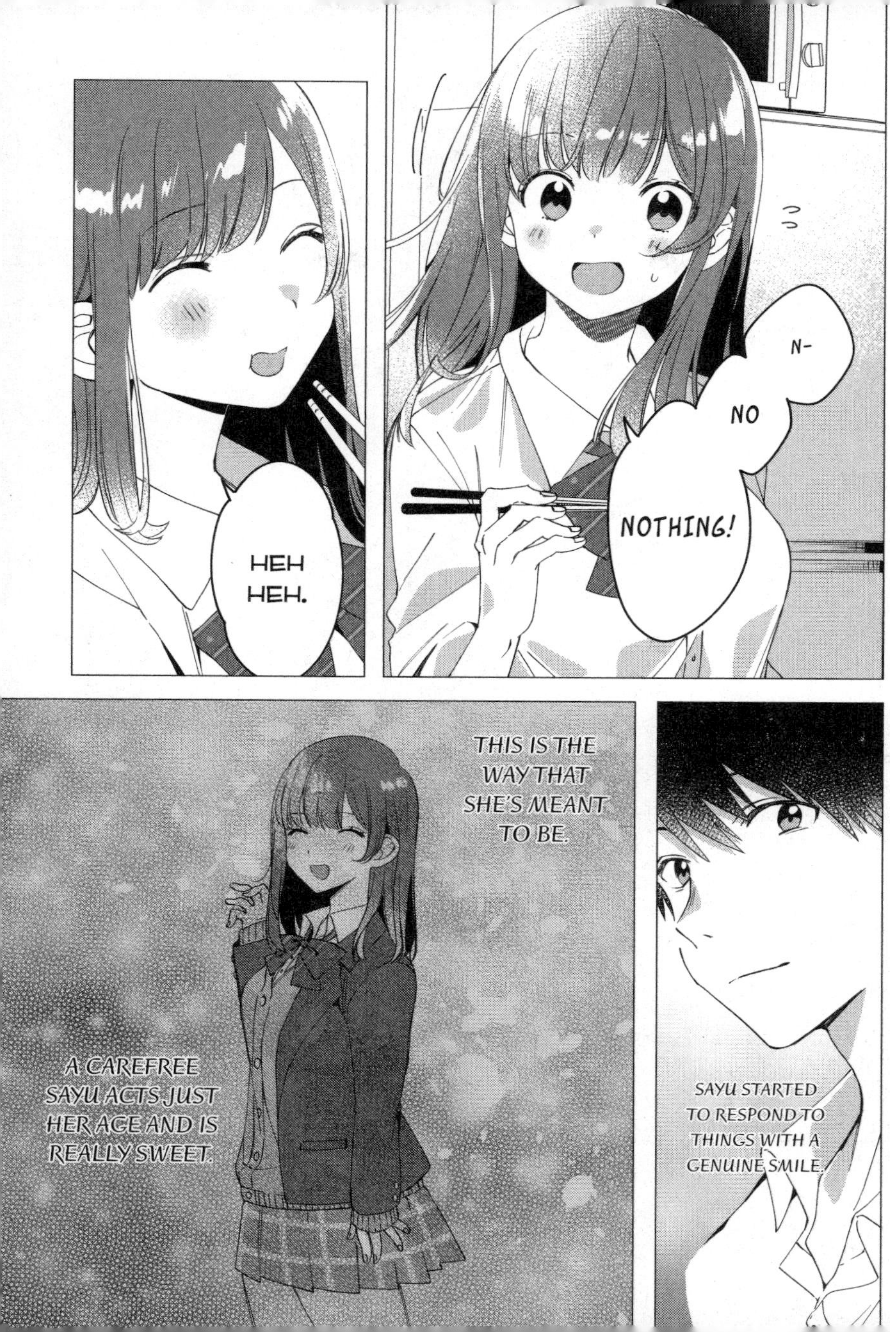
N-
NO
NOTHING!
HEH HEH.
SAYU STARTED TO RESPOND TO THINGS WITH A GENUINE SMILE.
THIS IS THE WAY THAT SHE'S MEANT TO BE.
A CAREFREE SAYU ACTS JUST HER AGE AND IS REALLY SWEET.

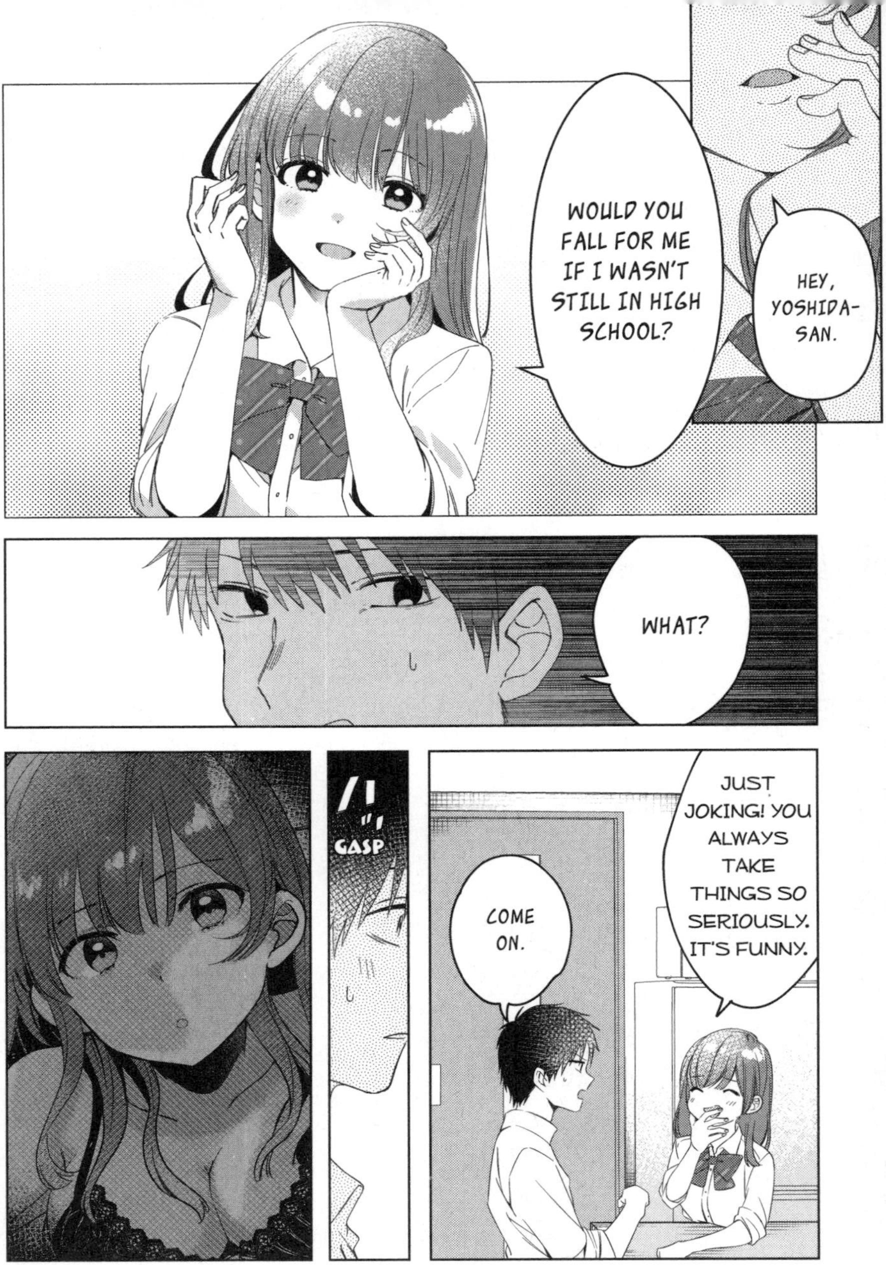
HEY, YOSHIDA-SAN.
WOULD YOU FALL FOR ME IF I WASN'T STILL IN HIGH SCHOOL?
WHAT?
JUST JOKING! YOU ALWAYS TAKE THINGS SO SERIOUSLY. IT'S FUNNY.
COME ON.
GASP

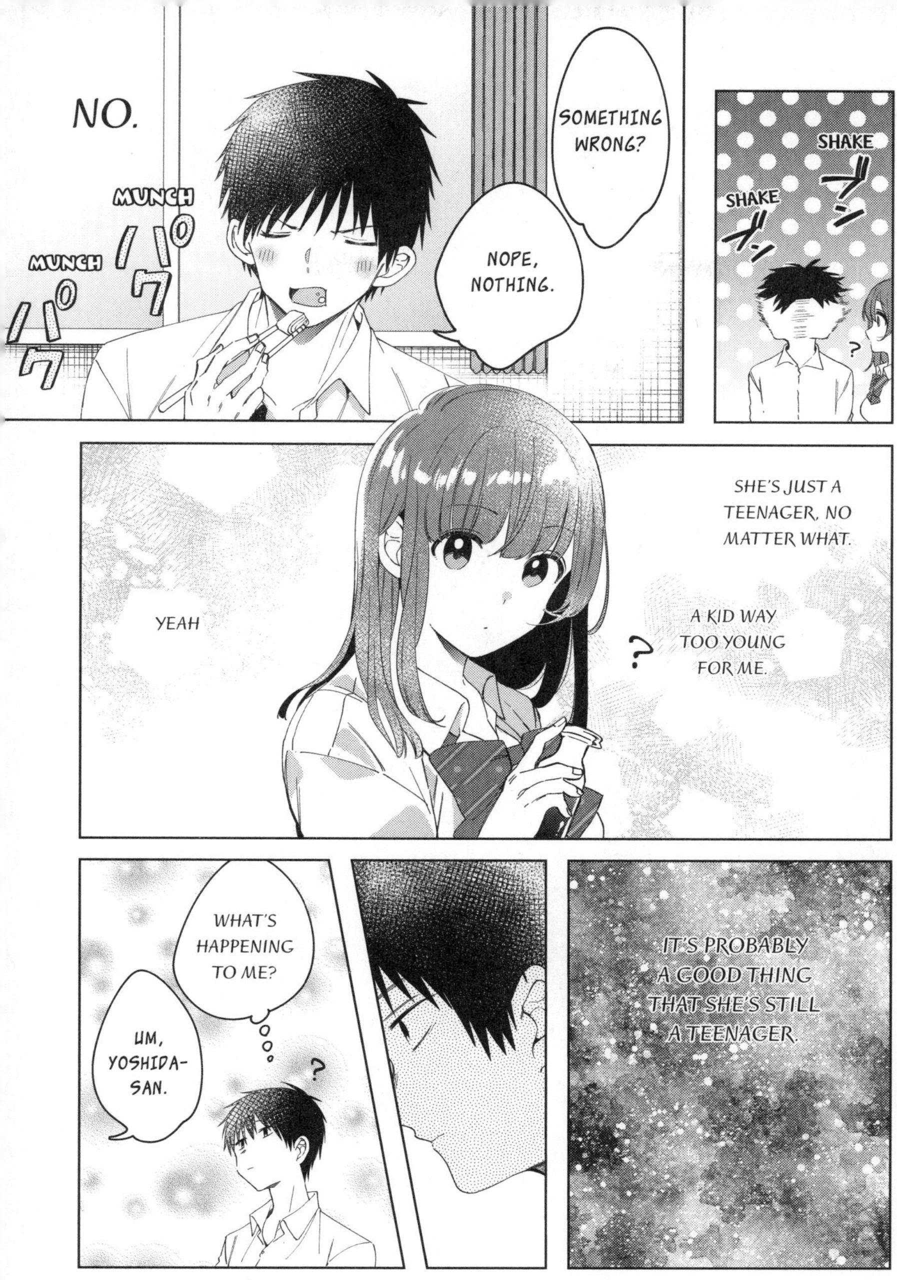
SHAKE
ブン
SHAKE
ブン
?
SOMETHING WRONG?
NOPE, NOTHING.
NO.
MUNCH
パク
MUNCH
パク
SHE'S JUST A TEENAGER, NO MATTER WHAT.
A KID WAY TOO YOUNG FOR ME.
?
YEAH
IT'S PROBABLY A GOOD THING THAT SHE'S STILL A TEENAGER.
WHAT'S HAPPENING TO ME?
UM, YOSHIDA-SAN.
?

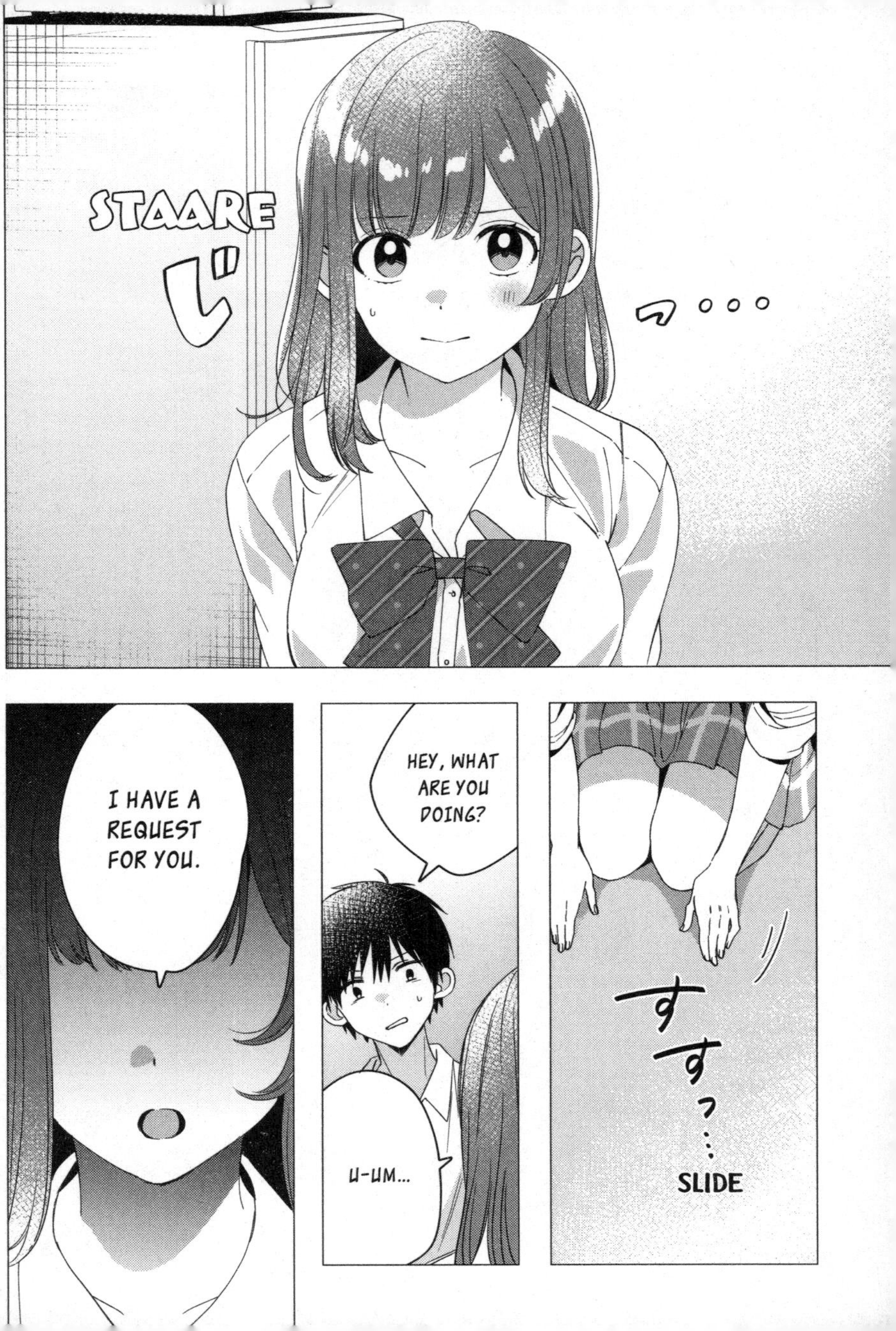

っ。。。
STAARE
じ
すすっ…
SLIDE
HEY, WHAT ARE YOU DOING?
U-UM...
I HAVE A REQUEST FOR YOU.

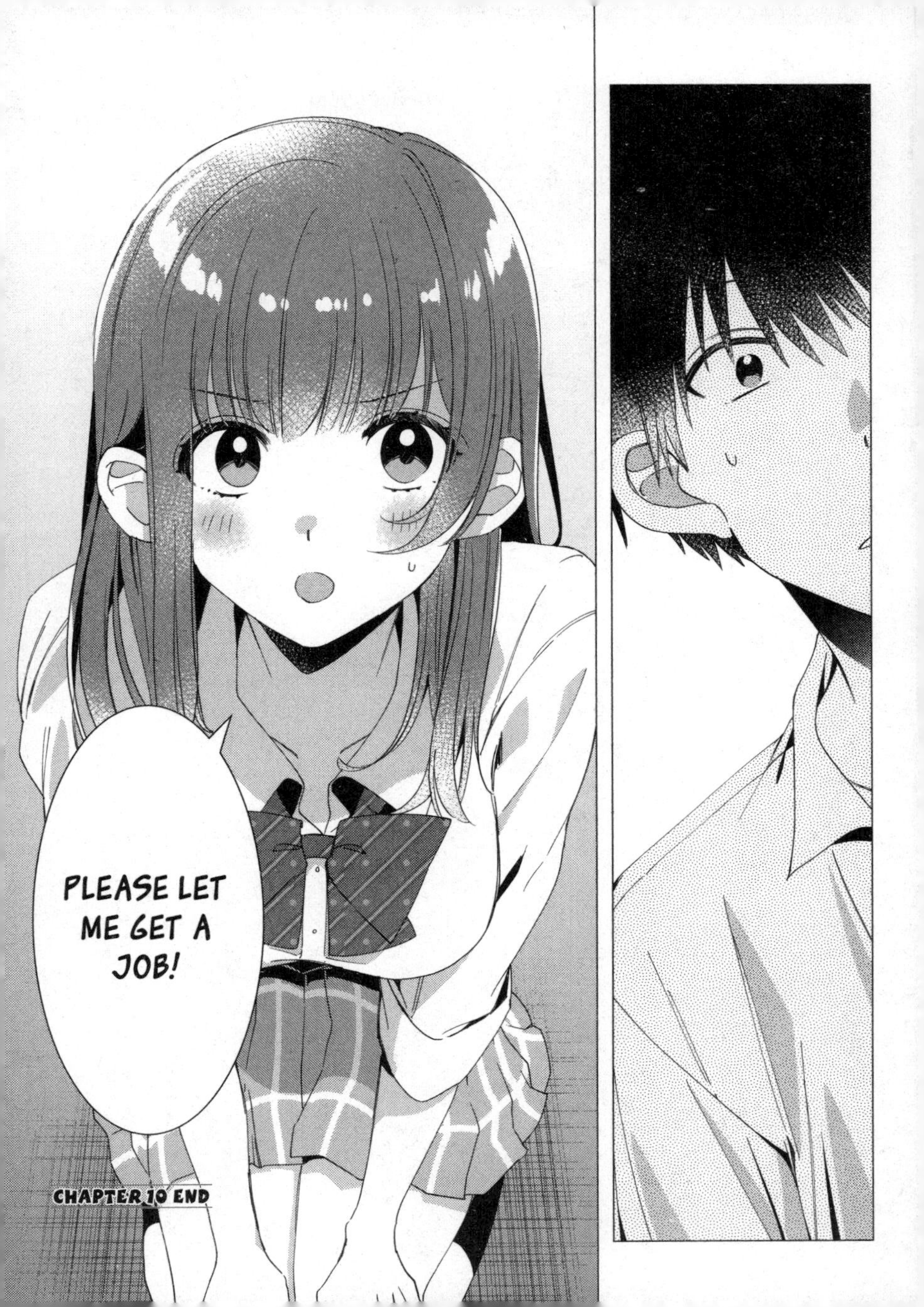
PLEASE LET ME GET A JOB!
CHAPTER 10 END

HIGEHIRO

After Being Rejected,
I Shaved and Took
in a High School Runaway

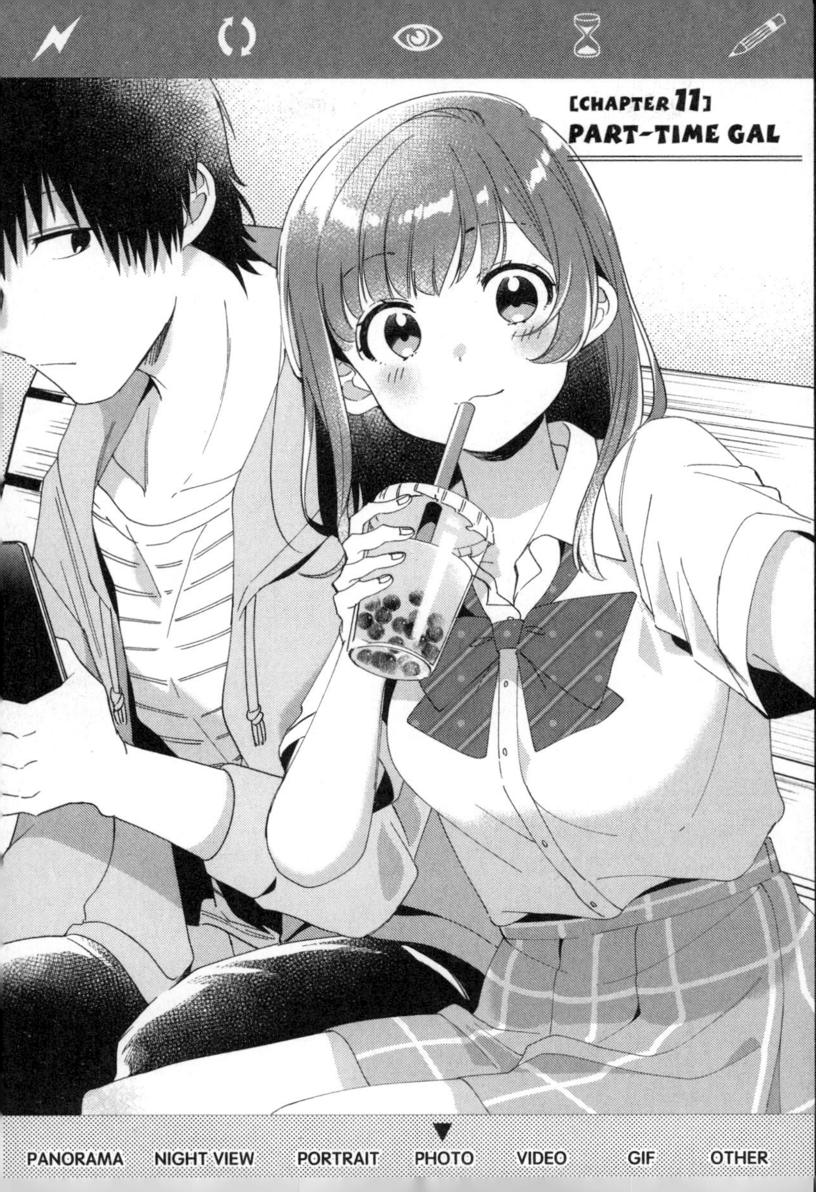
[CHAPTER 11]
PART-TIME GAL
PANORAMA
NIGHT VIEW
PORTRAIT
PHOTO
VIDEO
GIF
OTHER

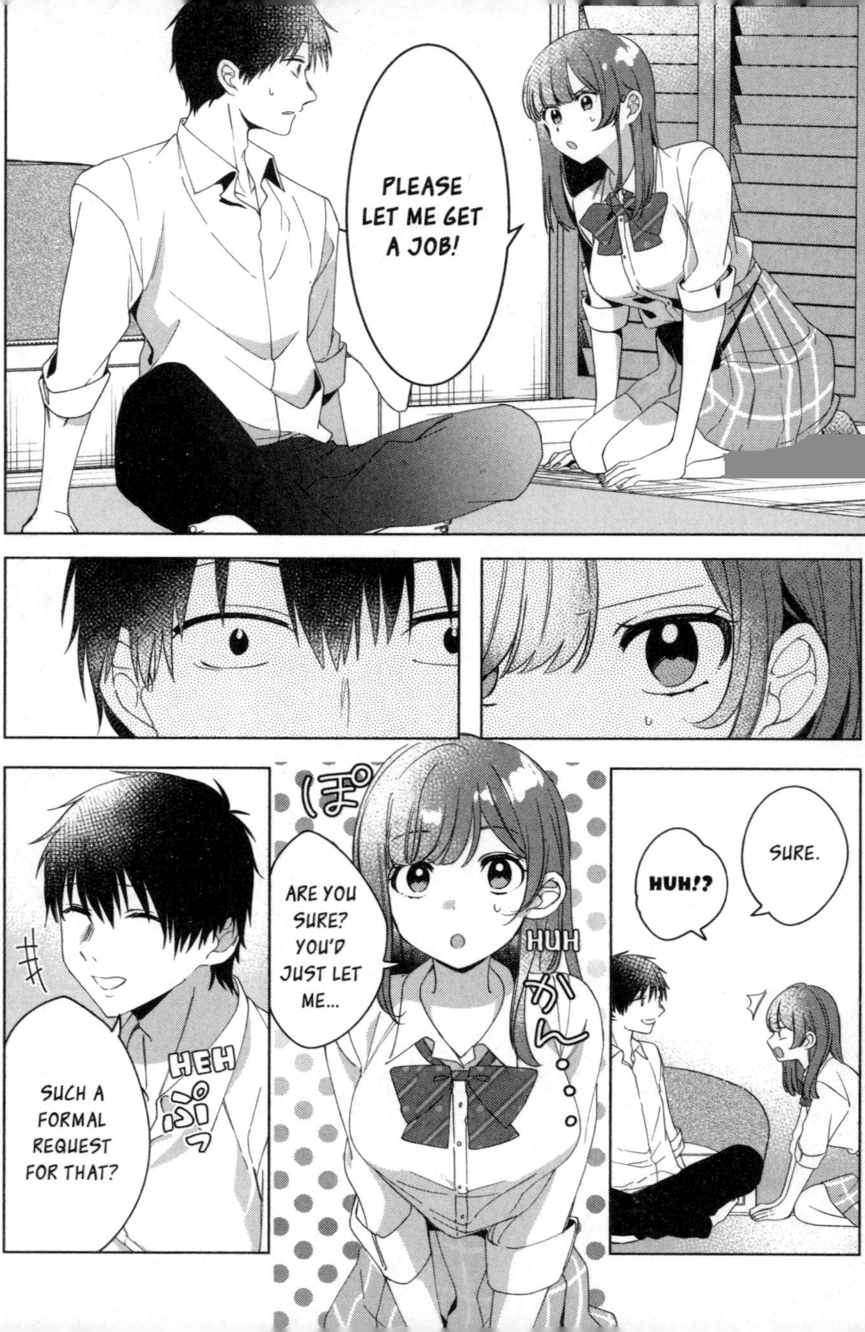
PLEASE LET ME GET A JOB!
SURE.
HUH!?
HUH
ARE YOU SURE? YOU'D JUST LET ME...
HEH
ぷっ
SUCH A FORMAL REQUEST FOR THAT?

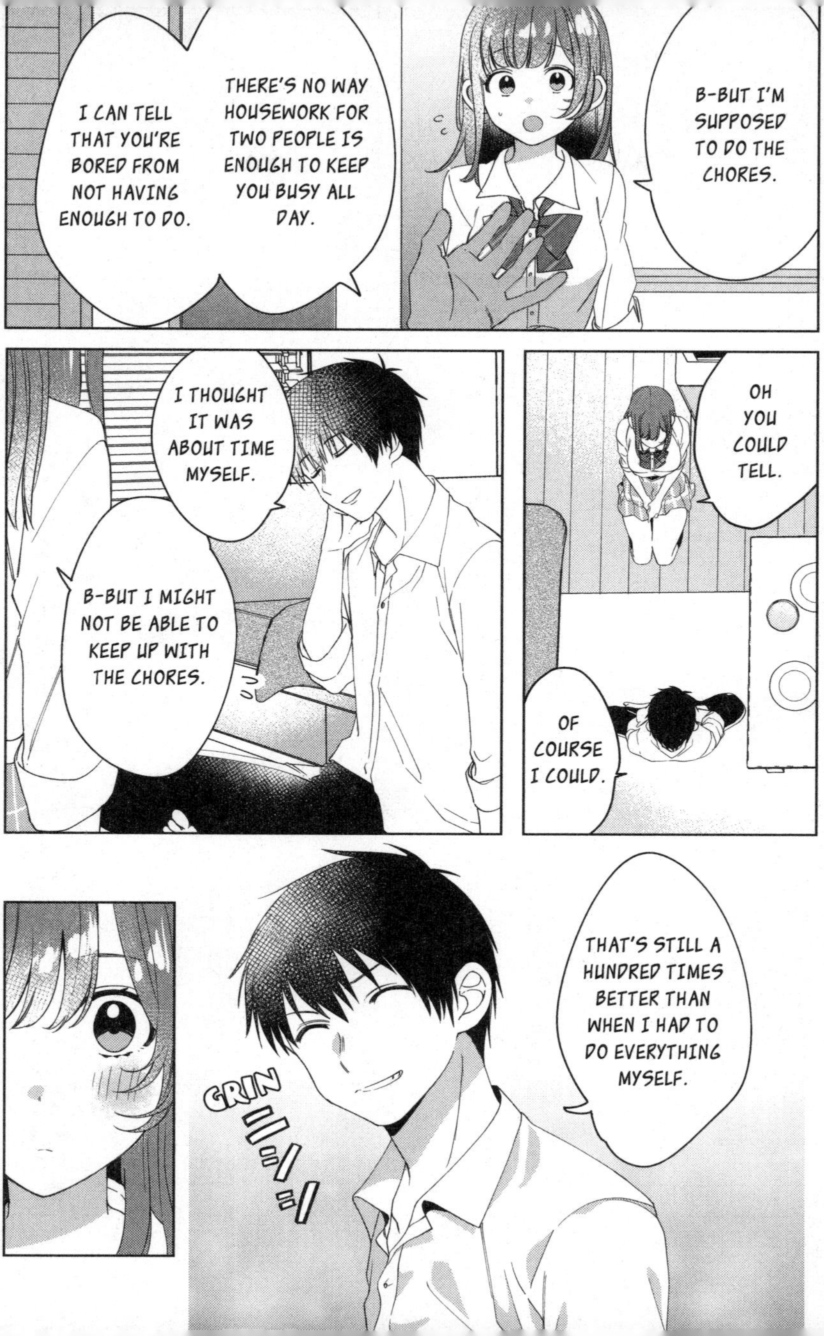
B-BUT I'M SUPPOSED TO DO THE CHORES.
THERE'S NO WAY HOUSEWORK FOR TWO PEOPLE IS ENOUGH TO KEEP YOU BUSY ALL DAY.
I CAN TELL THAT YOU'RE BORED FROM NOT HAVING ENOUGH TO DO.
OH YOU COULD TELL.
OF COURSE I COULD.
I THOUGHT IT WAS ABOUT TIME MYSELF.
B-BUT I MIGHT NOT BE ABLE TO KEEP UP WITH THE CHORES.
THAT'S STILL A HUNDRED TIMES BETTER THAN WHEN I HAD TO DO EVERYTHING MYSELF.
GRIN

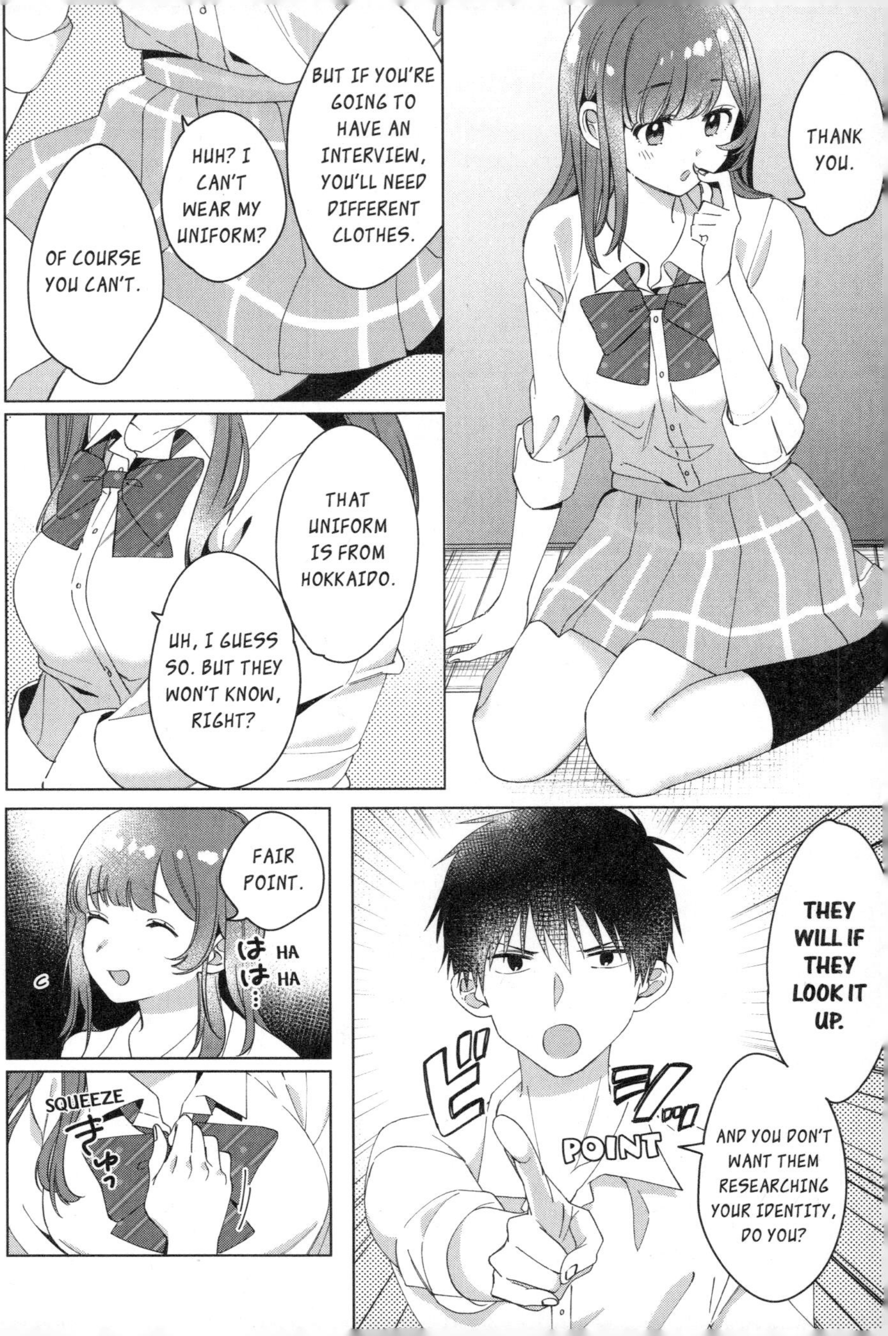
THANK YOU.
BUT IF YOU'RE GOING TO HAVE AN INTERVIEW, YOU'LL NEED DIFFERENT CLOTHES.
HUH? I CAN'T WEAR MY UNIFORM?
OF COURSE YOU CAN'T.
THAT UNIFORM IS FROM HOKKAIDO.
UH, I GUESS SO. BUT THEY WON'T KNOW, RIGHT?
THEY WILL IF THEY LOOK IT UP.
ビシッ
POINT
AND YOU DON'T WANT THEM RESEARCHING YOUR IDENTITY, DO YOU?
FAIR POINT.
はは…
HA HA
SQUEEZE
きゅっ

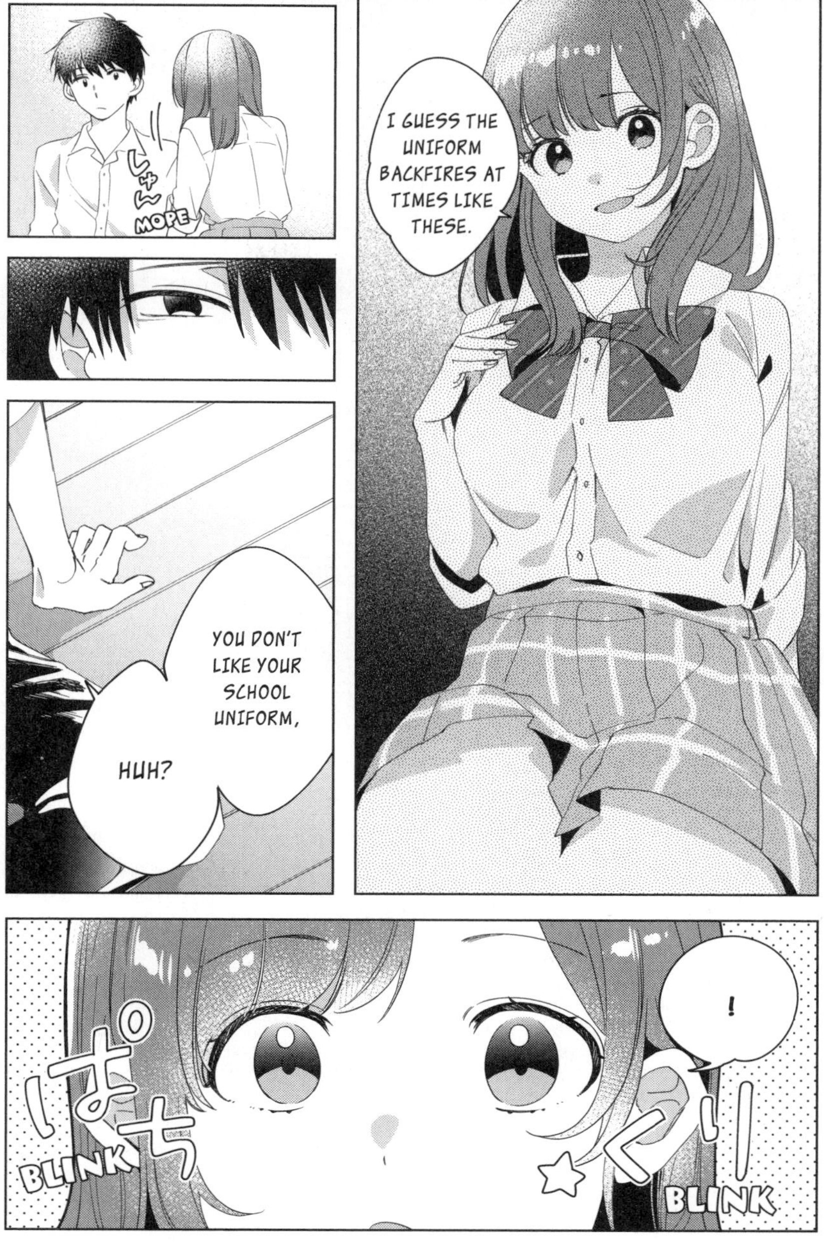
I GUESS THE UNIFORM BACKFIRES AT TIMES LIKE THESE.
しゅん
MOPE
YOU DON'T LIKE YOUR SCHOOL UNIFORM,
HUH?
!
くい
BLINK
ぱち
BLINK

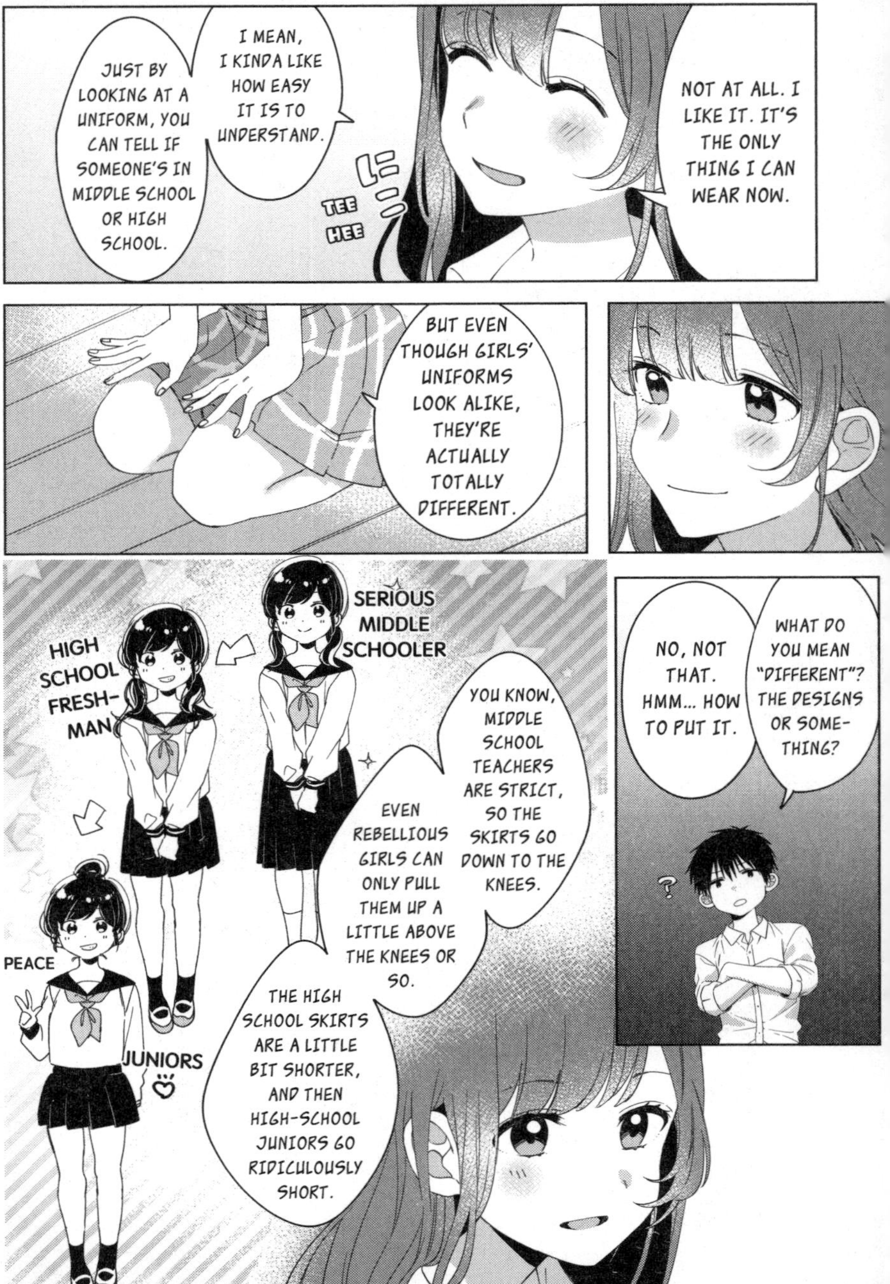
NOT AT ALL. I LIKE IT. IT'S THE ONLY THING I CAN WEAR NOW.
I MEAN, I KINDA LIKE HOW EASY IT IS TO UNDERSTAND.
TEE HEE
JUST BY LOOKING AT A UNIFORM, YOU CAN TELL IF SOMEONE'S IN MIDDLE SCHOOL OR HIGH SCHOOL.
BUT EVEN THOUGH GIRLS' UNIFORMS LOOK ALIKE, THEY'RE ACTUALLY TOTALLY DIFFERENT.
WHAT DO YOU MEAN "DIFFERENT"? THE DESIGNS OR SOME-THING?
NO, NOT THAT. HMM... HOW TO PUT IT.
SERIOUS MIDDLE SCHOOLER
YOU KNOW, MIDDLE SCHOOL TEACHERS ARE STRICT, SO THE SKIRTS GO DOWN TO THE KNEES.
HIGH SCHOOL FRESH-MAN
EVEN REBELLIOUS GIRLS CAN ONLY PULL THEM UP A LITTLE ABOVE THE KNEES OR SO.
PEACE
THE HIGH SCHOOL SKIRTS ARE A LITTLE BIT SHORTER, AND THEN HIGH-SCHOOL JUNIORS GO RIDICULOUSLY SHORT.
JUNIORS

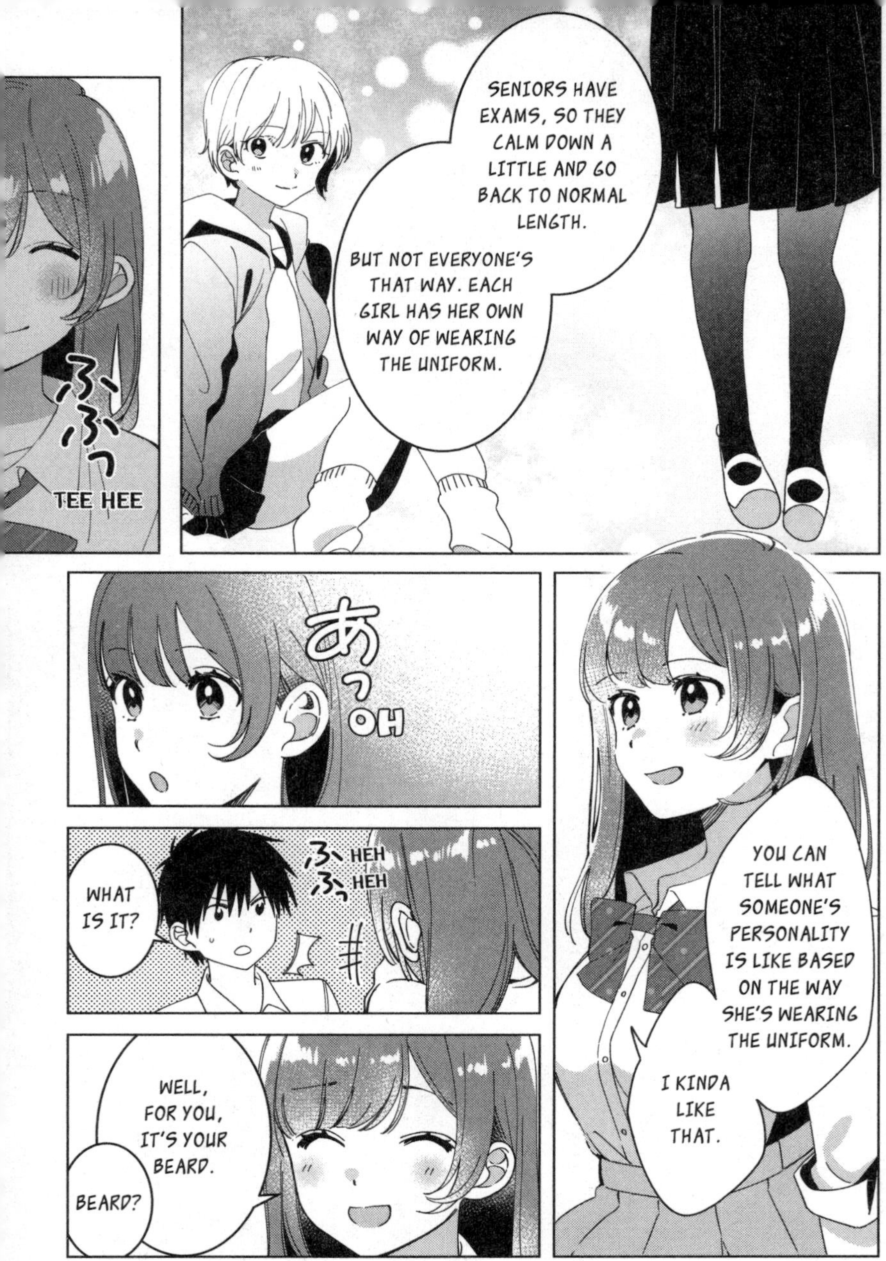
SENIORS HAVE EXAMS, SO THEY CALM DOWN A LITTLE AND GO BACK TO NORMAL LENGTH.
BUT NOT EVERYONE'S THAT WAY. EACH GIRL HAS HER OWN WAY OF WEARING THE UNIFORM.
ふふっ
TEE HEE
YOU CAN TELL WHAT SOMEONE'S PERSONALITY IS LIKE BASED ON THE WAY SHE'S WEARING THE UNIFORM.
I KINDA LIKE THAT.
あっ
OH
ふふっ
HEH HEH
WHAT IS IT?
WELL, FOR YOU, IT'S YOUR BEARD.
BEARD?

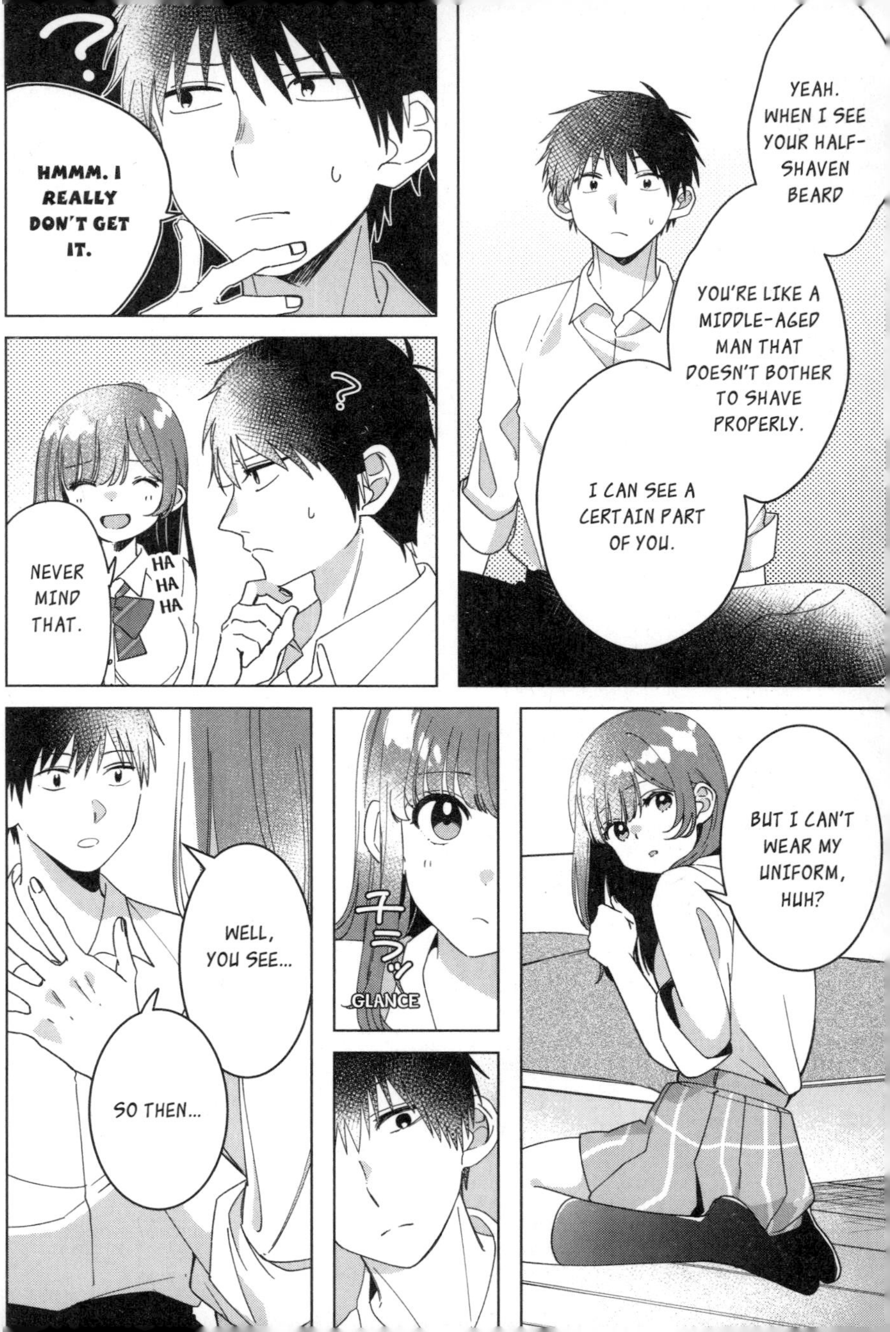
YEAH. WHEN I SEE YOUR HALF-SHAVEN BEARD
YOU'RE LIKE A MIDDLE-AGED MAN THAT DOESN'T BOTHER TO SHAVE PROPERLY.
I CAN SEE A CERTAIN PART OF YOU.
HMMM. I REALLY DON'T GET IT.
HA HA HA
NEVER MIND THAT.
BUT I CAN'T WEAR MY UNIFORM, HUH?
チラッ
GLANCE
WELL, YOU SEE...
SO THEN...

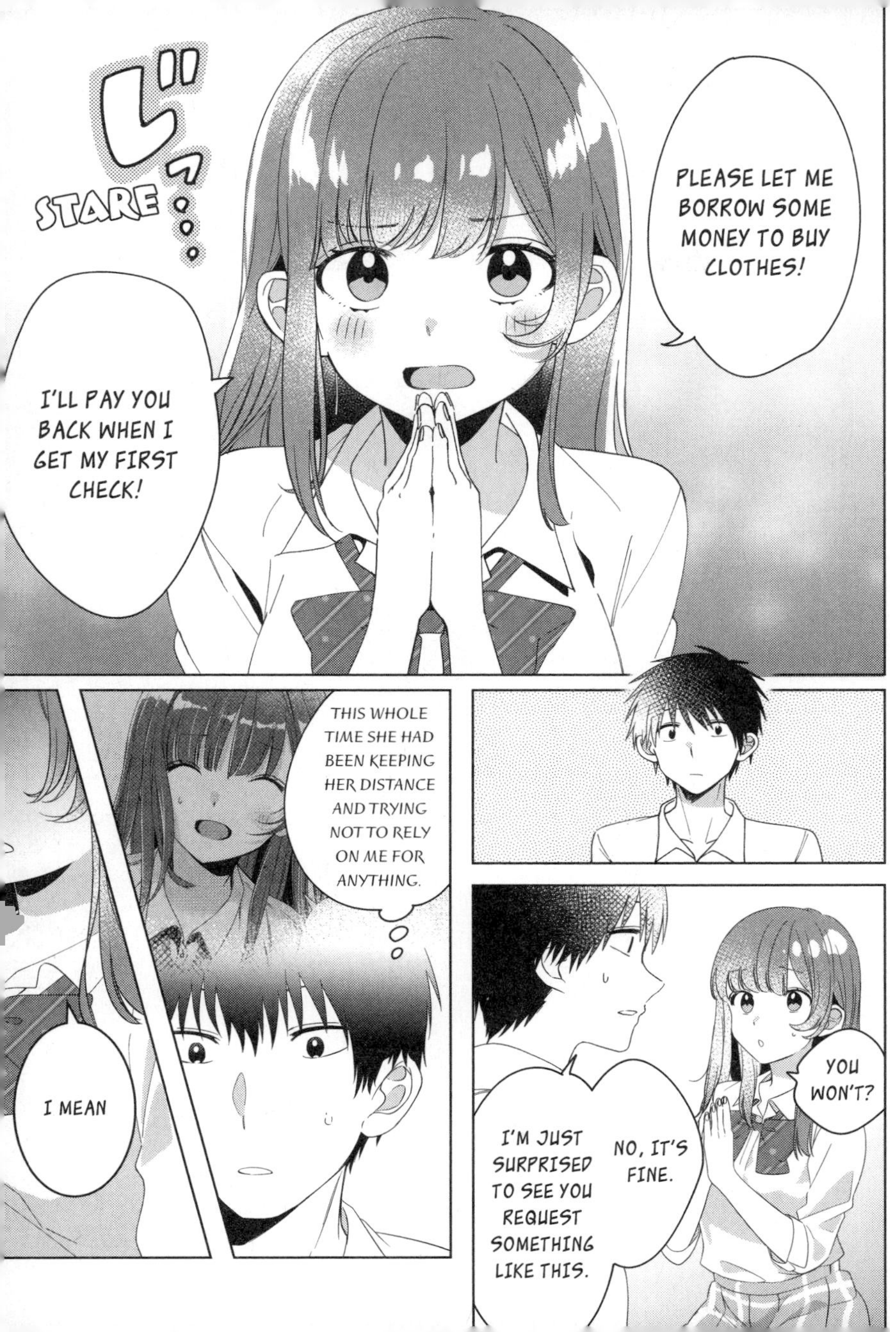
PLEASE LET ME BORROW SOME MONEY TO BUY CLOTHES!
STARE
I'LL PAY YOU BACK WHEN I GET MY FIRST CHECK!
YOU WON'T?
NO, IT'S FINE.
I'M JUST SURPRISED TO SEE YOU REQUEST SOMETHING LIKE THIS.
THIS WHOLE TIME SHE HAD BEEN KEEPING HER DISTANCE AND TRYING NOT TO RELY ON ME FOR ANYTHING.
I MEAN

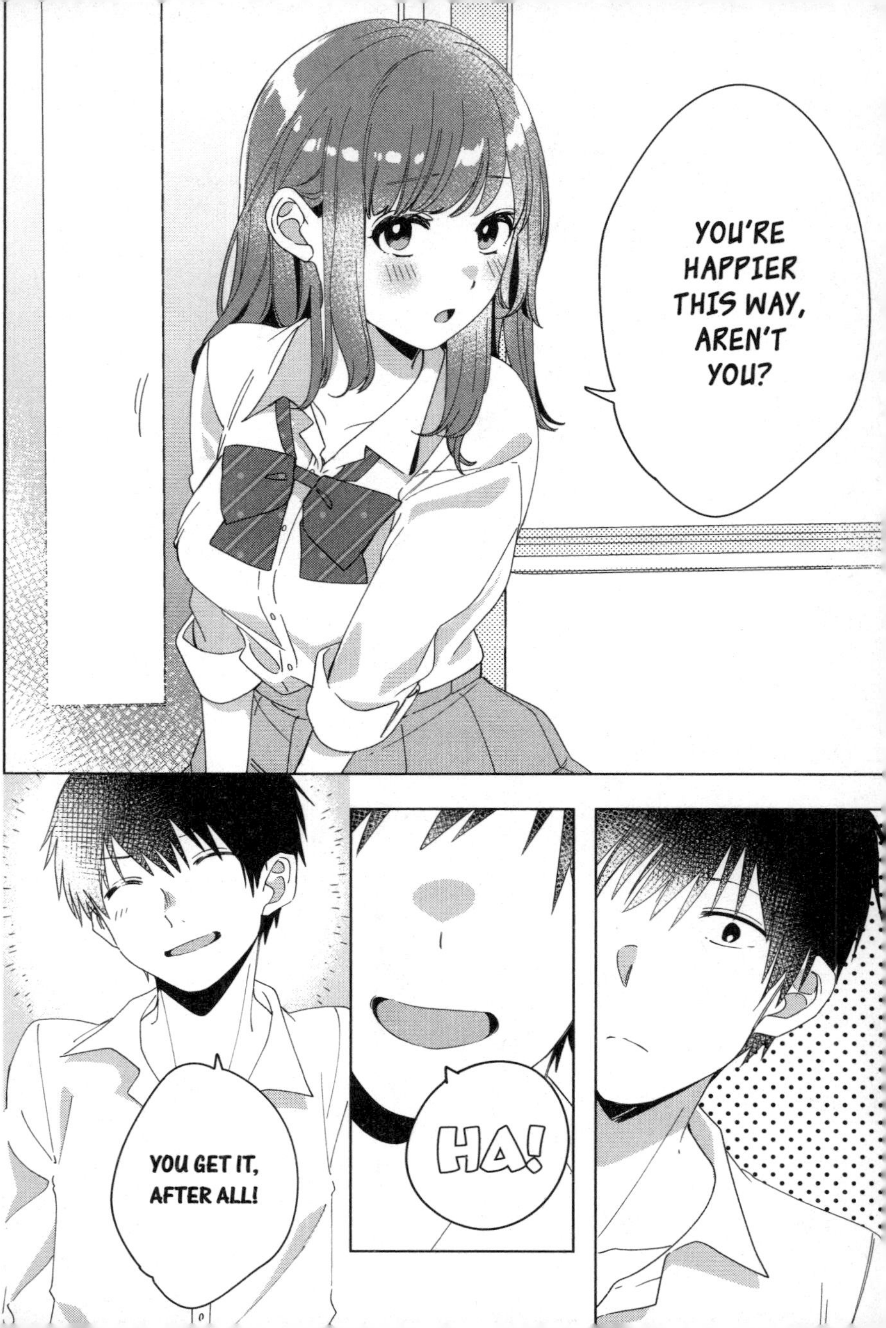
YOU'RE HAPPIER THIS WAY, AREN'T YOU?
HA!
YOU GET IT, AFTER ALL!

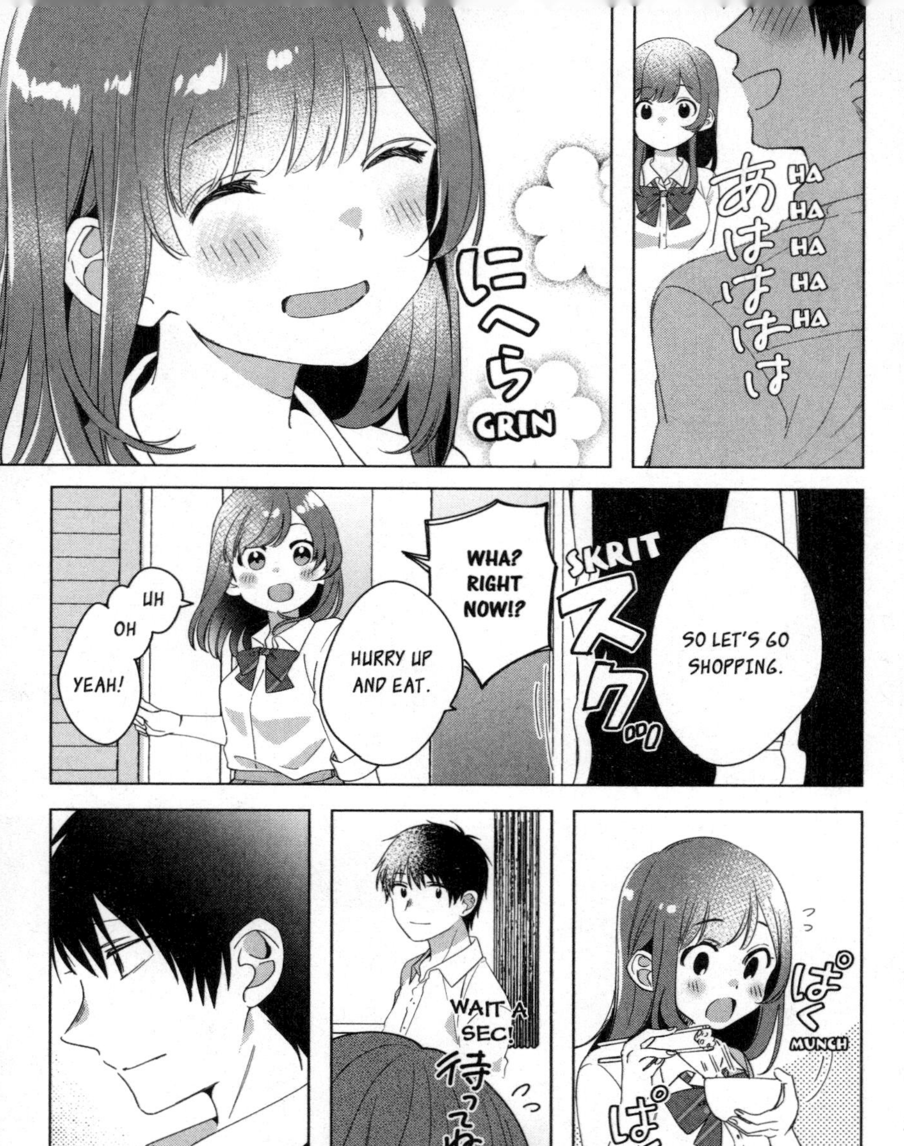

あははは
HA HA HA HA HA
にへら
GRIN
SO LET'S GO SHOPPING.
スクッ
SKRIT
WHA? RIGHT NOW!?
HURRY UP AND EAT.
UH OH YEAH!
ぱく
MUNCH
ぱく
MUNCH
WAIT A SEC!
待ってね～

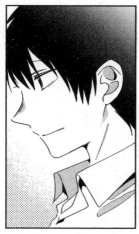

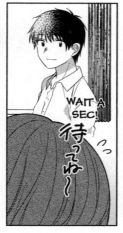

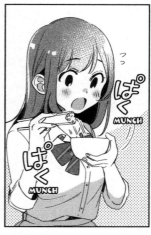

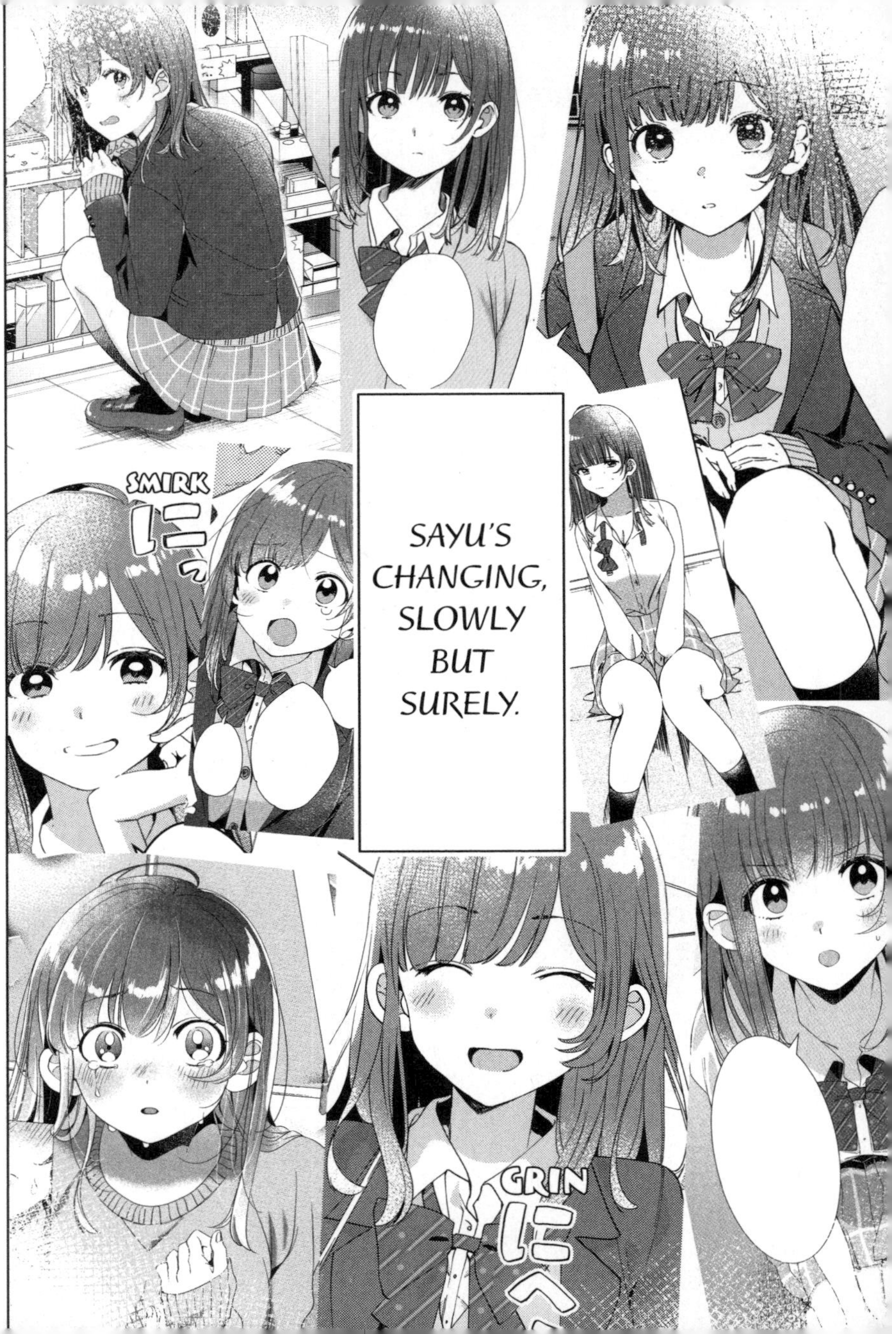
SAYU'S CHANGING, SLOWLY BUT SURELY.
SMIRK
にっ
GRIN
にへ

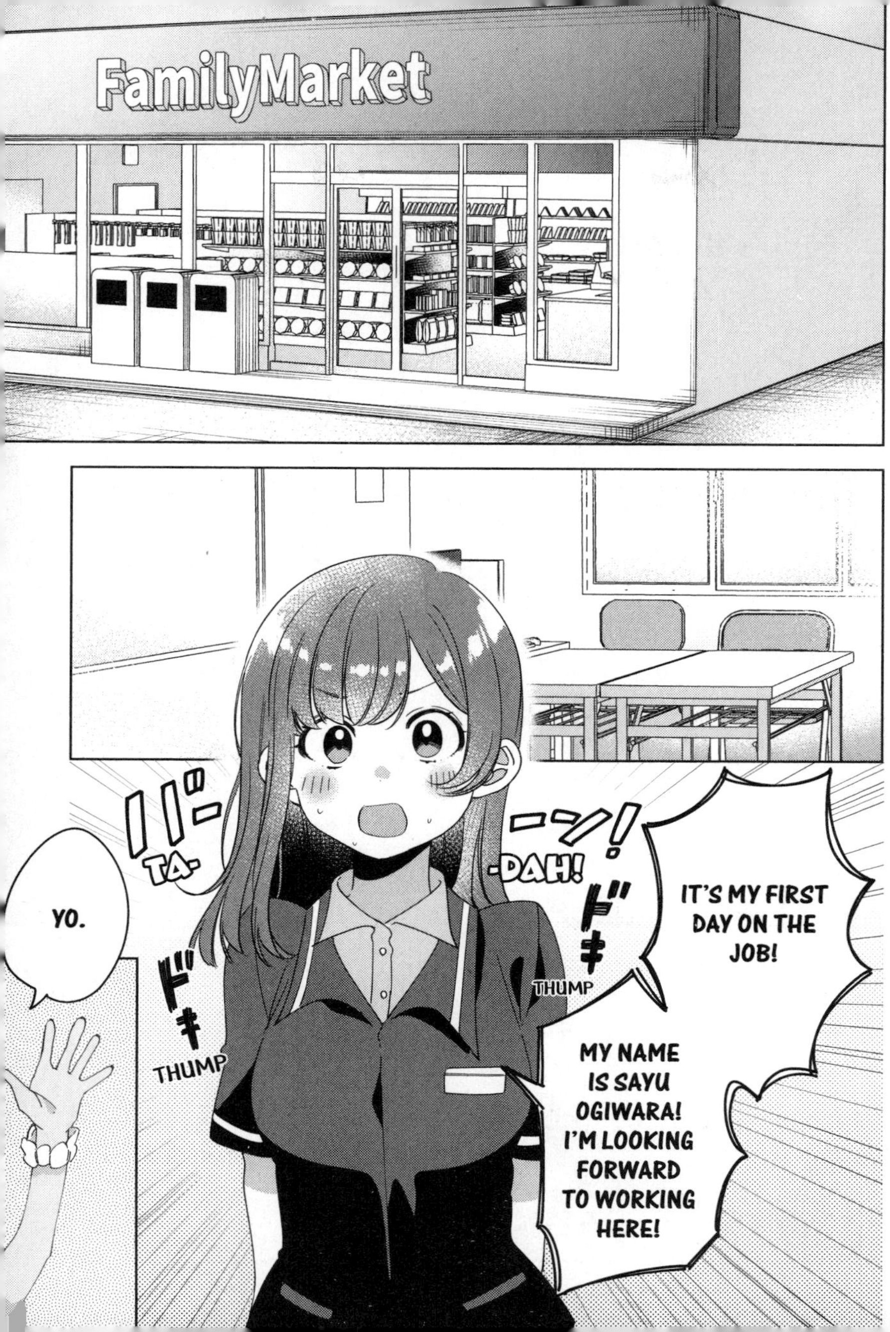
FamilyMarket
TA- -DAH!
IT'S MY FIRST DAY ON THE JOB!
THUMP
MY NAME IS SAYU OGIWARA! I'M LOOKING FORWARD TO WORKING HERE!
THUMP
YO.

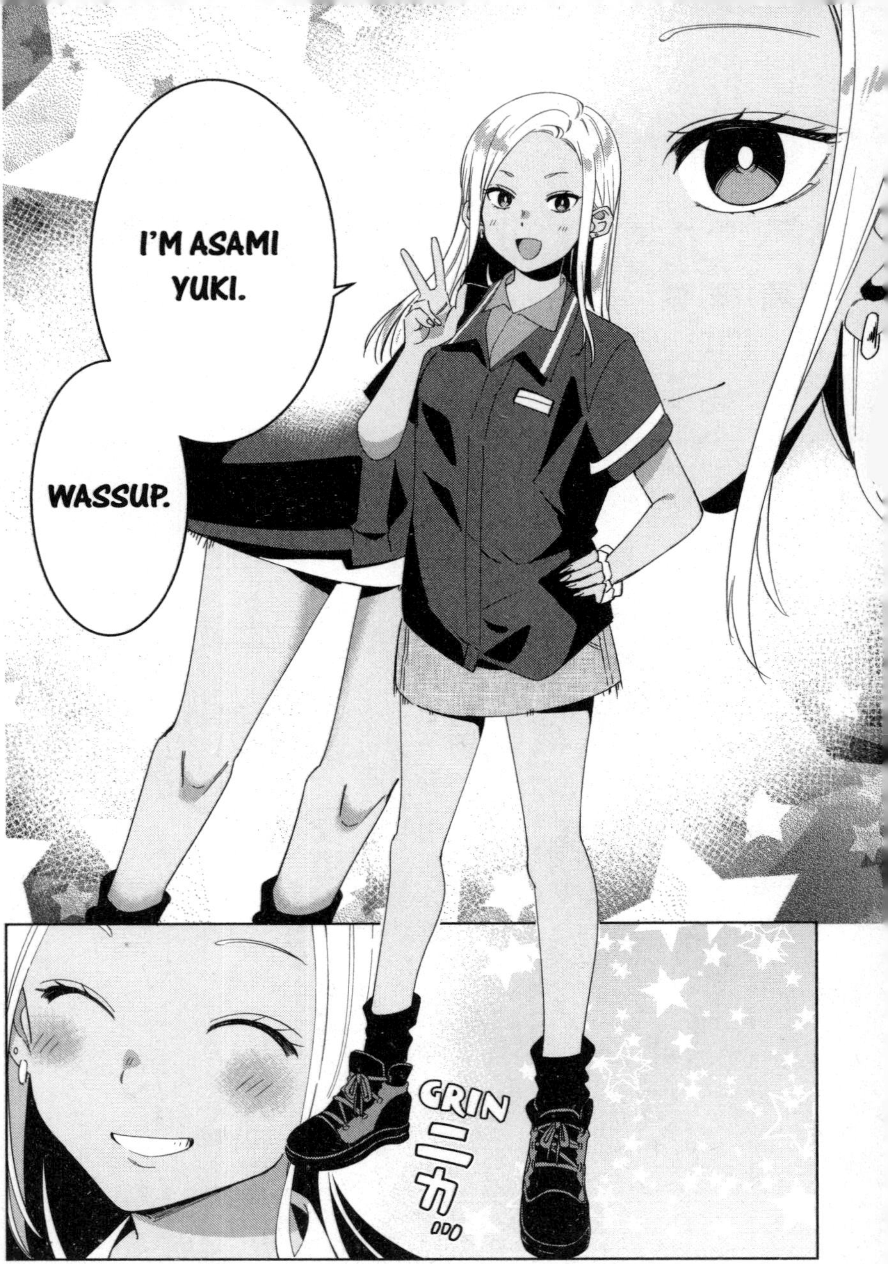
I'M ASAMI YUKI.
WASSUP.
GRIN
ニカ

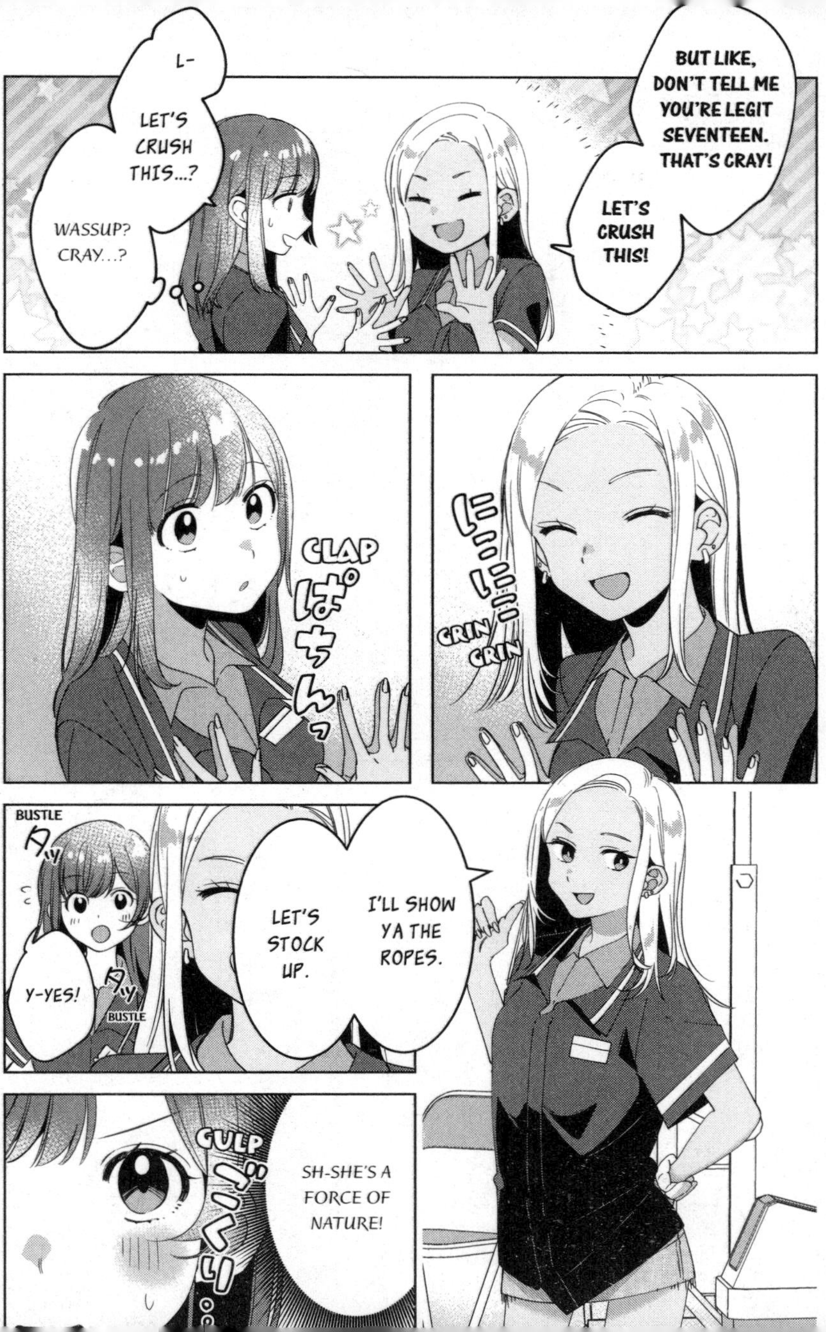
BUT LIKE, DON'T TELL ME YOU'RE LEGIT SEVENTEEN. THAT'S CRAY!
LET'S CRUSH THIS!
L-
LET'S CRUSH THIS...?
WASSUP? CRAY...?
にこにこ
GRIN GRIN
CLAP
ぱちんっ
I'LL SHOW YA THE ROPES.
LET'S STOCK UP.
BUSTLE
タッ
Y-YES!
タッ
BUSTLE
GULP
SH-SHE'S A FORCE OF NATURE!

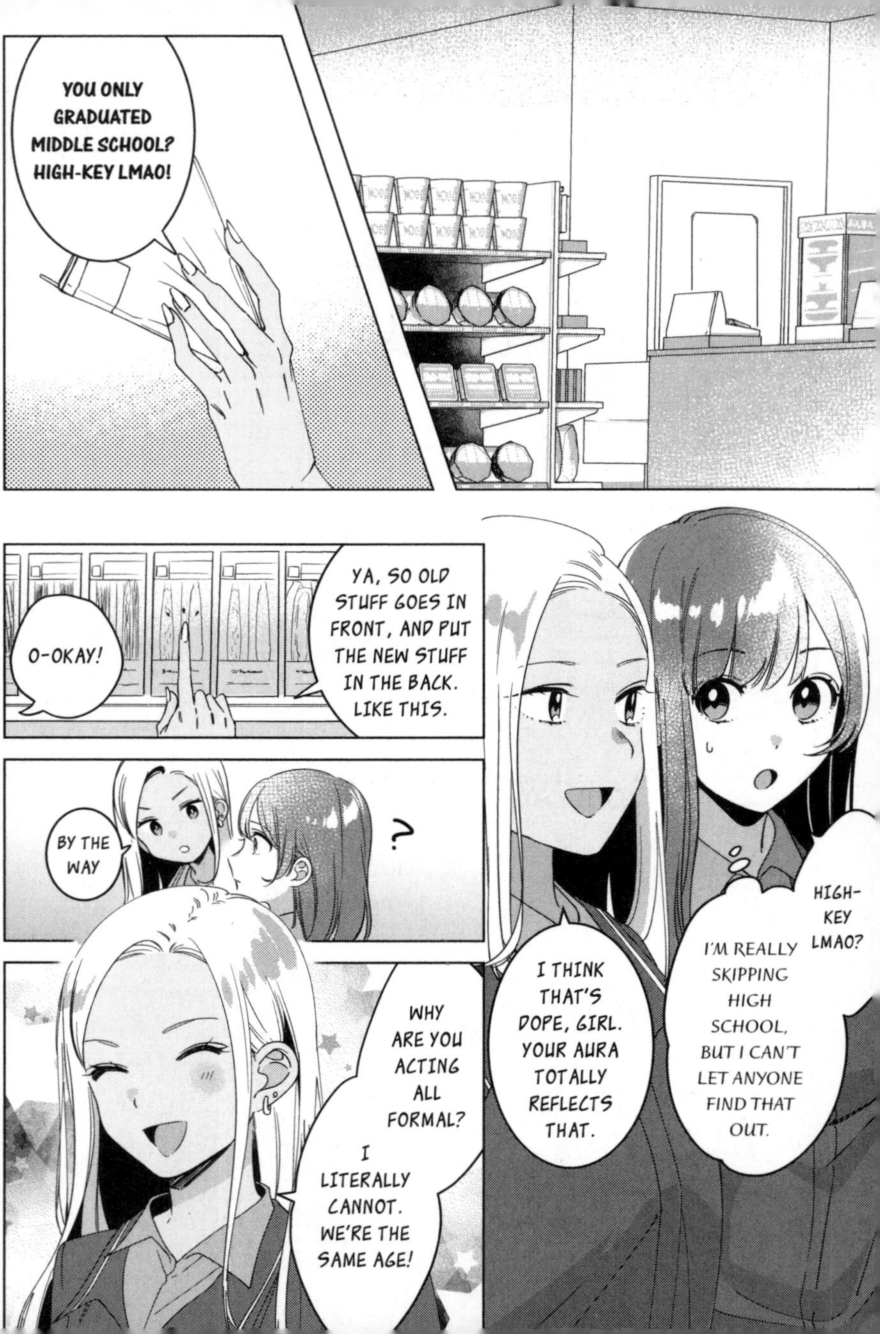
YOU ONLY GRADUATED MIDDLE SCHOOL? HIGH-KEY LMAO!
HIGH-KEY LMAO?
I'M REALLY SKIPPING HIGH SCHOOL, BUT I CAN'T LET ANYONE FIND THAT OUT.
I THINK THAT'S DOPE, GIRL. YOUR AURA TOTALLY REFLECTS THAT.
YA, SO OLD STUFF GOES IN FRONT, AND PUT THE NEW STUFF IN THE BACK. LIKE THIS.
O-OKAY!
?
BY THE WAY
WHY ARE YOU ACTING ALL FORMAL?
I LITERALLY CANNOT. WE'RE THE SAME AGE!

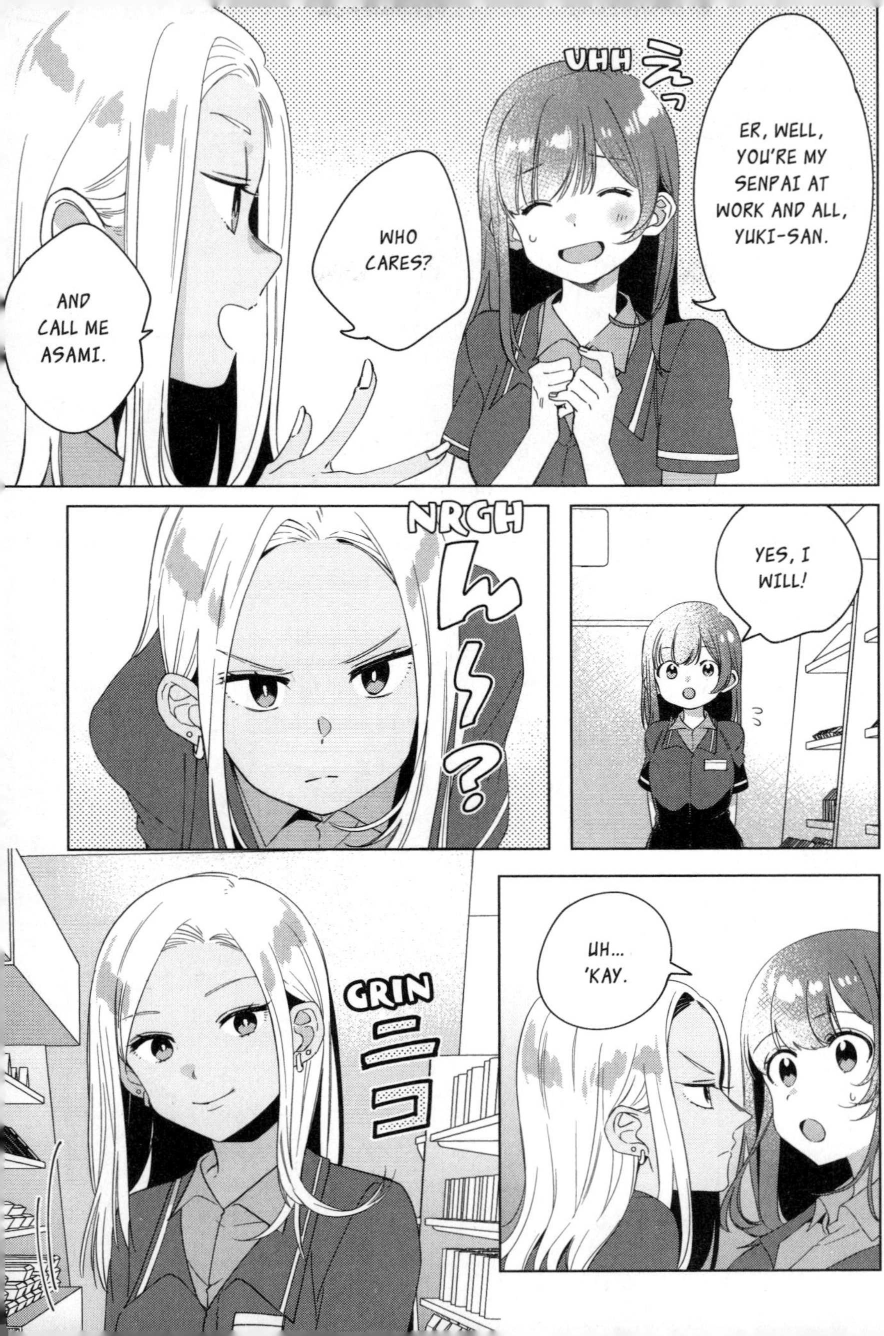
UHH えっ
ER, WELL, YOU'RE MY SENPAI AT WORK AND ALL, YUKI-SAN.
WHO CARES?
AND CALL ME ASAMI.
YES, I WILL!
NRGH
UH... 'KAY.
GRIN ニコ

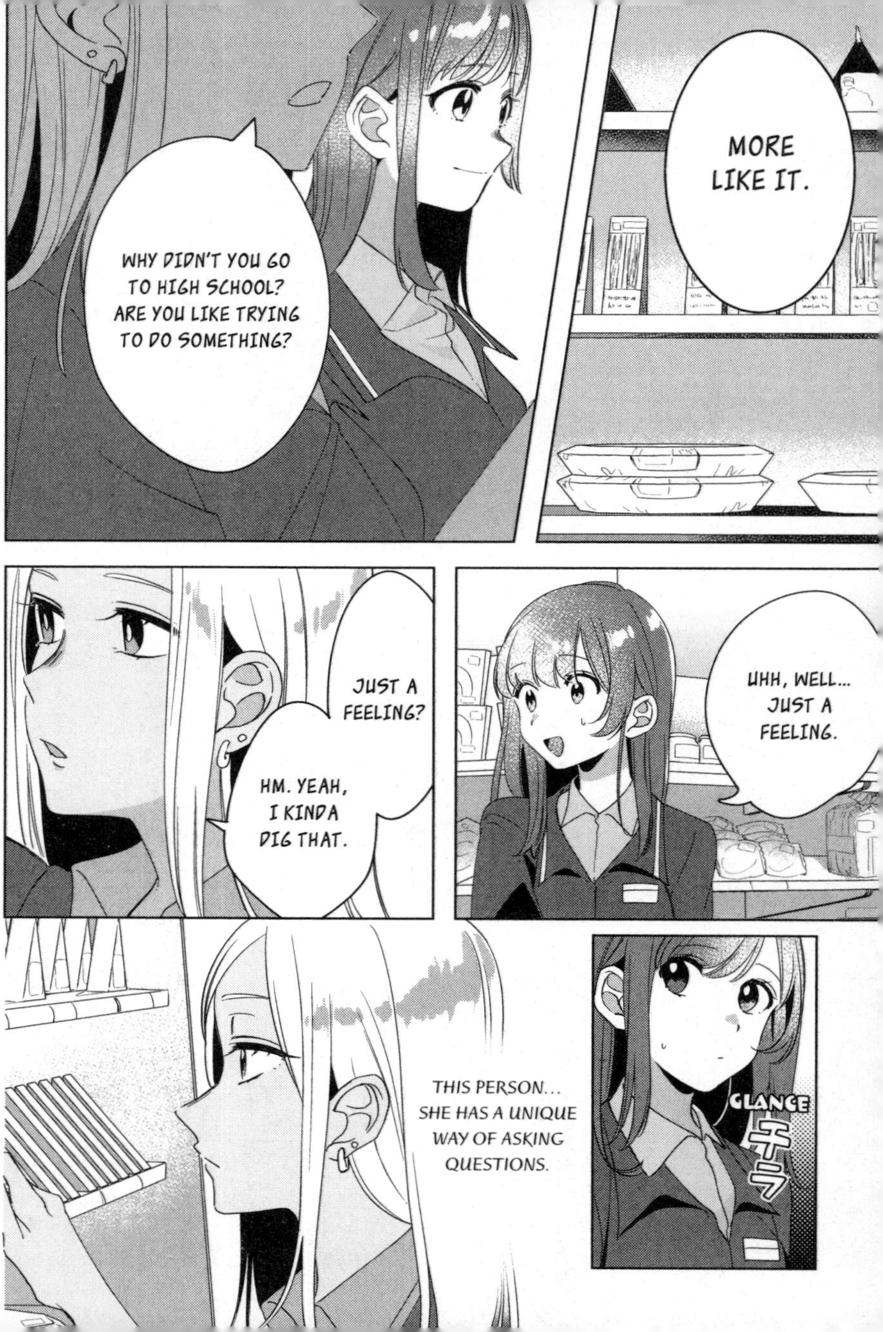
MORE LIKE IT.
WHY DIDN'T YOU GO TO HIGH SCHOOL? ARE YOU LIKE TRYING TO DO SOMETHING?
UHH, WELL... JUST A FEELING.
JUST A FEELING?
HM. YEAH, I KINDA DIG THAT.
GLANCE
チラ
THIS PERSON... SHE HAS A UNIQUE WAY OF ASKING QUESTIONS.

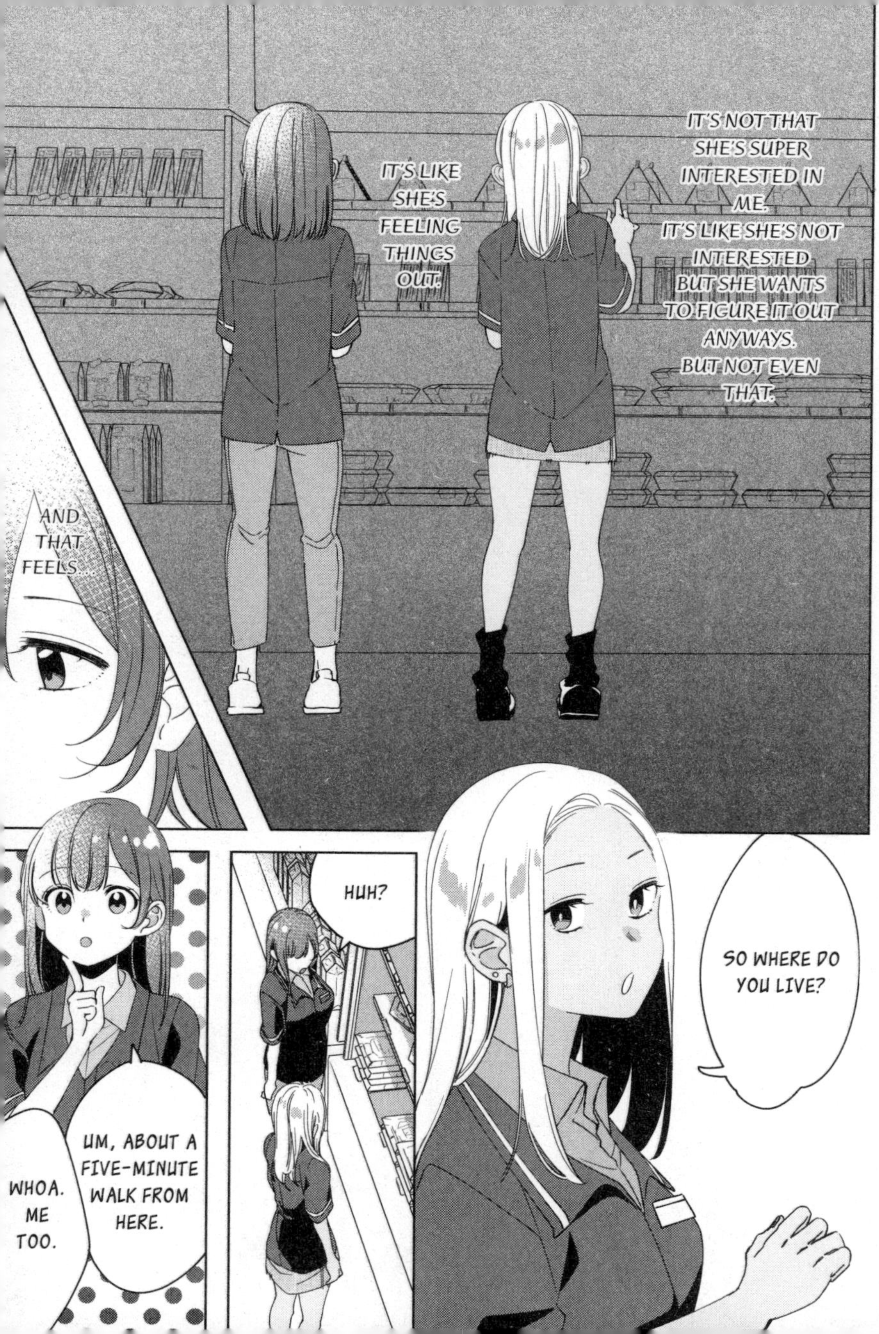
IT'S NOT THAT SHE'S SUPER INTERESTED IN ME. IT'S LIKE SHE'S NOT INTERESTED BUT SHE WANTS TO FIGURE IT OUT ANYWAYS. BUT NOT EVEN THAT.
IT'S LIKE SHE'S FEELING THINGS OUT.
AND THAT FEELS...
SO WHERE DO YOU LIVE?
HUH?
UM, ABOUT A FIVE-MINUTE WALK FROM HERE.
WHOA. ME TOO.

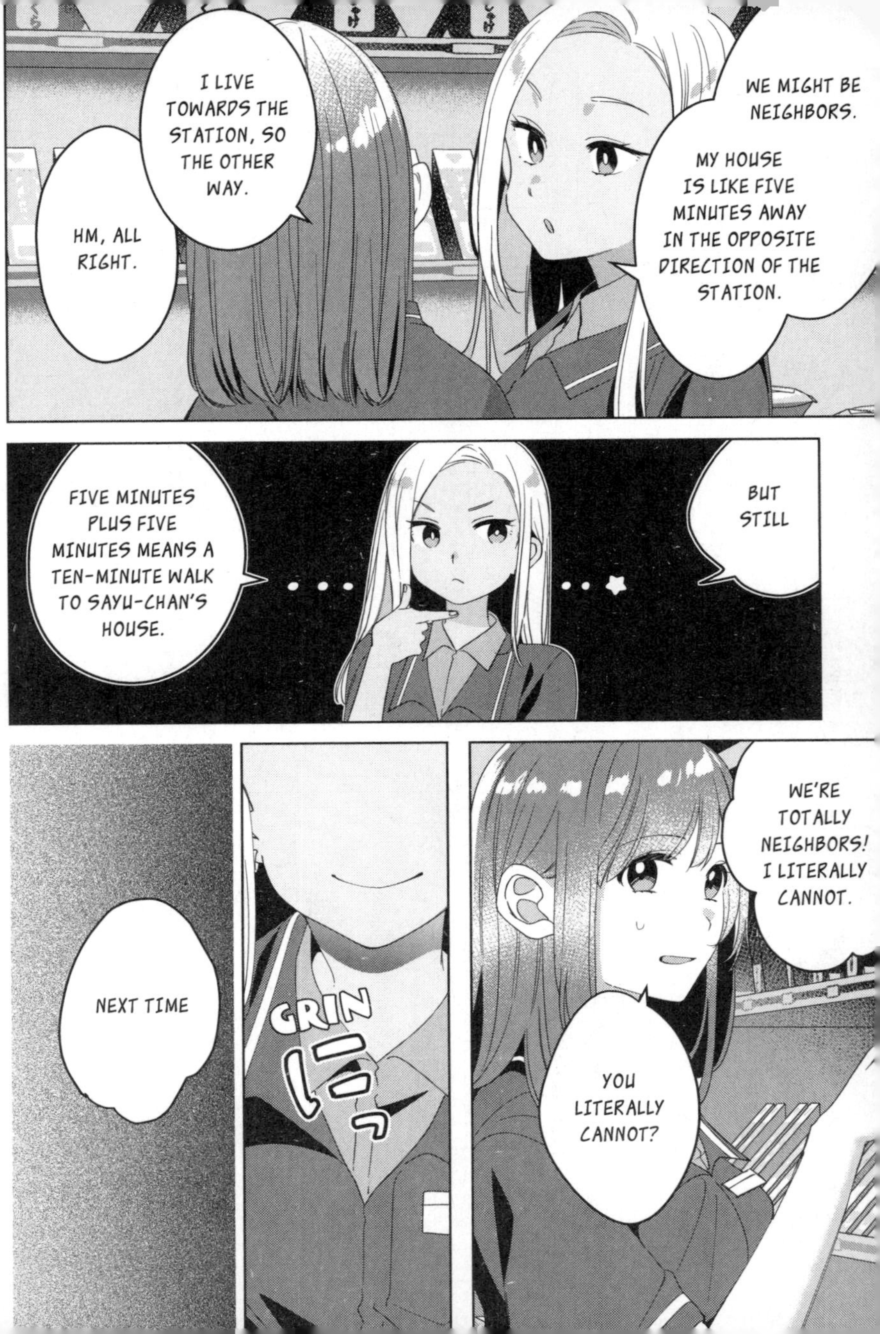

WE MIGHT BE NEIGHBORS.
MY HOUSE IS LIKE FIVE MINUTES AWAY IN THE OPPOSITE DIRECTION OF THE STATION.
I LIVE TOWARDS THE STATION, SO THE OTHER WAY.
HM, ALL RIGHT.
BUT STILL
FIVE MINUTES PLUS FIVE MINUTES MEANS A TEN-MINUTE WALK TO SAYU-CHAN'S HOUSE.
WE'RE TOTALLY NEIGHBORS! I LITERALLY CANNOT.
YOU LITERALLY CANNOT?
GRIN
NEXT TIME

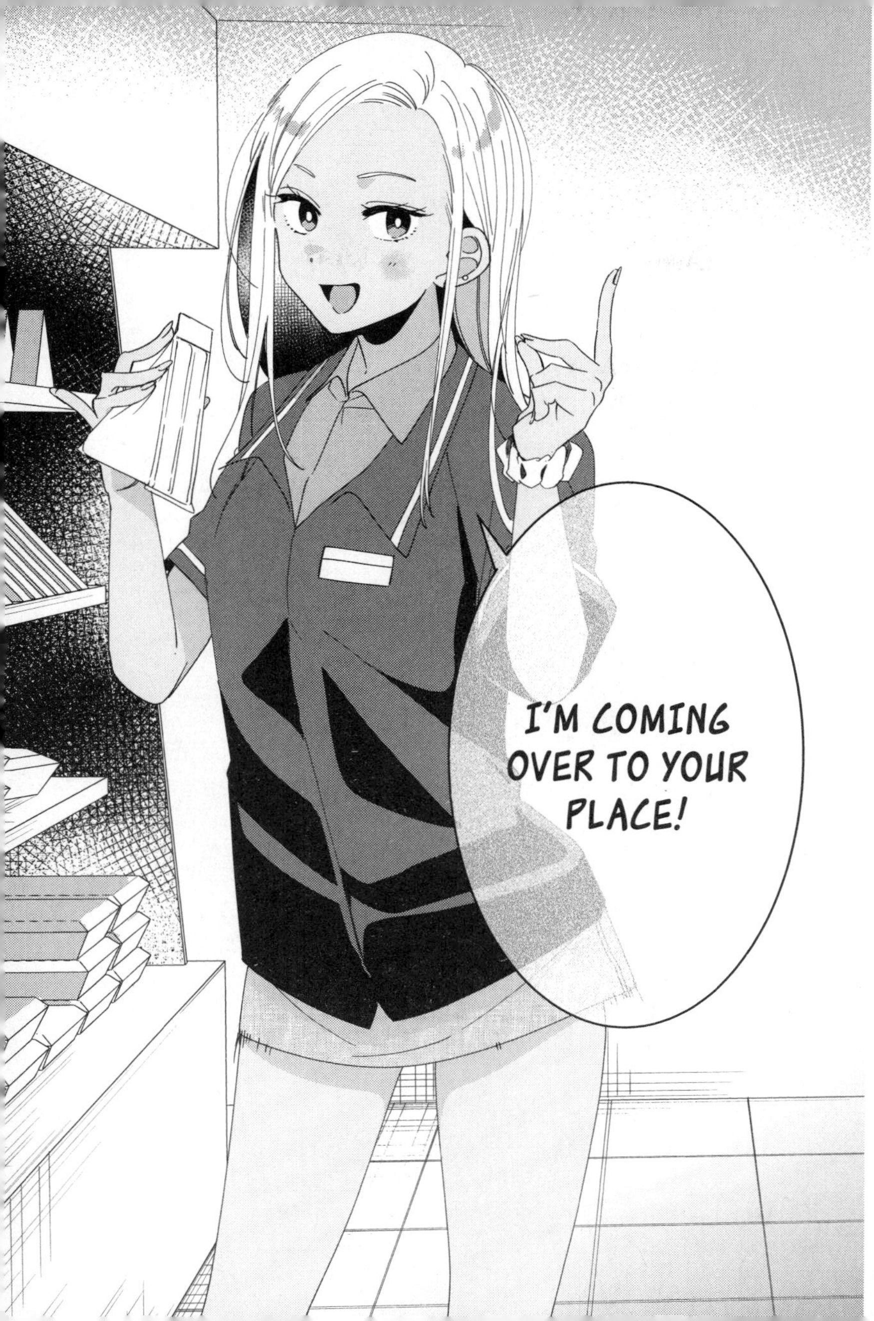
I'M COMING OVER TO YOUR PLACE!

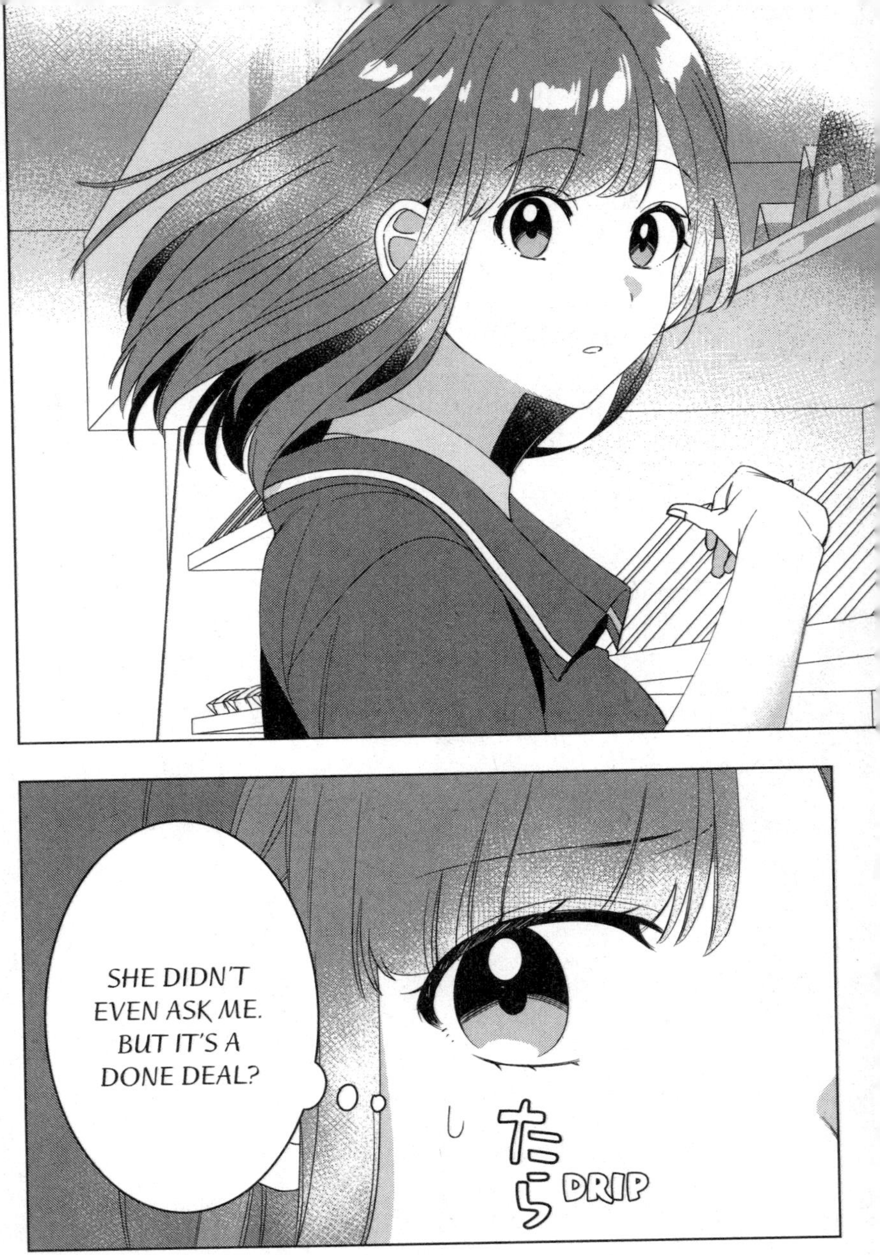
SHE DIDN'T EVEN ASK ME. BUT IT'S A DONE DEAL?
たら
DRIP

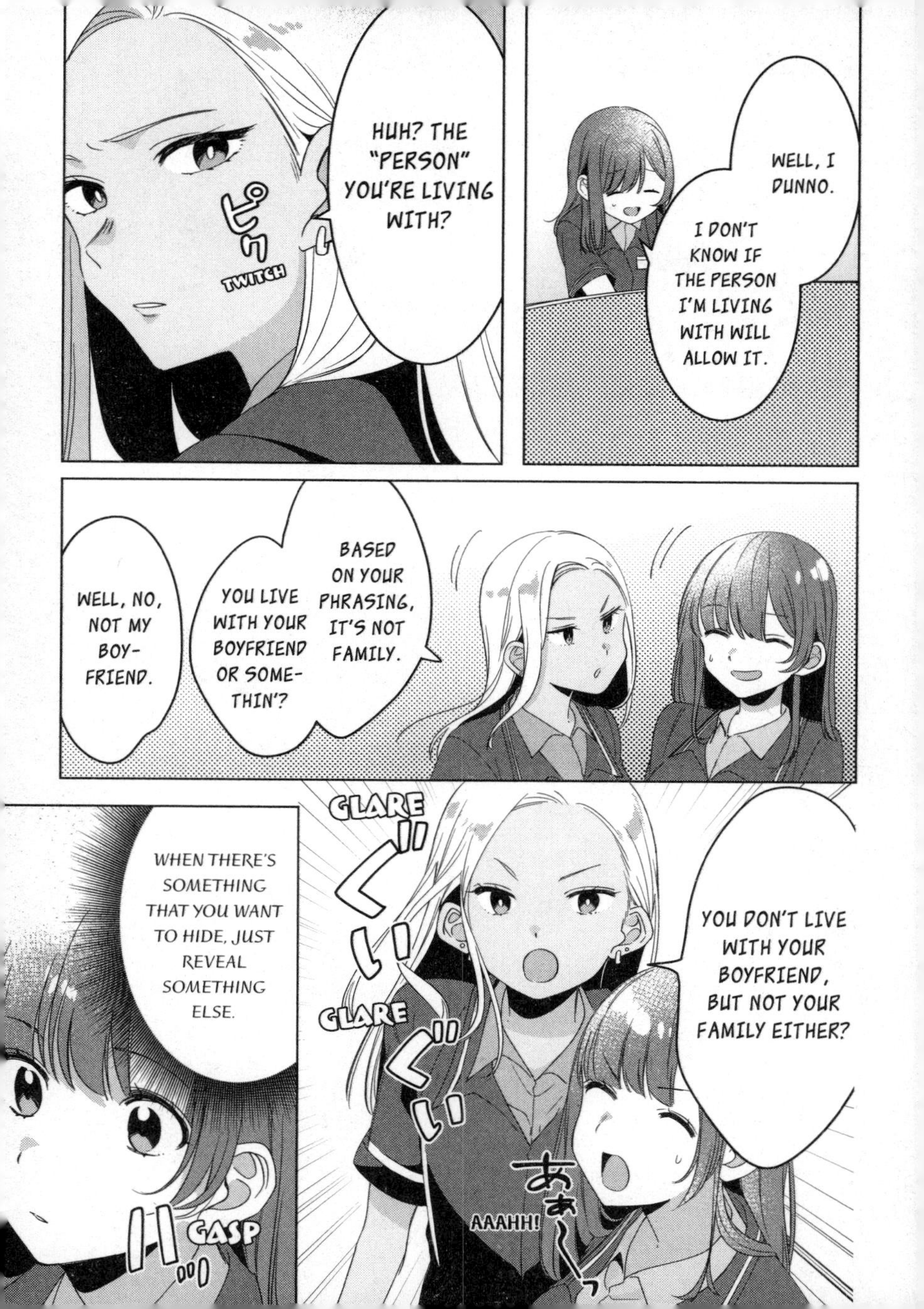
WELL, I DUNNO.
I DON'T KNOW IF THE PERSON I'M LIVING WITH WILL ALLOW IT.
ピク
TWITCH
HUH? THE "PERSON" YOU'RE LIVING WITH?
BASED ON YOUR PHRASING, IT'S NOT FAMILY.
YOU LIVE WITH YOUR BOYFRIEND OR SOMETHIN'?
WELL, NO, NOT MY BOY-FRIEND.
YOU DON'T LIVE WITH YOUR BOYFRIEND, BUT NOT YOUR FAMILY EITHER?
ぐい
GLARE
ぐい
GLARE
あぁ〜っ
AAAHH!
WHEN THERE'S SOMETHING THAT YOU WANT TO HIDE, JUST REVEAL SOMETHING ELSE.
はっ
GASP

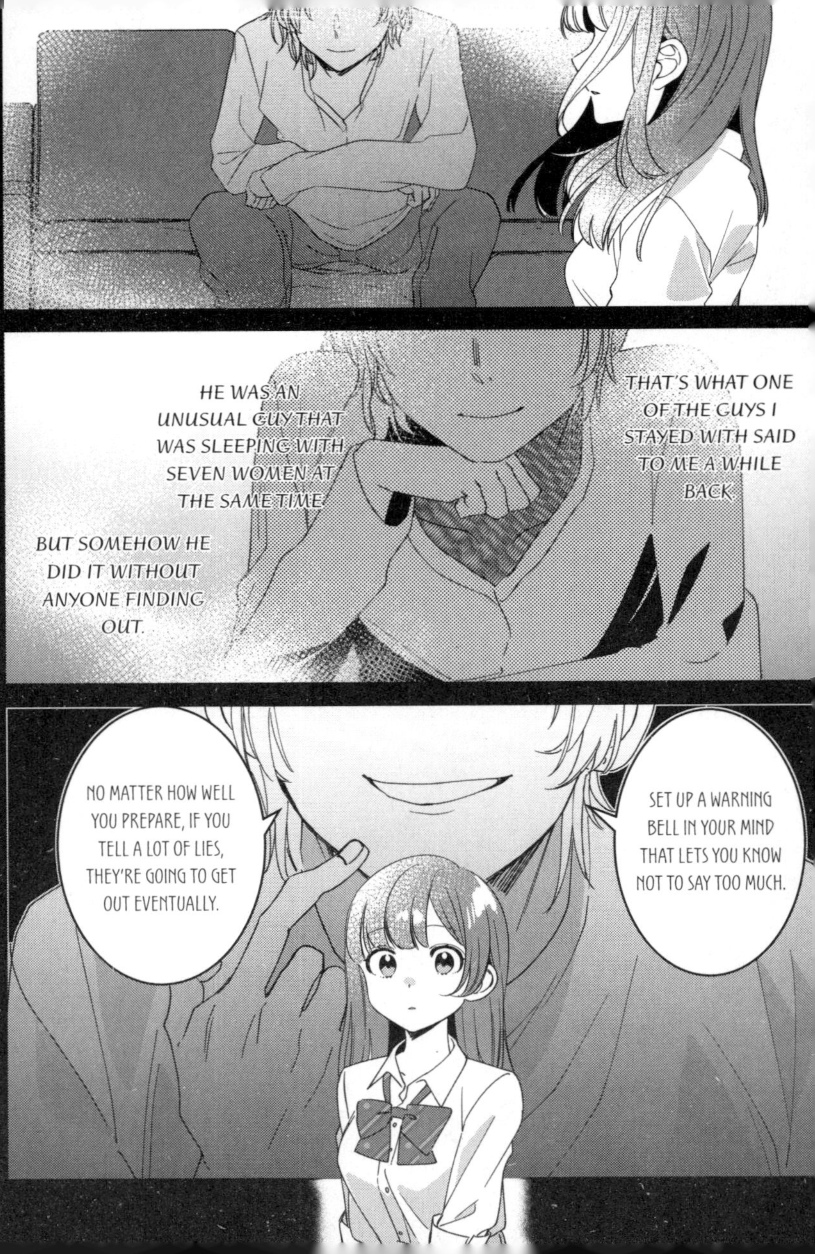
THAT'S WHAT ONE OF THE GUYS I STAYED WITH SAID TO ME A WHILE BACK.
HE WAS AN UNUSUAL GUY THAT WAS SLEEPING WITH SEVEN WOMEN AT THE SAME TIME
BUT SOMEHOW HE DID IT WITHOUT ANYONE FINDING OUT.
SET UP A WARNING BELL IN YOUR MIND THAT LETS YOU KNOW NOT TO SAY TOO MUCH.
NO MATTER HOW WELL YOU PREPARE, IF YOU TELL A LOT OF LIES, THEY'RE GOING TO GET OUT EVENTUALLY.

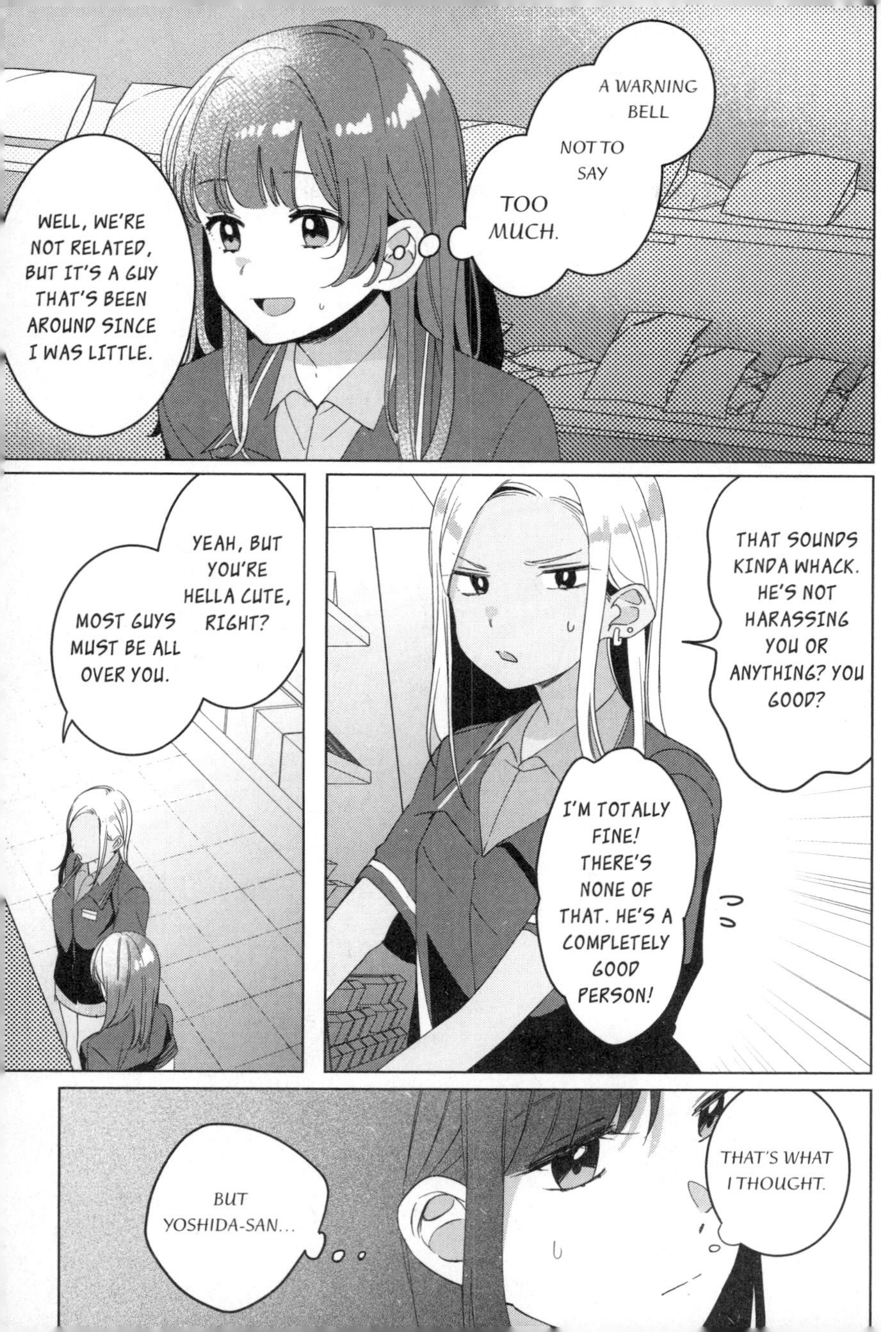
A WARNING BELL NOT TO SAY TOO MUCH.
WELL, WE'RE NOT RELATED, BUT IT'S A GUY THAT'S BEEN AROUND SINCE I WAS LITTLE.
THAT SOUNDS KINDA WHACK. HE'S NOT HARASSING YOU OR ANYTHING? YOU GOOD?
I'M TOTALLY FINE! THERE'S NONE OF THAT. HE'S A COMPLETELY GOOD PERSON!
YEAH, BUT YOU'RE HELLA CUTE, RIGHT?
MOST GUYS MUST BE ALL OVER YOU.
THAT'S WHAT I THOUGHT.
BUT YOSHIDA-SAN...

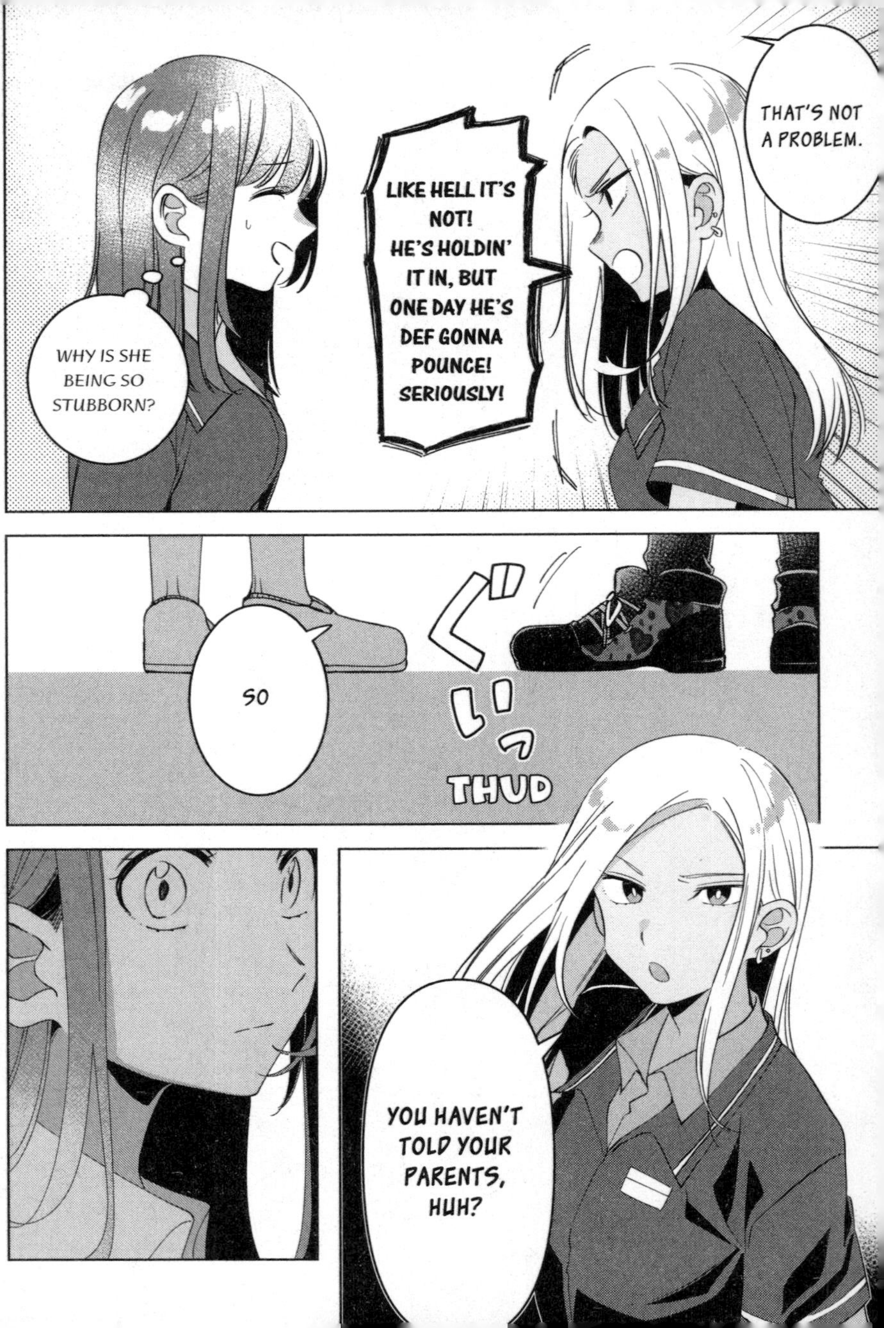
THAT'S NOT A PROBLEM.
LIKE HELL IT'S NOT! HE'S HOLDIN' IT IN, BUT ONE DAY HE'S DEF GONNA POUNCE! SERIOUSLY!
WHY IS SHE BEING SO STUBBORN?
ぐいっ
THUD
SO
YOU HAVEN'T TOLD YOUR PARENTS, HUH?

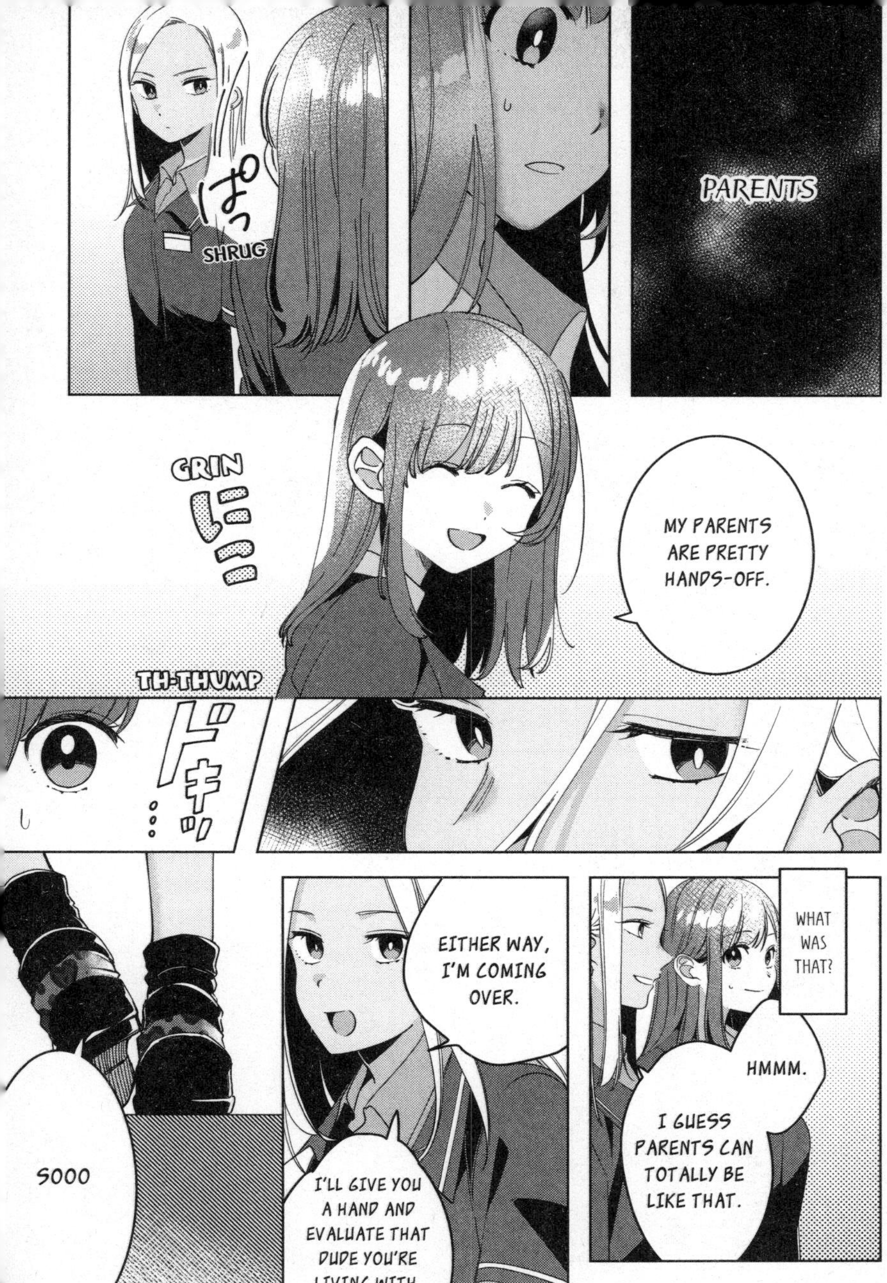
PARENTS
ぱっ
SHRUG
MY PARENTS ARE PRETTY HANDS-OFF.
GRIN
にこ
TH-THUMP
ドキッ...
WHAT WAS THAT?
HMMM.
I GUESS PARENTS CAN TOTALLY BE LIKE THAT.
EITHER WAY, I'M COMING OVER.
I'LL GIVE YOU A HAND AND EVALUATE THAT DUDE YOU'RE LIVING WITH.
SOOO

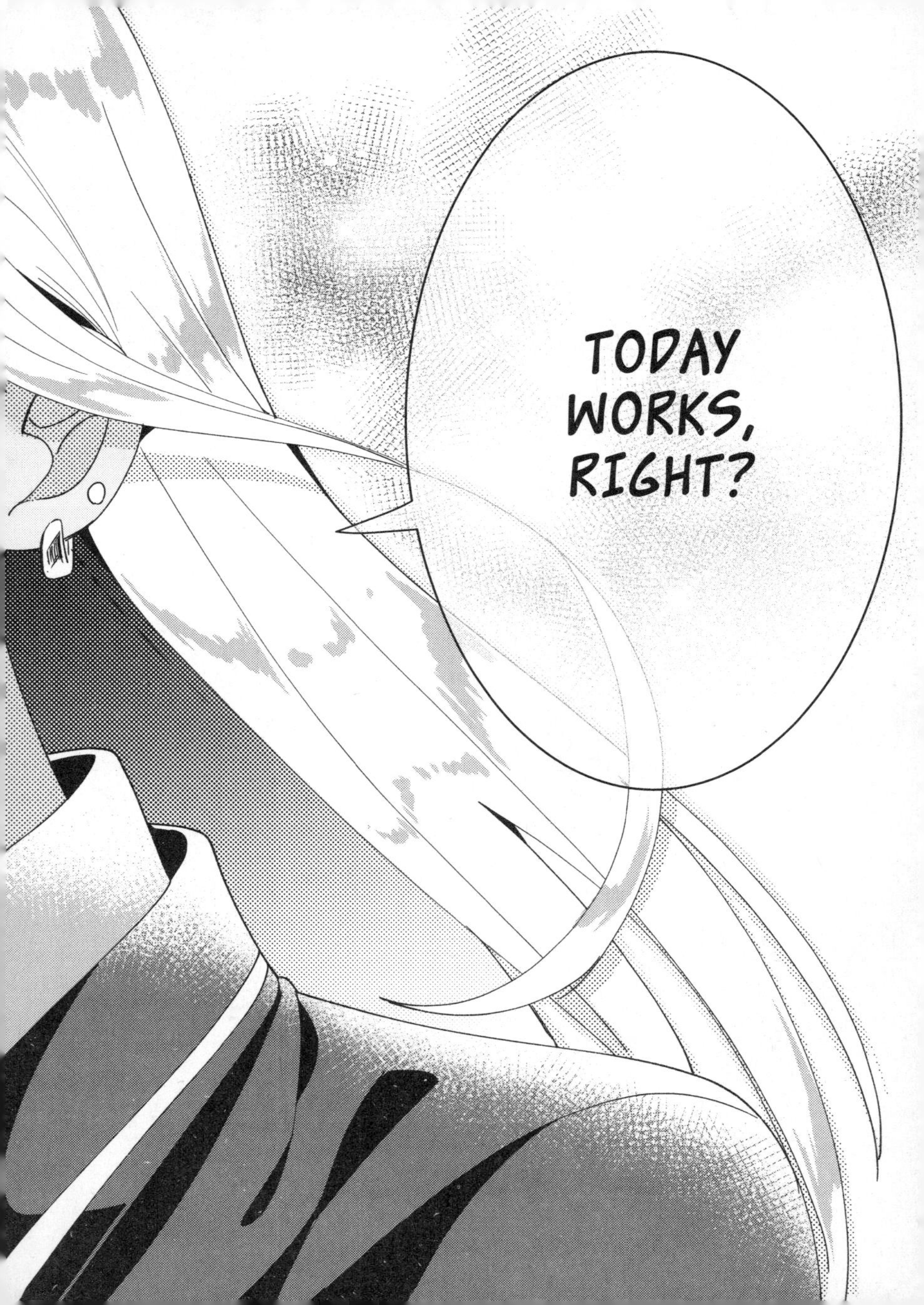
TODAY WORKS, RIGHT?

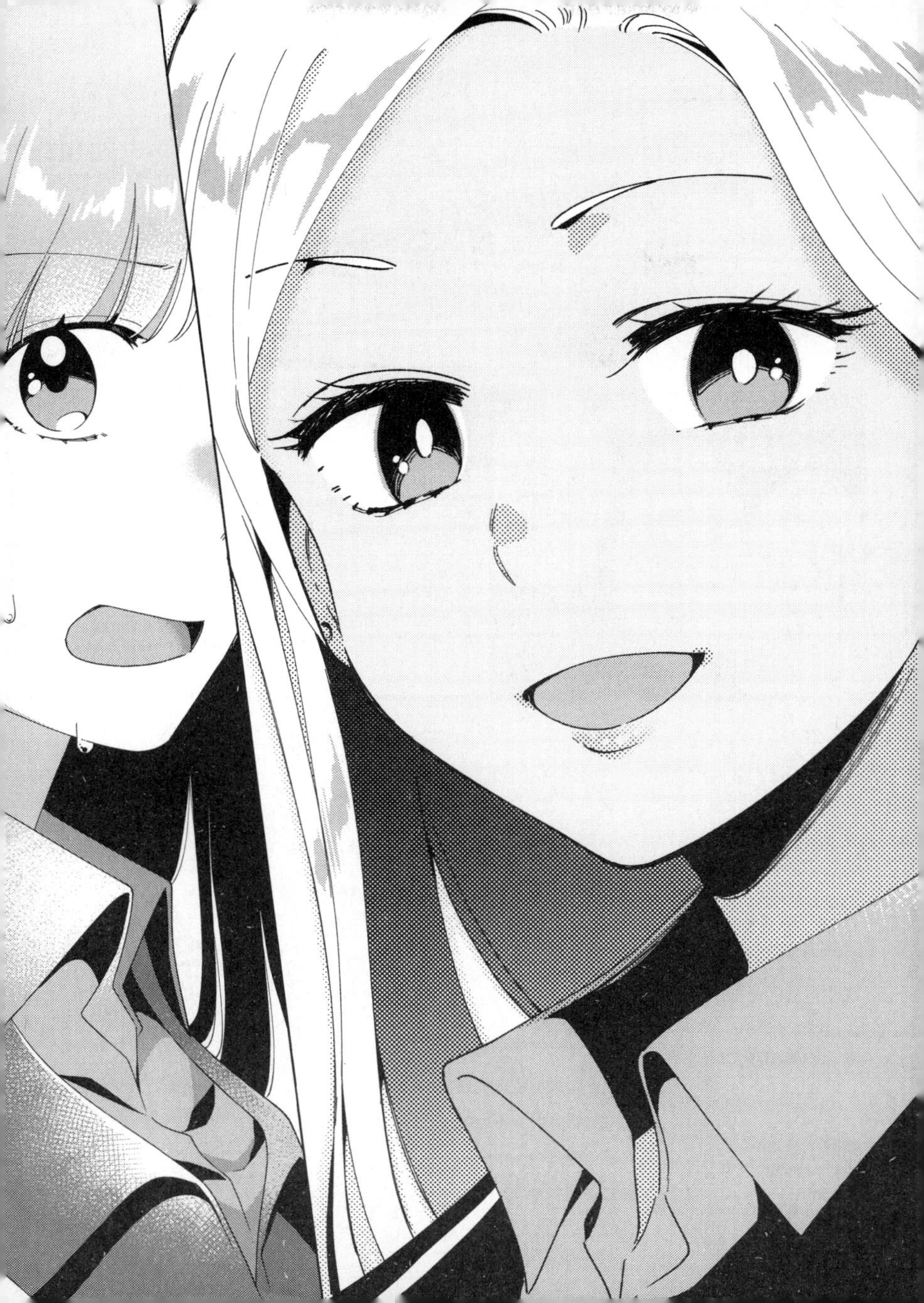

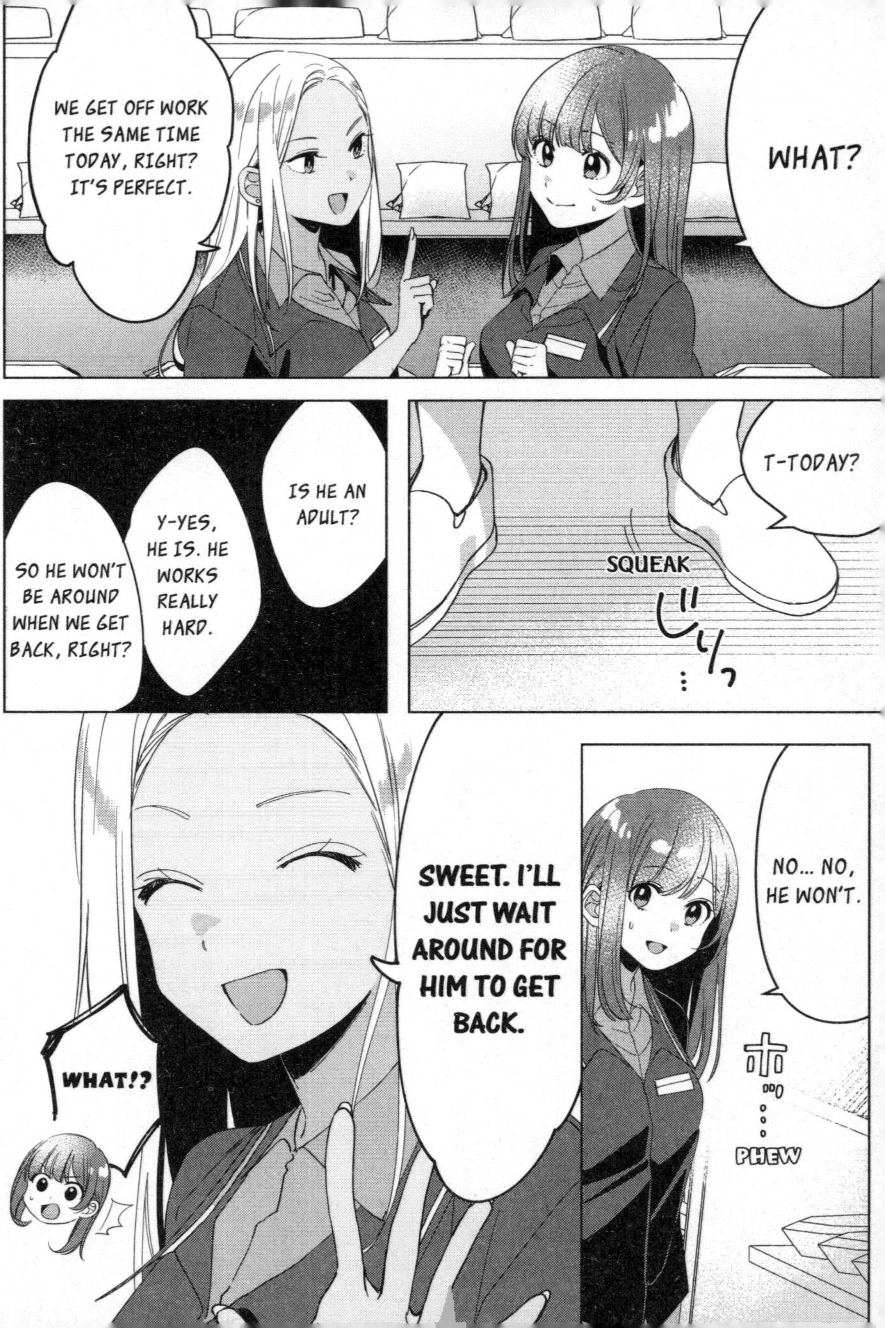
WHAT?
WE GET OFF WORK THE SAME TIME TODAY, RIGHT? IT'S PERFECT.
T-TODAY?
SQUEAK
IS HE AN ADULT?
Y-YES, HE IS. HE WORKS REALLY HARD.
SO HE WON'T BE AROUND WHEN WE GET BACK, RIGHT?
NO... NO, HE WON'T.
PHEW
SWEET. I'LL JUST WAIT AROUND FOR HIM TO GET BACK.
WHAT!?

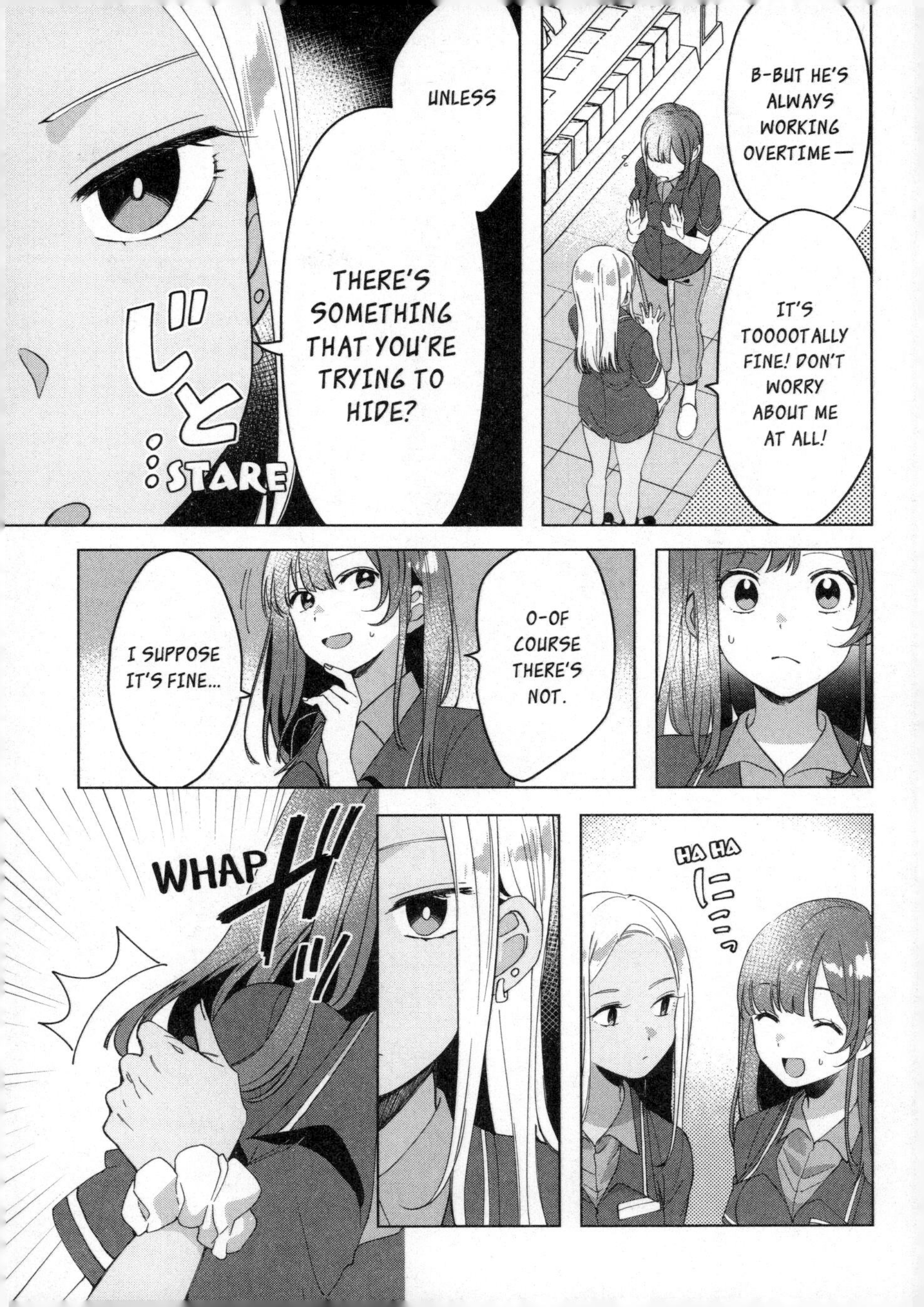
B-BUT HE'S ALWAYS WORKING OVERTIME—
IT'S TOOOOTALLY FINE! DON'T WORRY ABOUT ME AT ALL!
UNLESS
THERE'S SOMETHING THAT YOU'RE TRYING TO HIDE?
じと
STARE
O-OF COURSE THERE'S NOT.
I SUPPOSE IT'S FINE...
HA HA
WHAP
ガッ

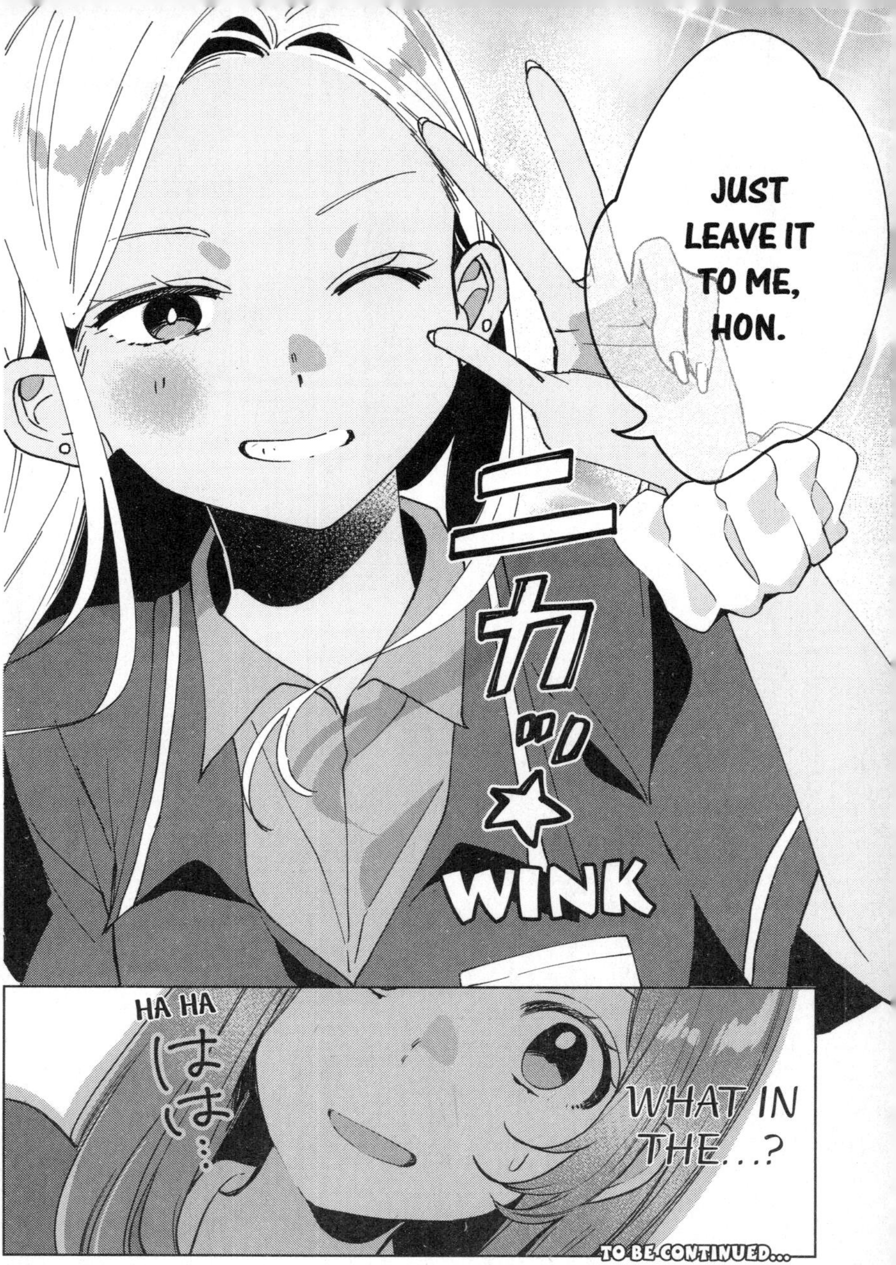
JUST LEAVE IT TO ME, HON.
ニカッ☆
WINK
WHAT IN THE...?
HA HA
はは…
TO BE CONTINUED...

HIGEHIRO

After Being Rejected,
I Shaved and Took
in a High School Runaway

VOLUME 2 BONUS
ADACHI IMARU'S CHARACTER DRAWINGS

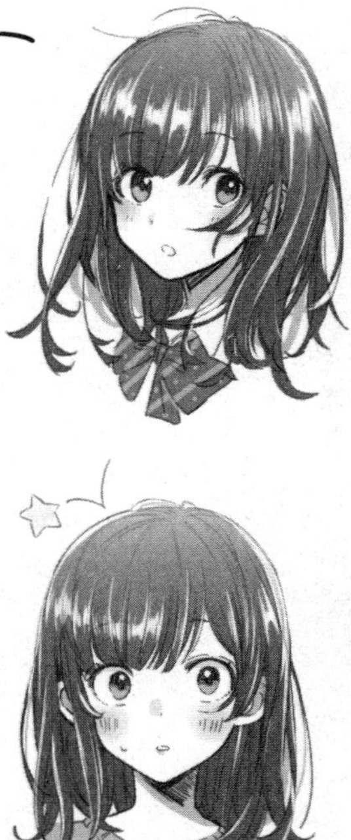

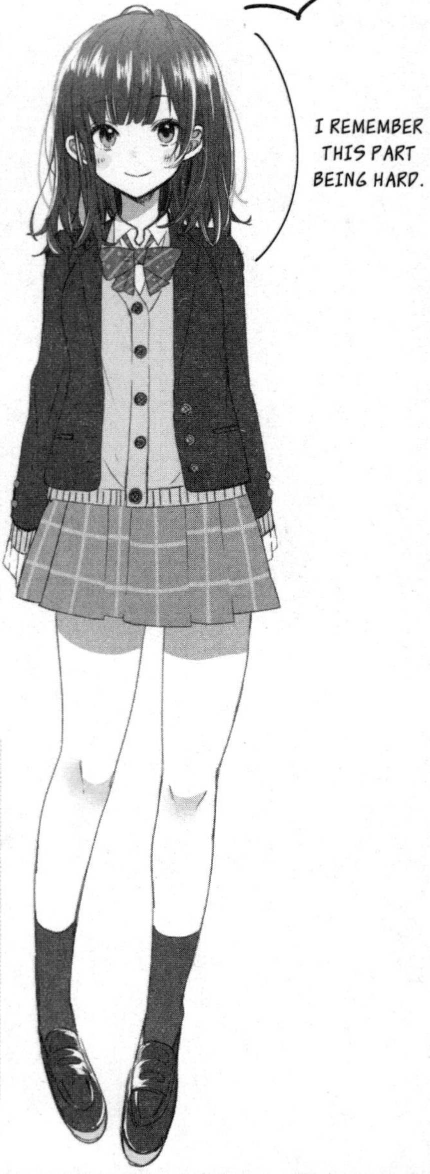
I REMEMBER THIS PART BEING HARD.

AT FIRST, SAYU-CHAN WAS THE HARDEST CHARACTER TO DRAW. I REMEMBER GOING BACK AND FORTH WITH MY MANAGER ON EARLIER DRAFTS. SINCE I DREW HER FACE COMPLETELY DIFFERENT FROM BOOOTA-SAN'S ORIGINAL DRAWINGS IN THE LIGHT NOVEL, IT WAS PRETTY TOUGH GETTING USED TO IT.

ADACHI IMARU

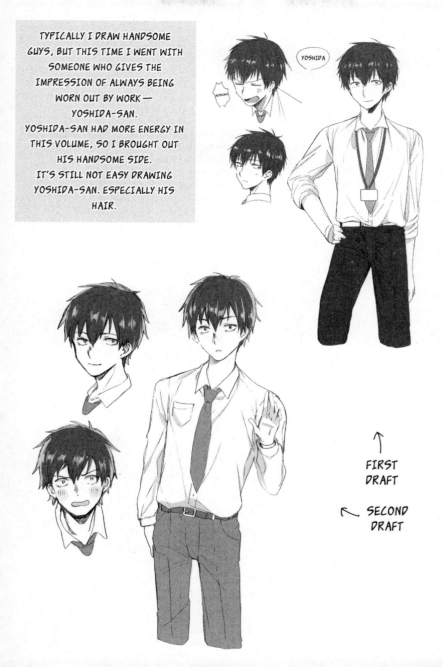

TYPICALLY I DRAW HANDSOME GUYS, BUT THIS TIME I WENT WITH SOMEONE WHO GIVES THE IMPRESSION OF ALWAYS BEING WORN OUT BY WORK—YOSHIDA-SAN.
YOSHIDA-SAN HAD MORE ENERGY IN THIS VOLUME, SO I BROUGHT OUT HIS HANDSOME SIDE.
IT'S STILL NOT EASY DRAWING YOSHIDA-SAN. ESPECIALLY HIS HAIR.

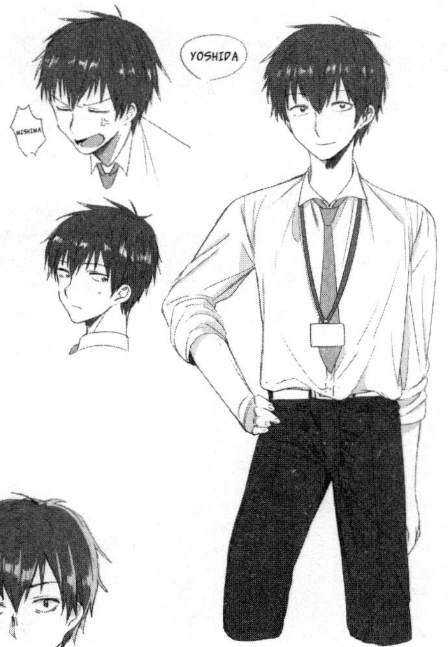
YOSHIDA
MISHIMA

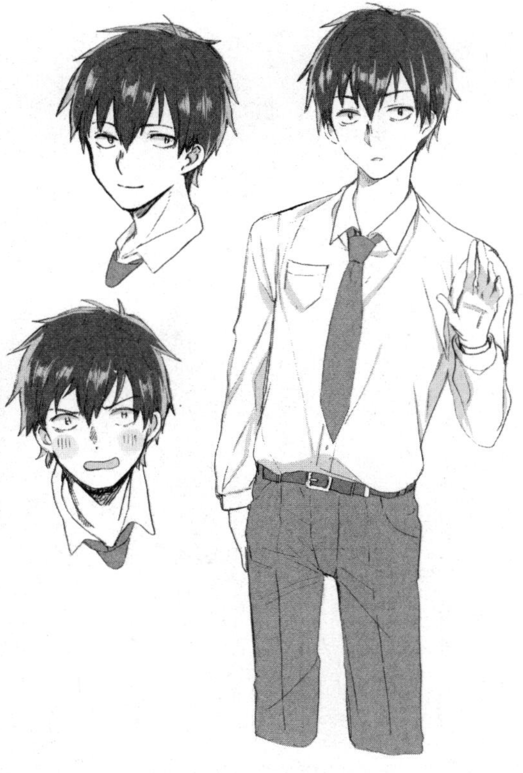

FIRST DRAFT

SECOND DRAFT

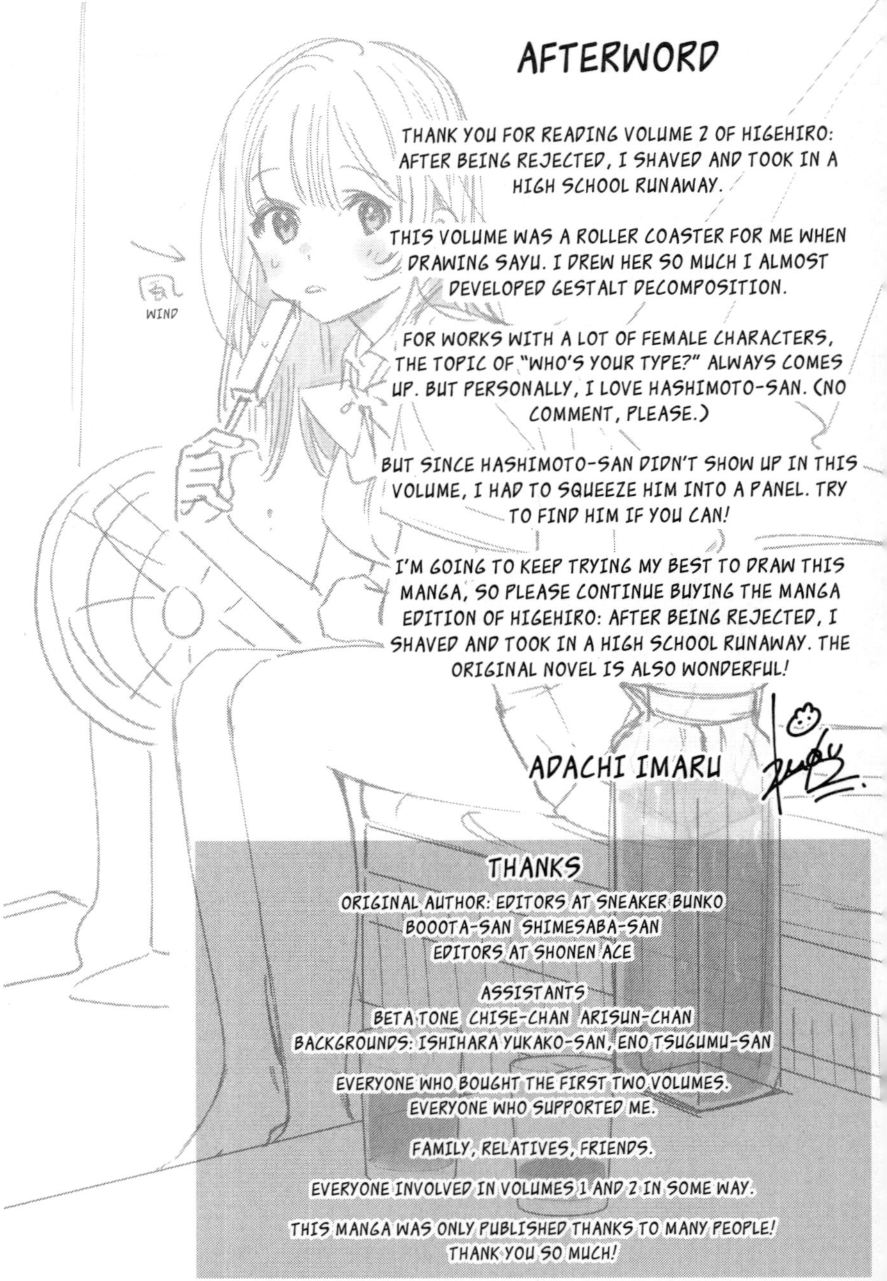
風
WIND

AFTERWORD

THANK YOU FOR READING VOLUME 2 OF HIGEHIRO: AFTER BEING REJECTED, I SHAVED AND TOOK IN A HIGH SCHOOL RUNAWAY.

THIS VOLUME WAS A ROLLER COASTER FOR ME WHEN DRAWING SAYU. I DREW HER SO MUCH I ALMOST DEVELOPED GESTALT DECOMPOSITION.

FOR WORKS WITH A LOT OF FEMALE CHARACTERS, THE TOPIC OF "WHO'S YOUR TYPE?" ALWAYS COMES UP. BUT PERSONALLY, I LOVE HASHIMOTO-SAN. (NO COMMENT, PLEASE.)

BUT SINCE HASHIMOTO-SAN DIDN'T SHOW UP IN THIS VOLUME, I HAD TO SQUEEZE HIM INTO A PANEL. TRY TO FIND HIM IF YOU CAN!

I'M GOING TO KEEP TRYING MY BEST TO DRAW THIS MANGA, SO PLEASE CONTINUE BUYING THE MANGA EDITION OF HIGEHIRO: AFTER BEING REJECTED, I SHAVED AND TOOK IN A HIGH SCHOOL RUNAWAY. THE ORIGINAL NOVEL IS ALSO WONDERFUL!

ADACHI IMARU

THANKS

ORIGINAL AUTHOR: EDITORS AT SNEAKER BUNKO
BOOOTA-SAN SHIMESABA-SAN
EDITORS AT SHONEN ACE

ASSISTANTS
BETA TONE CHISE-CHAN ARISUN-CHAN
BACKGROUNDS: ISHIHARA YUKAKO-SAN, ENO TSUGUMU-SAN

EVERYONE WHO BOUGHT THE FIRST TWO VOLUMES.
EVERYONE WHO SUPPORTED ME.

FAMILY, RELATIVES, FRIENDS.

EVERYONE INVOLVED IN VOLUMES 1 AND 2 IN SOME WAY.

THIS MANGA WAS ONLY PUBLISHED THANKS TO MANY PEOPLE!
THANK YOU SO MUCH!

HIGEHIRO'S ASSISTANTS' PAGE!

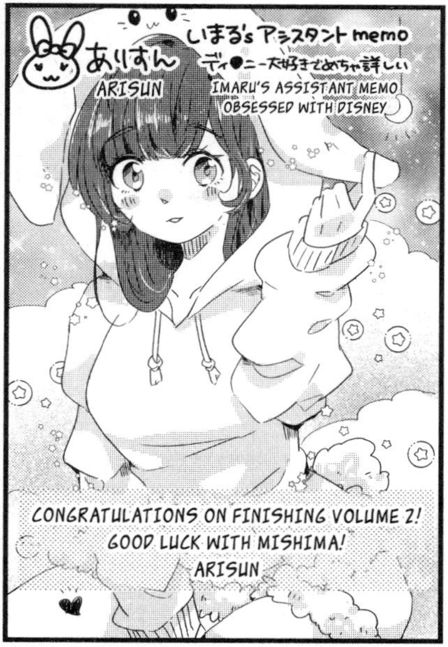

ありすん
ARISUN
いまる's アシスタント memo
ディ●ニー大好きでめちゃ詳しい
IMARU'S ASSISTANT MEMO
OBSESSED WITH DISNEY
CONGRATULATIONS ON FINISHING VOLUME 2!
GOOD LUCK WITH MISHIMA!
ARISUN

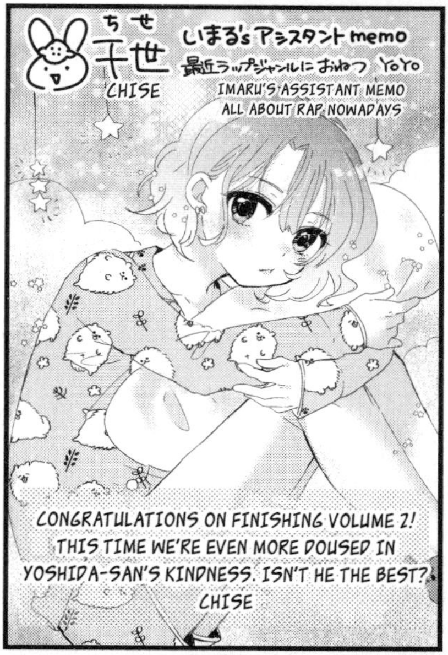

ちせ
千世
CHISE
いまる's アシスタント memo
最近ラップジャンルにおねつ YoYo
IMARU'S ASSISTANT MEMO
ALL ABOUT RAP NOWADAYS
CONGRATULATIONS ON FINISHING VOLUME 2!
THIS TIME WE'RE EVEN MORE DOUSED IN
YOSHIDA-SAN'S KINDNESS. ISN'T HE THE BEST?
CHISE

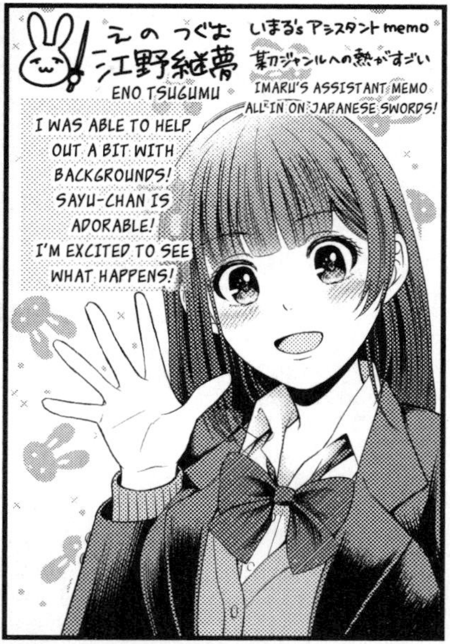

えの つぐむ
江野継夢
ENO TSUGUMU
いまる's アシスタント memo
某刀ジャンルへの熱がすごい
IMARU'S ASSISTANT MEMO
ALL IN ON JAPANESE SWORDS!
I WAS ABLE TO HELP OUT A BIT WITH BACKGROUNDS! SAYU-CHAN IS ADORABLE! I'M EXCITED TO SEE WHAT HAPPENS!

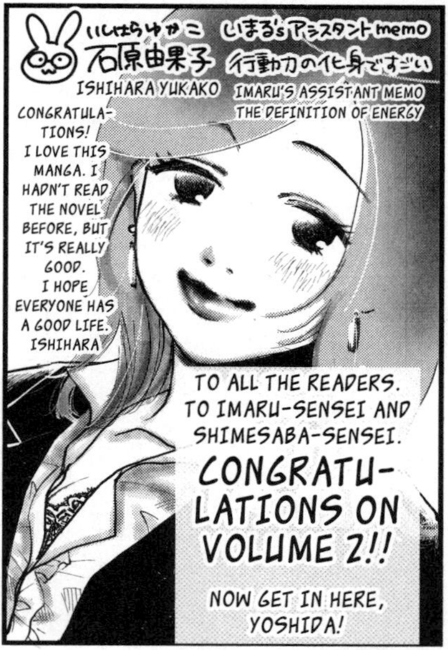

いしはらゆかこ
石原由果子
ISHIHARA YUKAKO
いまる's アシスタント memo
行動力の化身ですごい
IMARU'S ASSISTANT MEMO
THE DEFINITION OF ENERGY
CONGRATULATIONS! I LOVE THIS MANGA. I HADN'T READ THE NOVEL BEFORE, BUT IT'S REALLY GOOD. I HOPE EVERYONE HAS A GOOD LIFE. ISHIHARA
TO ALL THE READERS. TO IMARU-SENSEI AND SHIMESABA-SENSEI.
CONGRATULATIONS ON VOLUME 2!!
NOW GET IN HERE, YOSHIDA!

THANK YOU SO MUCH! WE APPRECIATE YOU!

Higehiro: After Being Rejected, I Shaved and Took in a High School Runaway Vol. 02
(HIGE O SORU. SOSHITE JOSHIKOSEI O HIRO. Vol.2)
© Shimesaba, Booota 2019
© Imaru Adachi 2019
First published in Japan in 2019 by KADOKAWA CORPORATION, Tokyo. English
translation rights arranged with KADOKAWA CORPORATION, Tokyo.

ISBN: 978-1-64273-145-3

Original story by Shimesaba
Manga by Imaru Adachi
Character design by booota
English Edition Published by One Peace Books 2021

Printed in USA
1 2 3 4 5 6 7 8 9 10

One Peace Books
43-32 22nd Street STE 204 Long Island City New York 11101
www.onepeacebooks.com